The
New
Youth
Justice

Edited by
Barry Goldson

D0529901

Russell House Publishing

First published in 2000 by:
Russell House Publishing Ltd.
4 St. George's House
Uplyme Road
Lyme Regis
Dorset DT7 3LS

Tel: 01297–443948
Fax: 01297–442722
e-mail: help@russellhouse.co.uk

British Library Cataloguing-in-publication Data:
A catalogue record for this book is available from the British Library.

ISBN: 1–89892472–4

Typeset by Saxon Graphics Ltd, Derby
Printed by Ashford Press

Russell House Publishing

is a group of social work, probation, education and youth and community work practitioners and academics working in collaboration with a professional publishing team. Our aim is to work closely with the field to produce innovative and valuable materials to help managers, trainers, practitioners and students.
We are keen to receive feedback on publications and new ideas for future projects.

Contents

Acknowledgements

Behind each and every contribution to this book there are many people, other than the named authors, who deserve special thanks. I do not know who they all are but I am certain that they are there. Less than twelve months have elapsed from the point at which this book was but an idea to the stage at which it has become a book. Such an achievement requires considerable effort, determination, commitment, talent and sheer hard work and I am very grateful to each of the contributors, and the many more 'anonymous' people behind them, who have made editing this collection of essays such a rewarding task. Thank you.

There are some less 'anonymous' people to whom I owe special thanks.

Geoffrey Mann at Russell House Publishing has been a delight to work with. The hospitality of Cal and Doug in New Zealand, and the tremendous joy of meeting Nick for the first time, provided precisely the 'shot in the arm' that I needed when my energy levels were beginning to wane. Nick's warm nature, interest in others and youthful exuberance inspired me, and I am hopeful that in the course of growing up he will never have to endure the adult hostilities and ambivalence that beset the children who are the core concern of this book. Sheena as always has been supportive and her patience, quite apart from everything else, is probably more than I deserve. Many other colleagues and friends have helped enormously by simply being who they are, and by being there of course.

Barry Goldson
Liverpool

Notes on Contributors

Sue Bandalli is a Lecturer in the Law School at the University of Birmingham. She has researched and published in relation to children and the criminal law.

Mark Drakeford is a Senior Lecturer in the School of Social Sciences at the University of Wales, Cardiff. His most recent book (with Kevin Haines) is *Young People and Youth Justice* which was published by Macmillan in 1999.

Barry Goldson is a Lecturer in the Department of Sociology, Social Policy and Social Work Studies at the University of Liverpool. He has researched and published widely in relation to the sociology of childhood, social policy and youth, state welfare services and youth crime. He is the editor of *Youth Justice: Contemporary Policy and Practice* which was published by Ashgate in 1999.

Kevin Haines is a Lecturer in the School of Social Sciences and International Development at the University of Wales, Swansea. He has a longstanding academic and professional interest in youth justice and is a Board Member of the International Network for Research in Juvenile Criminology. His most recent book (with Mark Drakeford) is *Young People and Youth Justice* which was published by Macmillan in 1999.

Richard Hester is a Lecturer in the Department of Social Policy and Social Work at the University of Birmingham and a National Executive Member of the National Community Safety Network. He has also researched and published in the area of policing and New Age Travellers.

Kerry McCarthy has undertaken post-graduate research at the University of Wales, Cardiff and currently works for the Probation Service in Inner London.

Geoff Monaghan is a Senior Policy Development Officer with the Youth Crime Section at the National Association for the Care and Resettlement of Offenders. He is an active commentator on youth justice matters and is the convenor of the Policy Committee, and Deputy Chairperson of the National Association for Youth Justice.

Sharon Moore has been a Probation Officer, a Youth Justice Manager and she is currently the National Co-ordinator of the Children's Society's National Remand Review Initiative. She has presented numerous conference papers and has written widely on child incarceration and the work of the Remand Review Initiative.

John Muncie is a Senior Lecturer in Criminology and Social Policy at the Open University. He has researched and published widely and his most recent books are *Criminological Perspectives*, 1996 and *The Problem of Crime*, 1996 both published by Sage/Open University Press, and *Youth and Crime: A Critical Introduction* published by Sage in 1999.

John Pitts is Vauxhall Professor of Socio-Legal Studies and Director of the Vauxhall Centre for the Study of Crime at the University of Luton. He has researched and published extensively in the areas of youth crime and youth justice and his most recent books are *Working with Young Offenders* (second edition), 1999 and *Discipline or Solidarity: the New Politics of Youth Crime*, 2000 both published by Macmillan.

David Smith is Professor of Social Work at Lancaster University. He has published extensively and he is currently researching racist violence, programmes for persistent juvenile offenders and electronic monitoring. He is the author of *Criminology for Social Work* which was published by Macmillan in 1995.

Brian Williams is Reader in Criminal Justice at De Montfort University, Leicester. His most recent book is *Working with Victims of Crime* which was published by Jessica Kingsley in 1999.

Editor's Introduction:
The New Youth Justice

Barry Goldson

In 1815 an august body was assembled in London to undertake a major social inquiry. One year later, the *Society for Investigating the Alarming Increase of Juvenile Delinquency in the Metropolis* reported that three principal 'causes' and two 'auxiliary causes' had been found which, taken together, accounted for the 'alarming increase' of juvenile crime in England's developing and industrialising capital city. Whether or not juvenile crime was actually 'increasing' at an 'alarming' rate was in fact uncertain as there were no reliable statistics. What was more certain however, was the sense of 'alarm' itself. The 'want of education', the 'want of employment' and the 'inadequate' state of parenting comprised the Society's principal 'causes'. The 'defective' state of the police and the 'over-severity' of the criminal code for children were thought to represent the 'auxiliary' counterparts.

Two centuries later and all of this sounds very familiar. The contested nature and unreliability of youth crime statistics continues to confound us. 'Moral panics' and 'respectable fears' (Cohen, 1972; Pearson, 1983) persist, and the quality of parenting, together with educational deficits and circumscribed employment opportunities, are still rooted at the core of aetiological accounts of juvenile crime. Recent concerns about the quality of policing – most notably found in the Macpherson report, (1999) – have endured over time, and the very fact that the UK locks up proportionately more children than most of our neighbour states in the European Union (Ruxton, 1996), reflects something of the 'severity of the criminal code'. Youth justice business continues as usual. So what's new? Why *The New Youth Justice* ?

Whilst it is true to say that the 'domain assumptions' (Gouldner, 1971), which underpin youth justice discourse have remained relatively constant over time, much has emerged in the past ten years or so that can legitimately be termed 'new'. In this sense the cross-party political consensus which has consolidated around the need for 'toughness' is notable (Goldson, 1997 and 1999). Indeed, Curtis (1999), has observed this 'new' consensus and has noted that the youth justice policies of New Labour are 'curiously alike' those of the previous Conservative administration. What is more striking however, are the policy developments and organisational changes in the youth justice system expressed through, and brought about by, the Crime and Disorder Act 1998 and the Youth Justice and Criminal Evidence Act 1999. Here we are witness to the most radical overhaul of the youth justice system in fifty years: it is here that the 'newness' with which this book is primarily concerned is to be found. The chapters that follow engage critically with the new youth justice at the levels of criminological theory, politics, policy and practice and they subject its underpinning priorities to analytical interrogation.

John Pitts opens this endeavour in Chapter 1 in setting out key features of New Labour's youth justice programme and locating them within a wider political context. Pitts argues that the new 'toughness' comprises an 'electoral hermetic' and 'above all else New Labour is a vehicle for the acquisition and retention of political power, and nowhere is this more evident than its position on crime and justice'. Pitts broadens his conceptualisation of the new youth justice as a new form of governance which 'designs out' the 'myopic banality' which lies at its core and emphasises crude correctional, regulatory and disciplinary priorities in its appeal to that prized electoral constituency that is middle-class middle-England. Electoral anxiety, as distinct from a considered and compassionate response to children in trouble, is the motor force of the new youth justice.

In Chapter 2, John Muncie picks up on a number of themes raised in the opening chapter which centre around political pragmatism. Muncie considers the means by which the state's gaze has steadfastly focussed upon blaming parents and 'failed' families, targeting 'incivilities', blurring the boundaries between crime and anti-social behaviour and emphasising 'risk management' and individualised forms of intervention. He identifies an awkward eclecticism combining neo-conservative and left-realist theoretical perspectives and argues that 'numerous criminological themes can be identified in New Labour's reinterpretation and reorganisation of youth justice'.

In Chapter 3, I initially shift the focus from the broader political and criminological analyses to a more specific critical assessment of interventionist priorities. My argument is that effective diversionary strategies have been replaced by policies and practices which emphasise early intervention in the new youth justice. By tracing the primary legislative elements which provide for early intervention, and reviewing key messages from theoretical analyses and empirical research, connections are formed with the opening two chapters and interventionist practices are exposed to critical scrutiny. Some emphasis is placed on the Referral Order as provided by Part 1 of the Youth Justice and Criminal Evidence Act 1999, and fundamental concerns relating to the violation of the child's right to justice are discussed.

Kevin Haines develops and consolidates the critique of the Referral Order and the Youth Offender Panel in Chapter 4 and locates the analysis within a restorative justice context. Haines argues that there is an evident disjuncture between the proposed 'restorative' policies and practices intrinsic to the Referral Order, and the intended outcomes of such interventions. Moreover, he posits that there can be no guarantee that the interests and rights of children will be given due weight within the deliberations of the Youth Offender Panels and herein lie profound tensions with international standards, treaties and rules. Building further upon the primary forms of political analysis that are considered in the opening three chapters, Haines argues that the new restorative approaches are 'more concerned with political objectives than the rights of children' before he concludes by making a number of proposals which might inform a model for a better practice.

Chapter 5 is the first of two chapters which explicitly examines the 'responsibilising' tendencies of the new youth justice. Sue Bandalli explores in detail the means by which the abolition of the long-established rebuttable presumption that a child is *doli incapax*, (as provided by the Crime and Disorder Act 1998), represents a fundamental erosion of legal safeguards in respect of children in criminal proceedings. Bandalli examines both the legal complexities of abolition, and the practical consequences for children and the courts, and she draws attention to the contradictions and inconsistencies between children's rights in civil proceedings and children's responsibilities in the criminal courts. Not dissimilar to Chapters 3 and 4, Bandalli situates her discussion alongside an analysis of international contexts where she considers the UK's conventional obligations and responsibilities in accordance with international standards, treaties and rules.

Mark Drakeford and Kerry McCarthy turn to an examination of parental responsibility in Chapter 6 and argue that the welfarist constructions of family support, treatment and rehabilitation have been supplanted by a set of new youth justice imperatives that emphasise correctional, retributive, punitive and parent-blaming tendencies. By drawing upon research findings, Drakeford and McCarthy contend that coercive responses to perceived parenting deficits are counter-productive, and by engaging a content analysis of pre-sentence reports they raise fundamental questions of justice and legitimacy in relation to the Parenting Orders as provided by the Crime and Disorder Act 1998. The authors conclude by suggesting that whilst the Parenting Orders might suit the government's political objectives they are unlikely to have any significant positive purchase either in off-setting family difficulties or in preventing youth offending.

Nowhere are the punitive dimensions of the new youth justice more visible than in the legal provisions and practical responses that lead to the incarceration of children. In Chapter 7, Sharon Moore develops a persuasive critique of child incarceration contending that it is expensive, damaging and utterly counter-productive. By tracing the key legal provisions of the Crime and Disorder Act 1998, and examining the new arrangements for the management and delivery of incarcerative responses, Moore argues that practices will be 'at loggerheads with the spirit and content of the United Nations Convention on the Rights of the Child' and other international standards, treaties and rules. Equally, by focussing upon the disadvantaged and damaged backgrounds of child remand prisoners, the chapter calls for a 'new agenda' within which the 'Youth Justice Board for England and Wales openly acknowledges that state policy since the early 1990s has been an expensive and damaging failure'.

David Smith examines the origins and development of corporate approaches within youth justice policy and practice alongside an analysis of the emergence and development of crime prevention strategies in Chapter 8. Smith assesses some of the practical difficulties and impediments that confront 'inter-agency co-operation', not least of which are the 'inherent structural and power differentials' between the primary youth justice agencies. The chapter considers 'benevolent' and 'conspiratorial' conceptualisations of corporatism, and, although acknowledging that the 'similarities of punitive policies are more apparent than the differences' between New Labour and the previous Conservative administration, Smith nevertheless detects attempts to recover the relative coherence and success of policies in the late 1980s and early 1990s within the corporatist flavour of the new youth justice at both the central and local levels.

From ministerial and agency corporatism Geoff Monaghan turns his attention to the courts in Chapter 9, where he explicitly develops a number of themes signalled in previous chapters. Monaghan carefully analyses the key implications of the new legislative framework for the courts and whilst recognising that many of the provisions from previous statute 'remain intact', he considers the 'array of new powers and orders' within which he identifies a 'trend towards the primacy of objectives other than the promotion of children's welfare and rights'. Monaghan predicts that increasing numbers of children, particularly black children, will be remanded into custodial settings, a major concern in the light of Moore's chapter, and he recommends practices which may offset this. He then systematically examines what he calls the 'sentencing arena' and the 'custodial arena' and raises a number of penetrating questions of the courts and the new youth justice.

Richard Hester engages with the very meaning of the terms 'youth justice' and 'community safety' in Chapter 10, and he begins to unravel the inherent complexities and tensions both within and between the concepts. Hester proceeds to subject the whole evaluative 'what works' project to critical scrutiny by locating it alongside pressing political imperatives and a 'target' economy. He argues that such a relation inevitably prioritises 'quick-fix' and 'short-term' 'solutions' which in turn displace initiatives with longer-term objectives, and adds that the 'toughness' emphasis so characteristic of the new youth justice is 'paradoxically detrimental to the development of community safety'. Against this difficult backdrop Hester attempts to develop an integrated model which 'synthesises' community safety imperatives and youth justice objectives and in so doing he offers a 'counterpoint to what appears to be an overall punitive and excluding discourse.'

Safer communities will be particularly welcomed by victims of crime and it is fitting that the book concludes with Brian Williams' analysis of the role of victims within the new youth justice. Williams opens Chapter 11 by noting that victims have become a 'politically popular group, and an increasingly powerful one'. By contextualising the burgeoning influence of victims within youth justice policy and practice and drawing upon research findings, Williams examines both the potential benefits and the problems of engaging victims perspectives and victim-oriented practice approaches. The chapter covers key areas of policy and practice including:

reparation orders; action plan orders; supervision orders; report preparation; racially aggravated offences; referral orders and witness protection initiatives. Williams concludes by contending that the potential to develop meaningful reparative approaches to practice are seriously undermined by the retributive and punitive tenor of the new youth justice and he suggests that 'victims have, once again, been cynically used to improve the presentation of punitive criminal justice policies'.

There are differences in content, interpretation and analysis that run across this book. There are also commonalities and coherent themes. Each and all of the contributors offer their reflections in good faith and hope that their collective efforts will make some contribution to enhancing an understanding of youth crime, and perhaps even securing a greater measure of justice for children.

References

Cohen, S., (1972), *Folk Devils and Moral Panics: The Creation of the Mods and Rockers.* New York, St Martin's Press.

Curtis, S., (1999), *Children Who Break the Law or Everybody Does It.* Winchester, Waterside Books.

Goldson, B., (1997), Children in Trouble: State Responses to Juvenile Crime pp124–145 in Scraton, P. *'Childhood' in 'Crisis'?* London, UCL Press.

Goldson, B., (1999), Youth (In)Justice: Contemporary Developments in Policy and Practice in Goldson, B.(Ed.) *Youth Justice: Contemporary Policy and Practice.* Aldershot, Ashgate.

Gouldner, A., (1971), *The Coming Crisis in Western Sociology.* London, Heinemann.

Macpherson, Sir W., (1999), *The Stephen Lawrence Inquiry.* London, The Stationery Office.

Pearson, G., (1983), *Hooligan: A History of Respectable Fears.* London, Macmillan.

Ruxton, S., (1996), *Children in Europe.* London, NCH Action for Children.

CHAPTER 1

The New Youth Justice and the Politics of Electoral Anxiety

John Pitts

Contemporary politics is similarly constrained by an unacknowledged impossibility. Tony Blair and Bill Clinton make minor changes to the style and presentation of public life but leave unanswered broader questions of how society should be governed ... genuine political action is virtually impossible now because capitalism has won the ideological war and nobody is seriously questioning its values or rules. But just like postmodern culture persuades itself that it lives in an age of freedom so politicians mask their limitations with a façade of energetic political activity.

(Slavoj Zizeck, 1999)

We will deliver on our pledge on court delays, just as we are cutting class sizes, reducing waiting lists, helping young people off benefit and into work and building a platform for long term growth and prosperity. We will work tirelessly to build the modern and fairer society that Express readers want.

('How we're fighting teenage tearwaways', Tony Blair,
The Sunday Express, March 7th, 1999)

Introduction

The broad contours of New Labour's youth justice strategy are easily described. It involves the induction of a new, younger population into the youth justice system, via pre-emptive civil measures which target 'incivilities' perpetrated by younger children, and the inadequacies of their parents. Informalism is abandoned in favour of earlier, formal, interventions by the police, via reprimands and final warnings. Diversion from custody into 'integrative' 'alternatives' gives way to community penalties, which may be imposed on a maximum of two occasions. After this, an expanded range of semi-indeterminate custodial penalties may apply. Moreover, the age at which such sentences may be imposed is lowered from 15 to 12.

Organisational unanimity

Above all else, 'New Labour' is a vehicle for the acquisition and retention of political power, and nowhere is this more evident than in its stance on crime and justice. However, in the run-up to the 1997 general election, New Labour's new-found toughness on law and order perplexed many of its supporters, particularly those ranged to the left of the party. The optimists amongst them speculated that, although in the short term political expediency required the Party to disguise its real intentions, it would all be different once they settled into government. This speculation was fuelled by 'winks and nods' from senior frontbench spokespeople to traditionally 'friendly' political and professional audiences. When the time was right, they appeared to be suggesting, New Labour would quietly implement the intelligent and progressive policies which all 'reasonable people' agree would work best.

But these covert assurances were accompanied by an implicit warning that, because any criticism of party policy from 'within' would be read by the party's 'enemies' as disunity or indiscipline, and exploited accordingly, it should be avoided. This attempt to defuse dissent went into overdrive following the 1997 election as 'behind the scenes' Home Office ministers attempted to pressurise or 'cut deals' with potentially critical civil liberties, penal and welfare rights pressure groups. Meanwhile, in the political foreground, the newly New Labour-friendly tabloids and Polly Toynbee, the party's premier broadsheet apologist, strove to keep an increasingly restive party faithful 'onside' by pointing to the government's success in reformulating traditional Labour values in ways which rendered them relevant to the radically changed realities of the modern age.

The real deal

This concerted attempt to persuade the rank and file that things could only get better continued, notwithstanding that, back in Millbank HQ, the in-house psephologists and spin doctors had already determined that a tough line on youth crime should be a central plank of New Labour's criminal justice policy. It was of course true, as shadow ministers never tired of insisting, that in some constituency surgeries, a number of constituents expressed various concerns about youth crime and disorder. However, like Margaret Thatcher, who famously observed that it was not she but 'the people of Britain' who were going to make the 'fight against crime' an issue at the next, (1979), general election, New Labour depicted itself as the only party prepared to respond to 'Middle England's' deepest fears. In reality, of course, it was the voting habits of 'Middle America' rather than the anxieties of 'Middle England' which had pushed the issue of youth crime into poll position as the 1997 election approached.

Following the Labour Party's defeat in the 1992 general election, party strategists turned their attention to the USA where Bill Clinton and his team had 'reinvented' an apparently defunct political party and built, and then held together, a political constituency which would elect it. Indeed, it was only three days after his return from the United States in January 1993, that Tony Blair, by now shadow

Home Secretary, first voiced his now-famous Clintonism: 'tough on crime and tough on the causes of crime', on BBC Radio 4's Today programme, (King and Wickham-Jones, 1999). As Jack Straw was later to confirm:

> *The two governments are learning more from one another all the time. There is now a deep ideological relationship but it is not all one-way traffic.*
>
> (The Observer 1/2/98 p20)

By 1998 the emerging ideological relationship to which Straw referred had coalesced into the *Third Way*. Yet, as many commentators have observed, (see Powell, 1999) what a politics of the third way actually means remains elusive:

> *The big idea is that there is no big idea. Instead, it appears to be used in an eclectic, negative and pragmatic manner. It has been claimed that it is defined like Herbert Morrison's famous definition of socialism, as what a (New) Labour government does. In this sense it is post-ideological and may best be summed up by the New Labour phrase 'what counts is what works'.*
>
> (Powell, 1999)

Nonetheless, within the intellectual and ideological mélange which was third way politics, crime and its control came to assume great symbolic significance. The logic of this, in as much as it can be inferred from the utterances of the Anglo-American centre-left political classes, derives from a particularly hard-nosed analysis of the imperatives of modern political life. This analysis holds that, with the decline in the size of the industrial working class, the diminishing power of the trades unions, and the widescale rejection of the electoral process by the urban poor, modern 'centre-left' parties must build new political constituencies. It follows that, because it is the more prosperous sections of the 'working' and 'middle' classes who remain politically engaged, it is in the suburbs, the small towns and the gentrified urban enclaves that elections will be won and lost. This new constituency of the centre is, the argument runs, 'post-political', in that it has rejected both right and left wing dogmatism, preferring governments which administer the state in accordance with the dictates of common sense, administrative and technical competence and value for money. This is, however, a constituency which, next to job security, is most concerned about the threat of criminal victimisation posed by an expanding 'underclass' which dwells in the 'unemployed ghettos' of the inner city. However, the imperatives of the 'free market' and the fiscal constraints placed upon national governments by the financial markets, (Hutton, 1995), the IMF and the European Central Bank, (Bordieu, 1998), have meant that governments lack both the means and the political mandate to protect society from the social dislocation generated by globalisation, or to embark upon economic and social reform on a scale sufficient to ameliorate the 'urban problem'. In these circumstances, in order to maintain political legitimacy, modern, centre-left governments must be seen to be intervening robustly, efficiently, and effectively, to control the types of low-level crime and the 'incivilities' which the new centre-left constituencies find most threatening to their quality of life and freedom of action.

Kicking 'ass' in Worcester

This was, of course, precisely the electoral strategy which helped secure the presidency for Bill Clinton in 1993 and 1996. Indeed, in 1992, in the midst of the crucial New Hampshire presidential primary campaign, Clinton returned to Arkansas, where he was governor, to personally supervise the execution of Rickey Ray Rector, a brain-damaged Black, double murderer and long-term resident of death row. For Clinton, 'youth crime' in general, and the implicit promise to contain the threat posed by socially and economically marginal African-American and Latino 'ghetto youth' to those in the social and economic 'mainstream', was an electoral hermetic which solidified an otherwise socially disparate political constituency.

John F. Kennedy knew that he could only win the presidency if, like his Republican predecessor Dwight D. Eisenhower, he could win the cities and this meant carrying the 'Black' and the 'blue collar' vote. Thirty years on, Bill Clinton's appeal was to the suburbs, not the cities, because the demographic changes which had occurred in the USA through the 1970s and 1980s meant that most of those who could leave the 'hollowed-out' inner-cities of the USA had done so, leaving behind a residual population of overwhelmingly poor, Black and Latino Americans, most of whom had given up on conventional politics and simply did not vote any more, (Wilson, 1987).

Although such spatial polarisation had not occurred in the UK on anything like the same scale, like Clinton, Tony Blair opted for an electoral strategy of 'suburbanisation'. New Labour calculated that to gain and hold political power they had to win 'Middle England'. Whereas Margaret Thatcher had successfully galvanised 'Essex Man', New Labour believed the key to electoral success lay with 'Worcester Woman'. And if 'Worcester Woman' was to change her voting habits, New Labour strategists reasoned, she must be made to feel that the government would contain the threat posed to her property, person and peace of mind, not to mention the educational opportunities of her children, by the 'roughly spoken', 'badly behaved', young people who haunted the streets of the inner city and the estates on its periphery.

A politics of nostalgia

In its 1997 election campaign New Labour elaborated a vision of the world which would be brought into being by its youth justice and community safety strategies. This was a vision of a 1950s municipal housing estate where fully-employed, skilled, solvent, working class artisans took care of their families and kept their children under control. This was a world of civility and propriety in which a young Jack Straw, for it was he, with the moral support of his admiring neighbours, famously drove a hapless *Mr Whippy* ice-cream salesman from the estate, 'with a flea in his ear', for waking sleeping children with his intrusive amplified bell. This municipal idyll was juxtaposed with images of irredeemable, 'hollowed-out', urban ghettos, and accompanied by grim warnings that this was the future we might expect if we were foolish enough not to vote New Labour. Here was an implicit promise that, if elected, New Labour would instil a new sense of order and discipline into those dwellers in social housing, who were the instigators of urban decline and, of course, their perfidious offspring. At the core of this strategy was the assumption that New Labour could achieve a low-crime future if only it could reassert the social and moral characteristics of a low-crime past.

It's a family affair

As New Labour's election campaign gained impetus, and the contours of its criminal justice and social policies became clearer, it was evident that 'the family', and its capacity to control its children, would have a central role to play. An early signal that the family was to become the target of New Labour's assault upon youth crime was the publication, by the Fabian Society in 1993, of *Crime and the Family* by Utting, Bright and Hendrickson. This booklet cited the *Cambridge Study of Delinquent Development*, undertaken by David Farrington and Donald West between 1961 and 1985, (Farrington and West, 1993), to demonstrate that the origins of youth crime lay within the family. This represented a somewhat selective reading of the data generated by the *Cambridge Study* which is rather more equivocal regarding the impact of 'inconsistent parenting' on youth crime than is commonly supposed. Moreover, although Farrington and West's data specifies some of the factors which correlate with youthful criminality, it does not, in fact, proffer a causal explanation of that criminality. This causal link has been inferred from subsequent commentaries on the *Cambridge* data (see, for example, Graham and Bowling, 1995, Audit Commission, 1996). Nonetheless, the authors of *Crime and the Family* concluded that 'the tangled roots of delinquency lie, to a considerable extent, inside the family'. By 1995, in New Labour circles, the problem of 'irregular' families and the problem of youth crime had become more or less synonymous. In his speech to the Labour Party conference of that year, Tony Blair declared that 'a young country that wants to be a strong country cannot be morally neutral about the family', and promised that he would give a high priority to supporting the family as 'an effective, caring and controlling social unit'.

A speeding flagship: politics, policy and practice

The centrality of 'youth crime' to New Labour's political project meant that it's youth justice legislation hit the statute books in record time. Following a brief consultation period in 1997, which changed very little, the *No More Excuses*

White Paper became the *Crime and Disorder Act* on July 31st, 1998. It took Harold Wilson's government five years to get the *Children and Young Persons Act* (1969) onto the statute books. Mrs Thatcher, her 'law and order' bluster notwithstanding, took three years to enshrine her ideas in the *Criminal Justice Act*, (1982). New Labour did it in 14 months.

The *Crime and Disorder Act*, (1998), epitomised the New Labour project. Its account of the problem attested to the Party's common sense hard-headedness, its commitment to 'evidence-based' solutions demonstrated its adherence to the thoroughly modern precepts of scientific rationality, while the new administrative arrangements were presented as the very model of economy, efficiency and effectiveness.

Centralising power, devolving responsibility

The 1980s had witnessed swingeing cuts in local authority budgets, a substantial redistribution of political power from local to central government and the parallel introduction of 'market forces' into public services, (Jenkins, 1995; Hutton, 1995). In this period, decisions about the goals to which public services should strive, their spending priorities, and the day-to-day conduct of their staff were increasingly taken by central government or the government's appointees in the burgeoning, and largely unaccountable, QUANGOcracy which progressively annexed public services in the 1980s. As the 1997 general election approached, and New Labour's distaste for 'Old Labour' and left-leaning local authorities became apparent, there was considerable speculation about what kind of relationship New Labour might attempt to establish with local government.

Having given its toughness on youth crime the highest possible political profile, New Labour placed responsibility for the realisation of its new youth justice system in the hands of local authority chief executives who were charged with establishing multi-agency Youth Offending Teams (YOTs) and producing a local Youth Justice Plan. However, responsibility for central direction, oversight, the promulgation and enforcement of national standards for youth justice, quality control and the auditing of the YOTs was placed in the hands of a new QUANGO, the Youth Justice Board for England and Wales (YJB). But this apparent shift of 'youth justice' from a political to an administrative arena did not, as those on the left of the Labour Party had hoped, signal a softening of the government's stance on youth crime. On the contrary, the political imperatives which had informed the policies now came to infuse the administration of the new youth justice. The YJB was composed of an advisory Board of public figures and senior justice system experts, chaired by a newly created Labour Lord, Lord Warner of Brockley, who moved swiftly from being Jack Straw's professional adviser on youth crime to this new post. The Board was serviced by a senior Treasury civil servant, Mark Perfect, who was also joint author of the Audit Commission's report on youth justice, *Misspent Youth*, (1996), which had, in effect, described the administrative contours for the new youth justice. The YJB employed regional advisors who worked to promote 'best practice' in the local authorities which were to 'deliver' the Act.

Thus, when New Labour handed responsibility for Youth Justice to local authorities it was handing them an additional administrative task rather than additional political authority. It was establishing a 'steering and rowing relationship', in which the local authorities rowed and central government in the shape of the YJB, emphatically steered, (Crawford, 1997). Political and strategic responsibilities, which in a previous era had been held by local government, now rested with the YJB which was accountable, via its chair, to the Home Secretary. Cynics might argue, of course, that such an arrangement is also politically attractive because it enables ministers to claim any successes for themselves while laying any failures at the door of local authorities, few of which were regarded as 'friends' of New Labour in the first place.

Managerialist governance

New Labour was quick to appropriate both the language and the technology of the new managerialism. Its emphasis upon the rationality of 'what works', 'joined-up solutions' and 'empowerment' fitted well with its avowed commitment to rational public policy and a 'communitarian' devolution of power to 'local people'. But the central appeal of the new managerialism was that it offered a template for a new form of governance in which a more restricted role for government as a provider of services was paralleled by a more extensive role in specifying the nature and aims of those services. However, having relinquished direct control for services, it was found that ministers and senior civil servants' under constant pressure from the Prime Minister and his inner circle to achieve a mounting list of 'targets', tended to grow very anxious.

Andrew Cooper and Julian Lousada, (2000), have argued that anxieties about the maintenance of political legitimacy and electoral credibility engendered by this new form of governance, leads to an unprecedented concern with policy implementation. As a result, it is described in such detail by central government departments that what, at first sight, might appear to be an exercise in the devolution of power appears, upon closer inspection, to be a franchising operation. Thus, 'product support' is provided via a steady flow of 'evidence-based' data about 'what works' and the results of 'pilot studies' of new administrative arrangements and court orders, while 'quality control' is vouchsafed by statutory audit.

In handing new responsibilities to local authorities and local multi-agency partnerships, the *Crime and Disorder Act*, (1998), prescribed the goals they should pursue, the structures they should erect, the intervention techniques they should develop, the targets they should achieve and the timescales in which they should achieve them. To this end, on the 7th March, 1999, Tony Blair announced new national targets for youth court delays in *The Sunday Express*, observing that whereas '(some) young offenders could wait months between arrest and sentence with an average delay of 142 days', the government's 'aim as a first step this year is to hit our target of 72 days for persistent offenders in 50 per cent of cases.' It was, of course, the local authorities, the police and the courts who were responsible, on pain of financial sanctions, for achieving these targets.

The incorporation of conflict

Anxieties about controlling systems which, while central to the political legitimacy of governments, are outside their day to day control also find expression in an unwillingness to tolerate any conflict within systems. This is a particular problem in the case of the youth justice system which, like all justice systems, exists precisely to provide a site upon which conflict can be enacted. The essence of this conflict is carved above the main entrance to the Central Criminal Court at the Old Bailey, in London. And it reads:

> *Defend the Children of the Poor and Punish the Wrongdoer*

This 'mission-statement', as we might now describe it, appears to recognise that, overwhelmingly, it will be the children of the poor who pass through the youth justice system and that, even though they might also be the 'wrongdoer', they will often need to be defended, not simply in the strict legal sense but also because in the world of crime and justice, they will be more vulnerable in a multiplicity of ways, (Goldson, 1997). Traditionally, the role of law has been to organise social expectations. It strives to render the world more predictable, manageable and therefore amenable to hard and fast judgements. The traditional role of the social welfare component of youth justice, by contrast, has been to respond to unpredictable, messy and invariably complex, human situations. The law generates certainties while the stock in trade of social welfare should be uncertainty. Thus a core task of youth justice systems throughout the world has been to provide a space where these two discourses, one concerning the establishment and reaffirmation of social expectations, rights and responsibilities, and the other concerning responses to, and the management of, a complex and sometimes chaotic social reality, can enter into dialogue and an argument; a place where the competing claims of rules and needs, guilt and suffering, justice and welfare can be confronted.

Yet New Labour's new youth justice appears to be built upon an assumption that the political, legal, managerial and professional imperatives of the multiplicity of agencies and actors who constitute the contemporary youth justice system are of a piece; that they are merely interlocking components of a complex whole which, when fitted together correctly by a competent manager, will 'deliver' an optimal and uncontentious youth justice system.

The reality of the youth justice system of England and Wales at the beginning of the 21st century is of youth justice policies, which are fashioned by governments with an eye to their political legitimacy and electoral advantage. Policing is, as always, shaped by police perceptions of disreputability, (Smith, 1984, Marlow, 1999) and leavened by Home Office performance indicators and league tables, and a series of high profile 'scandals'. Youth court magistrates, like police officers, operate in accordance with their personal lay criminologists, and their perceptions of the nature of the problem of crime in the neighbourhoods in which they sit. These necessarily idiosyncratic views tend to be reflected in their sentencing, (Parker et al., 1989). With the introduction of market forces into public services, 'correctional' agencies have taken to making ever bolder claims for their correctional interventions; as have the academic criminologists who market the intellectual nostrum which underpin their endeavours, (Young, 1999; Pitts, 2000). Meanwhile, the professionals employed by correctional agencies must struggle to square an essentially 'person-centred', professional ethos with their involvement in and increasingly 'output' driven youth justice system.

There are inevitable tensions in such a system, as the organisations, agencies, and professionals pursue their legitimate but different, and not infrequently incompatible goals, which reflect their different ethical, legal and administrative responsibilities and, importantly, the different interests represented within the system. However, New Labour finds such conflict uncomfortable and threatening, and so it acts as if such conflicts have been 'designed out' of the new youth justice system it has brought into being.

Those who criticise the new arrangements, like the heads of the large voluntary child care agencies who refused to tender for the contracts to administer the government's new Secure Training Centres on the grounds that they were ill-considered, ill-conceived, politically inspired and inimical to the interests, and a threat to the well-being, of the troubled younger offenders for whom they were designed, get particularly short shrift. Indeed, on hearing these criticisms, a senior figure in the YJB publicly opined that these people should 'grow up' and get to grips with the political realities of what New Labour aficionados have taken to calling 'the real world'.

A 'bureaucratic social science'

One important source of conflict within, and around youth justice systems is that between a legal/administrative perception of the problems to which the system is a response, and those proffered by the social sciences. New Labour's new youth justice strategy has striven to erase important distinctions between political, managerial, intellectual and professional imperatives and, in the process, the range of ideas and theories which may be operationalised, and the range of professional practices which may be deployed, is sharply reduced. Now, it appears that only the least contentious, commonsensical theories of causality, the research findings and professional practices sanctioned by the Home Office and the YJB may inform the practices of the YOTs and the interventions of local community safety partnerships. The appeal of these 'theories' and practices for New Labour is fairly clear. In a time when politicians are unwilling to countenance robust social and economic intervention to counter social problems, and eager to demonstrate that they are 'tough on crime', an analysis which identifies poor child-rearing practices and weak parental control as the fundamental problem, and a strategy which targets families and classroom regimes and their capacity to inculcate self-control in unruly and disruptive children and, moreover, resonates closely with the moral sensibilities of New Labour's new constituencies in Middle England, is a political godsend.

The 'new' professional practices in the form of cognitive-behavioural treatment, reparation and mediation and mentoring all strive to make good those deficits in the behaviour, beliefs and attitudes of individual offenders and their parents, and to instil in them a new, disciplined, capacity for self-regulation. And while it is, of course, true that at some times, in some places, with some people, these practices have 'worked', their incorporation into policy is determined not by their demonstrable efficacy but by pre-scientific, ideological imperatives. Indeed, it often appears that it is the political project, to which these measures lend an air of scientific and technological proficiency, which is paramount, and around which the science and technology has had to fit. As C. Wright Mills reminds us, the subordination of science to governance, to produce what Jack Straw is pleased to call 'all the serious research', has a long pedigree. Writing in the 1950s, when the type of social science discussed here was at its zenith, he observes:

> *The New Social Science refers not only to abstracted empiricism but also to the new and illiberal practicality. The phrase refers to both method and use and quite correctly so; for the technique of abstracted empiricism and its bureaucratic use are now regularly joined. It is my contention that, so joined, they are resulting in a bureaucratised social science.*
>
> (C. Wright Mills, 1959)

Electoral anxiety

Ironically, of course, as a result of the anxiety which pervades its ranks, New Labour's new finely-tuned, scientistic 'evidence-based' structures can be subverted at a stroke if the opinion polls mirror back that the party, or its leader, is no longer regarded by the electorate as 'the fairest of them all'. Having snatched the issue of law and order from the Tories, New Labour has been desperate not to be shunted back into the political ghetto of penal reform where it languished for two decades. When the spin-doctors decree that a burst of vote-catching toughness is required from government ministers, the precepts of scientific management go 'onto the back burner'. Thus in 1999, the Home Secretary suddenly introduced Michael Howard's 'three strikes and out' sentencing policy for juvenile burglars, notwithstanding that it had been a spectacular failure in the USA. For all the talk of radicalism, newness and rationality, the default setting of New Labour's new youth justice is 'discipline' and, faced with electoral anxiety, it is to discipline that it reverts.

The new youth crime

The new politics of youth justice notwithstanding, contemporary youth crime presents us with problems undreamt of when the theories of delinquent causality and the technologies for its correction, which inform the Crime and Disorder Act, (1998), first saw the light of day. In February, 1999, the gap between the Gross Domestic Product of the poorest and the richest regions in the UK was the widest in the European Union. Between 1981 and 1991 the average household income of families in social housing in the UK fell from 79 per cent to 45 per cent of the national average. By 1995, over 50 per cent of council households had no bread-winner. By 1997, 20 per cent of the children and young people in the UK lived in these neighbourhoods, (Dean, 1997).

This remarkable redistribution of wealth was paralleled by an equally remarkable redistribution of crime and victimisation. Successive British Crime Surveys show that council and housing association tenants are amongst the most heavily victimised people in the UK, (Hope, 1994). In the areas of highest victim-isation, young people are heavily represented as both victims and perpetrators. Here, the crime is implosive and symmetrical, perpetrated by and against local residents. It is repetitive, the same people tend to be victimised again and again, and their victimisation is more likely to be violent. This crime is also more likely to be drug-related, if not drug induced, than crime in other areas because it is in these neighbourhoods that opiate addiction has taken hold, (Pearson, 1988). This is, of course, the crime profile which characterises what are now called 'winner-loser societies', in which a conglomeration of mutually-reinforcing social problems are increasingly concentrated in impoverished neighbourhoods. The Americans call it ghettoisation.

Notwithstanding Jack Straw's assertions about the primacy of the family in the onset of youth offending, what the 'serious research' actually reveals is that whereas in medium and high socio-economic status (SES) neighbourhoods, family-related risk factors are fair predictors of future criminality, in low socio-economic status neighbourhoods, 'neighbourhood factors' will often overwhelm the best efforts of the best parents. Wikstrom and Loeber, (1997), in their exem-plary Pittsburgh study, found that in the lowest SES neighbourhoods, youngsters with very low or no familial risk factors were involved in serious crime. Indeed, it appears that in these areas the correlation between familial risk-factors and youth offending breaks down. This is the reality which must be managed if New Labour is to make a dent on the worsening problem of youth crime and youth victimisation in the UK at the beginning of the 21st century.

Conclusion

Not least of the ironies of the New Labour project is that, while it presents itself as the party of the 'future', in its criminal justice policies it finds its precedents for action in the past. A concern with the past, a willingness to learn from it, and a commitment to preserve that which is true and beautiful about it, is utterly commendable. However, the seismic social and cultural shifts through which we are living pose crucial questions about how we are to absorb a rising generation of socially and economically marginal children and young people into this radically changed world. More than ever before, and perhaps more than anything else, we need to counter the myopic banality at the heart of such populist youth justice policies with a perspective and a politics which recognises the need to offer the children and young people on the social margins who get caught up in the youth justice system, a political status, a stake in, and a hand in, shaping their futures. Founded upon the principles of inclusivity, reciprocity, appreciation, tolerance and a positive indifference to difference, such an approach to children and young people on the social margins, backed by economic, social, criminal justice and employment policies which also embody these values, would quickly prove itself superior to New Labour's nostalgic attempt to recover an imagined past in which there were only good and bad children and commonsensical ways of making the bad ones behave themselves.

References

Audit Commission, (1996), *Misspent Youth*, London, The Audit Commission.

Bordieu, P., (1998), *Acts of Resistance: Against the New Myths of Our Time,* Cambridge, Polity Press.

Cooper, A. and Lousada, J., (2000), *The Meaning of Welfare*, London, Venture Press.

Crawford, A., (1997), *The Local Governance of Crime: Appeals to Community and Partnerships*, Oxford, Clarendon.

Dean, M., (1997), Tipping the Balance, *Search*, No. 27, Spring, York, Joseph Rowntree Foundation.

Farrington, D., (1996), *Understanding and Preventing Youth Crime*, York, Joseph Rowntree Foundation.

Farrington, D. and West, D., (1993), Criminal, Penal and Life Histories of Chronic Offenders: Risk and Protective Factors and Early Identification, *Criminal Behaviour and Mental Health*, 3, pp 492–523

Goldson, B., (1997), Children, Crime, Policy and Practice: Neither Welfare nor Justice, *Children and Society,* Vol.11 pp 77–88.

Graham, J. and Bowling, B., (1995), *Young People and Crime*, London, Home Office.

Hope, T., (1994), *Communities, Crime and Inequality in England and Wales*, Paper presented to the 1994 Cropwood Round Table Conference, *Preventing Crime and Disorder*, Sept. 14–15, Cambridge.

Hutton, W., (1995), *The State We're In*, London, Jonathan Cape.

Jenkins, S., (1995), *Accountable to None: the Tory Nationalisation of Britain*, London, Hamish Hamilton.

King, D. and Wickham-Jones, M., (1999), Bridging the Atlantic: The Democratic (Party) Origins of Welfare to Work, Powell M., (Ed.), *New Labour, New Welfare State: The Third Way in British Social Policy*, Bristol, The Policy Press.

Marlow, A., (1999), Youth, Minorities, Drugs and Policing: a Study of Stop and Search, Marlow, A. and Pearson, G., (Eds.), (1999), *Young People, Drugs and Community Safety*, Lyme Regis, Russell House Publishing.

Mills, C. W., (1959), *The Sociological Imagination*, Harmondsworth, Penguin.

Parker, H., Sumner, M. and Jarvis, G., (1989), *Unmasking the Magistrates*, Milton Keynes, Open University Press.

Pearson, G., (1987), *The New Heroin Users*, London, Batsford.

Pitts, J., (2000), *The New Politics of Youth Crime*, Basingstoke, Macmillan.

Powell, M., (Ed.), *New Labour, New Welfare State: The Third Way in British Social Policy*, Bristol, The Policy Press.

Smith, D., (1984), *Police and People in London*, London, Policy Studies Institute.

Utting, W., Bright, J. and Hendrickson, P., (1993), *Crime and the Family*, London Fabian Society.

Wikstrom, K. and Loeber, R., (1997), Individual Risk factors, Neighbourhood SES and Juvenile Offending, Tonry, M., (Ed.), *The Handbook of Crime and Punishment*, New York, Oxford University Press.

Wilson, W. J., (1987), *The Truly Disadvantaged: the Inner City, the Underclass and Public Policy*, Chicago, University of Chicago Press.

Young, J., (1999), *The Exclusive Society*, London, Sage Publications.

Zizeck, S., (1999), Attempts to Escape the Logic of Capitalism, *London Review of Books, Vol. 21, 28th October pp. 3–7.*

CHAPTER 2

Pragmatic Realism? Searching for Criminology in the New Youth Justice

John Muncie

Introduction

The 1998 Crime and Disorder Act has been described by sections of the media as 'the biggest shake-up for 50 years in tackling crime', (*The Guardian*, 26 September, 1997) and by some academics as 'a veritable paradigm shift in the discourse of social control', (Charman and Savage, 1999, p192). The now familiar New Labour soundbite, 'tough on crime, tough on the causes of crime' does indeed seem to herald a dramatic shift in emphasis away from an exclusionary punitive justice and towards an inclusionary restorative justice capable of recognising the social contexts in which crime occurs and should be dealt with. In addition, the repeated claims that previous law and order policies have failed, that 'enough is enough', and that there will now be 'no more excuses', holds the promise that a 'line can be drawn under the past' and a new era of rational policy and practice ushered in.

Close inspection of the Crime and Disorder Act however reveals as much continuity with the past as it does divergences. Firstly, a familiar blaming of irresponsible parents, together with the requirement that offenders should be held personally responsible for their actions, are the key persistent themes underpinning both Conservative and New Labour assessments of crime causation. However, initially at least, Labour's approach did seem prepared to open the debate to acknowledge the relevance of such social contexts as unemployment and recession.

Secondly, there are distinct continuities in the insistence that incivilities such as begging, rowdyism, nuisance neighbours, should be as much a target as crime itself. But whereas the Conservatives were reluctant to legislate on such matters for fear of undermining the sacred principle of individual freedom, New Labour has placed notions of anti-social behaviour on a statutory basis.

Thirdly, much has been made of New Labour's chosen pathway to control crime through crime prevention and community safety rather than a 'prison works' deterrence. Yet it was the Conservatives in the late 1980s who recognised that the criminal justice agencies could not be expected to control crime alone.

They too, at least up to 1993, advocated more community ownership of the problem through partnerships and multi-agency collaboration.

Finally, Labour has continued with a growing disillusionment with traditional rehabilitative justifications for criminal justice in favour of pragmatic assessments of risk management. Criminal justice over the past ten years has become more and more dominated by 'evidence-based' research whereby the problem of crime is to be managed, rather than necessarily resolved. Moral debate about the purpose of intervention has been shifted to the sidelines in the search for 'value for money' and cost-effective, measurable outcomes.

This chapter explores the traces of criminological theory and research that underpin and inform the 1998 Crime and Disorder Act. As we have already seen, many of these traces might be found in those elements of neo-conservative criminology that informed the Conservatives' reforming agenda from 1979 to 1997. There are, however, significant diversions from this orthodoxy, emanating in part from a left realist school of criminology, which came to fruition in the early 1980s. As a result, as in many other areas of New Labour's public and social policy there is a distinct merging and borrowing from both left and right in an attempt to mark out a distinctive 'third way'. But in criminological terms it is a borrowing from those theories and perspectives which clearly occupy one particular and narrow terrain in the criminological agenda: that of realist criminologies.

Realist criminologies

Against a backcloth of spiralling recorded crime rates, industrial unrest and urban disorders, Conservative politicians in the 1970s and 1980s depicted crime as the outcome of a broader decline in moral values. In Britain and the United States 'law and order' was a key electoral issue, which fuelled and fed off a growing public concern for, and fear of, crime. Both Reaganism and Thatcherism's rise to power were built on an appeal to the logic of social authoritarianism, in which free market economics, reduced state welfare intervention and increased state punitive intervention were paramount. The most manifest outcome of such economic and political doctrines was long-term unemployment, economic marginalisation of particular groups and attempts to reduce crime by strengthening the deterrent impact of the criminal justice system. Within this context, police powers were extended, tougher sentencing options were given to the courts and the use of imprisonment expanded, so that by the 1980s the United States could claim the highest incarceration rate in the world and Britain the highest in Western Europe. On both sides of the Atlantic the rhetoric of the radical right presented a popularly received picture that criminality was freely chosen – a course of action taken by pathological individuals with no self or parental control and who threatened the very moral fabric of society. Public political debate about crime came to be focused almost exclusively on images of youth lawlessness in which it made no sense to treat or rehabilitate offenders, but merely secure the means for their vindictive punishment. Neo-conservative 'realist' criminologists, such as Van den Haag, (1975) and Wilson, (1975), departed from the prevailing liberal consensus by simply claiming that crime emanates from wicked, evil people who are insufficiently deterred from their actions by a criminal justice system deemed to be chaotic and ineffective. Thus, in their view, the only remedy lay in the strengthening of penal sanctions.

The almost wholesale capture of the political terrain of law and order by the 'new right' did nevertheless force sections of the left to rethink their position, and to move closer to the mainstream in an attempt to counter some of its more reactionary policies. In particular, a school of left realism attempted to formulate alternative law and order policies in which crime would be 'taken seriously' and recognised as a problem that disproportionately affects the most vulnerable in the community, (Lea and Young, 1984). Politically, this necessitated the forging of alliances with centrist Labour or Democratic parties and the overcoming of any latent reluctance for those on the left to become engaged in day-to-day issues of crime and criminal justice policy. Such sentiments clearly impacted upon New Labour discourse as it sought to convince those communities that suffer most from street and property crime that it was prepared to act in their interests.

'Realist' criminologies, whether of the right or the left, claim their legitimacy by arguing that they are rational responses to a perceived intensity in the public's fear of crime. They take an increase in crime and an increase in fear for granted. As a result, they concentrate more on those crimes which have been made visible through media and political concern like youth crime, street crime, violence and burglary, than on those crimes that are rendered largely invisible, including corporate corruption and health and safety crimes, or those 'crimes' and 'violences' perpetrated by the state, such as genocide and the denial of basic human rights. Similarly, they are more concerned with developing effective measures of crime control and prevention, rather than exploring issues concerned with the power to criminalise and how it is that only certain harmful acts are defined as crime whilst the invisibility of more serious harms, like poverty, malnutrition, pollution and so on, is maintained, (Muncie, 2000). Indeed, it has been claimed that the import of 'realism', whether left or right, necessarily narrows the crime debate by their broad acceptance of legal definitions of crime, (Cohen, 1988, p9). As a result, the focus remains solely on those visible, intra-class and youthful crimes of the street. However, there are certain crucial differences between left and right realism. Whilst both are critical of utopianism and claim to be simply responding to increased levels of public fear, left realism insists that neo-conservatism is part of the problem, and not its solution. Both share an understanding that crime fundamentally involves moral choice. For right realism such 'choice' is driven by failures in parental and self-control. For left realism a range of 'restricting circumstances' such as marginalization and relative deprivation always mitigates moral choice. As a result, while right realism prioritizes order through exclusionary and retributive means of crime control, left realism seeks social justice and inclusion via community based crime prevention. Merging these polar views is just one of the many contradictions to be found in New Labour's reforming programme.

Causes of crime 1: irresponsibility and the parenting deficit

The single most important factor in explaining criminality is the quality of a young person's home life, including parental supervision.

(Home Office, 1997b, p5)

Recognising that there are underlying causes of crime is in no way to excuse or condone offending. Individuals must be held responsible for their own behaviour, and must be brought to justice and punished when they commit an offence.

(Straw and Michael, 1996, p6)

Tony Blair first coined the 'realist' slogan 'tough on the causes of crime' in January 1993 in an attempt to wrestle the law and order agenda away from the Conservatives. Since then, New Labour has continually promised that its policies would be based on a recognition of the underlying causes of crime. These 'causes' were first spelt out in detail in the consultation document, *Tackling the Causes of Crime*, (Straw and Michael, 1996). The key social and economic conditions of crime were then considered to be parenting, truancy, drug abuse, lack of facilities for young people, homelessness, unemployment, low income and recession. However, a year later, when the White Paper *No More Excuses* was published, these 'causes' were significantly contracted to provide a more limited focus on parenting, truancy and peer groups. Now the key factors were deemed to be: being male, being brought up by criminal parents, living in a family with multiple problems, poor parental discipline, school exclusion and associating with delinquent friends, (Home Office, 1997b, p5).

A major preoccupation with the family and crime has dominated Labour's legislative initiatives. This rather narrow interpretation of crime causation is in no small part derived from multi-variate correlational analyses, which have identified the quality of parent-child relationships as a key 'risk factor' in the onset of offending, (Graham and Bowling, 1995). A major influence has been the empirical longitudinal study of 'delinquent families' that has been conducted by the Cambridge Institute of Criminology since the 1960s, (Farrington and West, 1990). In 1961 a sample group of 411 working class (mainly white) boys aged eight was selected from six primary schools in Camberwell, London. They were contacted seven times over the next 24 years to examine which of them had developed a 'delinquent way of life' and why some had continued a 'life of crime' into adulthood. About a fifth of the sample had been convicted of criminal offences as juveniles and over a third by the time they were 32. But half of the total convictions were amassed by only 23 young men – less than six per cent of the sample. Most of these 'chronic offenders' shared common childhood character-istics. They were more likely to have been rated as troublesome, impulsive and dishonest at primary school. They tended to come from poorer, larger families and were more likely to have 'criminal parents'. They also had experienced harsh or erratic parental discipline. Six variables were eventually suggested as predictors of future criminality, (Farrington, 1996):

- socio-economic deprivation (e.g. low family income/poor housing)
- poor parenting and family conflict
- criminal and anti-social families
- low intelligence and school failure
- hyperactivity/impulsivity/attention deficiency
- anti-social behaviour (e.g. heavy drinking, drug taking, promiscuous sex)

Within this seemingly broad range of social and personality 'risk factors', a particular reading of 'failed families' becomes central:

> *... children from poorer families are likely to offend because they are less able to achieve their goals legally and because they value some goals (e.g. excitement) especially highly. Children with low intelligence are more likely to offend because they tend to fail in school. Impulsive children ... are more likely to offend because they do not give sufficient consideration and weight to the possible consequences. Children who are exposed to poor child rearing behaviour, disharmony or separation on the part of their parents are likely to offend because they do not build up internal controls over socially disapproved behaviour, while children from criminal families and those with delinquent friends tend to build up anti-authority attitudes and the belief that offending is justifiable. The whole process is self-perpetuating ...*
>
> (Farrington, 1994, pp558–9)

Using the same sample, Farrington, Barnes and Lambert, (1996), subsequently maintained that if children had a convicted parent by the time they were ten then that was the 'best predictor' of them becoming criminal and anti-social them-selves. Criminal behaviour, it was argued, was transmitted from parents to children; crime runs in the family.

Despite the emphasis given to choice, this theme of a 'parenting deficit' also continually surfaces in neo-conservative criminology. For example, James Q. Wilson, a political scientist who served on numerous presidential task forces and advisory commissions on crime in the United States, has consistently opposed the view that crime has social or economic causes. He has argued forcibly that poverty is not related to crime because the most dramatic increase in recorded crime occurred during the period of post war economic growth and relative prosperity in the United States. Criminality is simply accounted for by the existence of 'lower class' people who, 'attach little importance to the opinion of others'; are 'preoccupied with the daily struggle for survival'; and are 'inclined to uninhibited, expressive conduct', (Wilson, 1975, p 41–2).

In a later work, *Crime and Human Nature*, Wilson and Herrnstein, (1985), conclude a lengthy survey of causal and correlational factors by arguing that 'personality traits' such as impulsiveness and lack of regard for others are key factors in criminality. But significantly it is in 'discordant families' that these traits are largely to be found. However, it is also stressed that criminality rests on choice: a choice, mediated by the perceived consequences of the costs and benefits of such action. In a similar vein Gottfredson and Hirschi, (1990), contended that the key factor underlying criminal behaviour is lack of self control. In turn, self control derives from factors affecting calculation of the consequences of one's acts and most crucially on effective socialisation. Thus the major 'causes' of low self control, it is argued, are ineffective child rearing, poor parental supervision, working mothers and broken families, in short, a lack of discipline in the home.

However, as Labour's new approach revealed, notions of 'responsible parenting' and the dangers of a 'parenting deficit' need not be confined to Conservative ideologues. On coming to power Tony Blair argued:

> *We cannot say we want a strong and secure society when we ignore its very foundations: family life. This is not about preaching to individuals about their private lives. It is addressing a huge social problem ... Nearly 100,000 teenage pregnancies every year; elderly parents with whom families cannot cope; children growing up without role models they can respect and learn from; more and deeper poverty; more crime; more truancy; more neglect of educational opportunities, and above all more unhappiness. Every area of this government's policy will be scrutinised to see how it affects family life. Every policy examined, every initiative tested, every avenue explored to see how we strengthen our families.*
>
> (*The Guardian*, 1 October, 1997).

In this rhetoric strong families fit the traditional image of conjugal, heterosexual parents with an employed male breadwinner. Single parenting and absent fathers are key harbingers of social disorder. Indeed, one of Labour's key formative influences in defining a 'third way', Etzioni's communitarian agenda, also emphasises that the root cause of crime lies within the home and that it is in the domestic sphere that the shoring up of our moral foundations should begin, (Etzioni, 1995, p11). It is such a communitarianism which speaks of parental responsibility and moral obligation that clearly lies at the heart of Labour's reforming agenda, (Hughes, 1996, p21). As a result, concerns over irresponsibility and lack of parental discipline underpin many of the powers of the 1998 Act.

Causes of crime 2: the underclass and social exclusion

There is no more dreadful testimony to the last decade and a half than the position of the young unemployed and never employed. This lost generation is adrift from the working population, with no stake in society but with the same material aspirations as their contemporaries, and can easily become alienated from society.

(Straw and Michael, 1996, p12)

Notions of a parenting deficit are also clearly present in 'new right' versions of underclass theory. The American social policy analyst, Charles Murray, in his influential work *Losing Ground*, (1984), argued that much of the federal welfare system should be abolished because it encourages state dependency and feck-lessness and undermines communal sources of social solidarity. In particular, he maintained that welfare benefits have enabled young mothers to live independ-ently of fathers and thus increasing numbers of young people have grown up without viable male role models. This culture is then passed on to the next gener-ation. Young men who by nature are 'essentially barbarians' until they are civilised by marriage turn to drugs and crime and a vicious circle is created. For Murray, it is not poverty or unemployment that creates an underclass, but rather the 'affluence' and independence afforded to young women through their welfare entitlement.

In 1990 Murray applied this argument to the situation in Britain and claimed that increasing rates of illegitimacy, violent crime and drop-out from the labour force were clear signs that an underclass was emergent. These three factors, he argued, were intimately related:

... when large numbers of young men don't work, the communities around them break down, just as they break down when large numbers of young unmarried women have babies ... Men who do not support families find other ways to prove that they are men, which tend to take various destructive forms ... young males are essentially barbarians for whom marriage – meaning not just the wedding vows but the act of taking responsibility for a wife and children – is an indispensable civilising force. Young men who don't work don't make good marriage material. Often they don't get married at all; when they do they haven't the ability to fill their traditional role. In either case, too many of them remain barbarians.

(Murray, 1990, p37)

In a subsequent analysis Murray, (1994), focused more directly on illegitimacy. The restoration of the two-parent family, through marriage, he argued, was the only way to ensure the survival of 'free institutions and a civil society'. His view of Britain in the mid 1990s was even bleaker than that presented earlier. Noting an increasing rate of illegitimacy throughout British society, but particularly in the working classes, he conjured up a future vision of increasing segregation between the 'New Victorians', characterised by a levelling off of illegitimacy among the upper middle classes, and the 'New Rabble', characterised by increasing rates of illegitimacy among the working classes. Affluent, well-educated sections of the population will edge back towards traditional morality; poorer sections will continue to degenerate into an underclass characterized by more crime, more widespread drug addiction, fewer marriages and more unemployment. As before, Murray's solution to this 'crisis' was to reduce welfare benefit levels for single, unmarried mothers in order to encourage the avoidance of pregnancy for those women who have no husband.

In Britain this analysis was largely shared by such self styled 'ethical socialists' as Norman Dennis and George Erdos. They argued that children from 'fatherless families' would grow up without appropriate role models and supervision and would thus reduce their own chances of becoming competent parents. For Dennis and Erdos, (1992) it is 'commonsense' that family breakdown and rising crime will go hand in hand. Indeed, an image of wilfully negligent parents colluding with, or even encouraging, misbehaviour was popularised by the Conservatives in the 1980s as the inevitable result of a 1960s permissive culture. A breakdown of the nuclear family unit, high divorce rates and increases in single parenting, it was argued, were the root causes of a moral decay epitomised by increased crime rates, homelessness and drug taking. In addition, excessive welfare dependency had encouraged families to rely on state benefits rather than each other. In the process children's moral development had been eroded.

However, whilst for observers on the right the underclass is young, homeless, criminal and welfare dependent, for some of those on the left the 'underclass' is a pejorative label to describe those who have been systematically excluded from the labour market. They point out that a succession of such labels has been consistently attached to the poorest members of society in order to mark them out as either politically dangerous or as marginal outsiders – from the 'undeserving poor', 'dangerous classes' and 'social outcasts' of the nineteenth century to the 'culture of poverty ', 'scroungers' and 'workshy' of the twentieth, (Mann, 1991). Broadly speaking, 'the left' has employed the term 'underclass' to emphasise industrial decline, recession, political marginalisation and deprivation. It is not welfare dependency, but cuts in welfare provision, the widening of class differentials and the exclusion of the poor that account for the existence of an underclass, (Jordan, 1996).

Indeed, there is now convincing international evidence of a direct relationship between economic circumstances and rates of crime, (Pyle, 1998). Dickinson, (1995), for example, notes that in periods of relatively full employment, pre-1970, there may be little statistical relationship between crime and unemployment rates, but that after 1970, when unemployment began to rise, recorded crime exhibits cyclical fluctuations in line with the numbers out of work. Moreover, for certain crimes, such as domestic burglary committed by men under the age of 25, there appears to be a close and contemporaneous relationship with unemployment levels. Dickinson concludes that whilst this is no simple relationship, being out of work must be regarded as a major factor motivating crime. Field's, (1990), Home Office research also argued that economic factors have a major influence on trends in property and personal crime. Using levels of personal consumption, (i.e. the amount that people spend on average during a year), he found that when personal consumption falls, property crimes rise. Conversely, when consumption levels rise, so do personal offences. What this research suggests is that it is not absolute poverty or deprivation that necessarily causes crime, but a sudden loss of income or increasing levels of social inequality between the 'haves' and 'have-nots'.

Advocates of left realism have most forcefully promoted this notion of 'relative deprivation'. Access to the labour market is seen as vital to the working class in general, and a black 'underclass', in particular. When such access is denied, young people in particular are pushed to the margins of society, as peripheral to the economic process of production and consumption and to the political process of democratic representation. Whilst rejecting any direct causal link between deprivation and crime, Lea and Young, (1984, p81) stress that it is the *perception* of injustice, when expectations are not met by real opportunities, that is central. This situation is used to explain the assumed growth of street crime and disorder amongst the most relatively deprived section of the working class, namely young, inner city, African-Caribbean males, (Lea and Young, 1984, p 166).

Again, there are limited traces of such an approach in New Labour discourse and policy, (Charman and Savage, 1999, p197; Brownlee, 1998, pp318–21). Measures to assist single parents back to work, to tackle social exclusion, to provide a universal nursery education, to prevent drug use through education classes in primary schools and to ensure all 18–24 year olds are either in work, education or training have all been justified as 'ways of helping to tackle the roots of juvenile crime', (Home Office, 1997b, p10). But as Hope, (1998) notes, Labour's crime prevention legislation generally 'fails to acknowledge, let alone provide a means to tackle the social roots of disorder'. The risks associated with poverty, poor housing and income inequality are significant in their absence. New Labour appropriates only one part of left realism's dictum that crime involves 'moral choice in certain restricting circumstances', (Young, 1994, p109). Therefore, a key plank of left realism is ignored. Moreover, Labour's logic of 'compulsory inclusion' has strong authoritarian undertones. The welfare to work 'new deal' is designed to take a quarter of a million under 25 year olds off the dole but stipulates that if claimants refuse to take up the proposed employment and training options they will lose all right to claim welfare benefits. The general right to welfare benefit for 16 to 18 year olds had of course already been removed in 1988. Further, the withdrawal of benefit for those who fail to comply with community sentences, announced in the 1999 Queen's Speech, heralds a further negation that poverty and immiseration may be significant factors in continued offending.

The welfare to work strategy has always been touted, 'as much an anti-crime as it is an economic policy', (Straw and Michael, 1996, p9). But for left realists a key means of controlling relative deprivation and perceptions of inequality, and thereby crime, lies in opening up opportunities through developing a 'radical meritocracy', (Young, 1999). Similarly, crime will be endemic in societies built on principles of competition, conflict and individualism. To attack the roots of the crime problem 'we must build a society that is less unequal, less depriving, less insecure, less disruptive of family and community ties and less corrosive of co-operative values', (Currie, 1985, p225). In short, an effective crime control strategy lies outside of the criminal justice system and in the fields of education and employment, through which fundamental economic, social and political inequalities can be challenged. In contrast, Labour's limited attempts to bring the excluded 'back in' fails to recognise that their inclusion would only be to a world that continues to be dominated by market exploitation, discrimination and a widening gap between rich and poor, (Levitas, 1996).

Crime and disorder: misbehaviour, incivilities and the anti-social

The rising tide of disorder is blighting our streets, neighbourhoods, parks, town and city centres. Incivility and harassment, public drunkenness, graffiti and vandalism all affect our ability to use open spaces and enjoy a quiet life in our own homes . . . crime and disorder are linked.

(Straw and Michael, 1996, p4)

Children under ten need help to change their bad behaviour just as much as older children.

(Home Office, 1997a, p18)

The 1998 Act is the first piece of criminal justice legislation in England and Wales to act against legal *and* moral/social transgressions. New Labour's acceptance that crime runs in certain families and that anti-social behaviour in childhood is a predictor of later criminality has opened the door to a range of legislative initiatives which target 'disorderly' as well as criminal behaviour. It also draws children below the age of criminal responsibility into formal networks of social control. Much of this is justified through notions of 'child protection' or 'nipping crime in the bud' and is exemplified in the powers for local authorities to enforce local child curfews and for courts to deliver child safety orders. Both are designed to restrict the movement of those under ten years old whose behaviour is considered troublesome, (Goldson, 1999).

The idea of creating environments that discourage 'incivility' was imported into Britain from the United States by the Conservatives and became a key part of New Labour's campaigning agenda. For the Conservatives, a ready connection between homelessness and crime – shoplifting, petty theft, begging, prostitution, drug taking – had already been made. For 'homeless' travellers and squatters, the 1994 *Criminal Justice and Public Order Act* had effectively limited their ability to live within the law. In 1994 John Major, then Prime Minister, launched an attack on 'offensive beggars' – claiming that 'it is not acceptable to be out on the street' and 'there is no justification for it these days', (*The Guardian*, 28 May, 1994). He urged more rigorous application of the law – begging is an offence under the 1824 *Vagrancy Act* and sleeping rough is punishable by a £200 fine. A year later the then Shadow Home Secretary, Jack Straw, echoed such sentiments by calling for the streets to be cleared of the 'aggressive begging of winos, addicts and squeegee merchants', (*The Guardian*, 5 September, 1995). Since being returned to power, Labour has consistently backed the idea that low level disorder, which may not necessarily be criminal, should be a priority target. Misbehaviour and crime are conflated. The 1998 Act also introduces Anti-Social Behaviour Orders to be applied to any behaviour, by either youth or adult, that is 'likely to cause harassment to the community'. The court can order an offender to cease their behaviour and comply with any number of measures, such as curfew, exclusion, restriction of movement and so on, in order to protect the community from further anti-social acts. Although the order is a civil rather than criminal matter, violation carries a maximum sentence of five years imprisonment.

The order draws heavily on a series of intensive community policing strategies that were introduced in New York in 1994. These were based on the principle that by clamping down on minor street offences and incivilities, begging, under age smoking and drinking, unlicensed street vending, public urination, graffiti writing, and by arresting 'aggressive beggars', 'fare dodgers', 'squeegee merchants', 'hustlers', 'abusive drunks' and 'litter louts', then many of the more serious offences will be curtailed. In part, the strategy is a mutation of Wilson and Kelling's, (1982), highly influential neo-conservative theory that claimed that if climates of disorder are allowed to develop, then more serious crime would follow in their wake. Merely leaving a broken window unrepaired, they argued, will quickly encourage outbreaks of vandalism. Failure to combat vandalism will see an escalation in the seriousness of crimes:

> *The citizen who fears the ill smelling drunk, the rowdy teenager, or the importuning beggar is not merely expressing his distaste for unseemly behaviour, he is also giving voice to a bit of folk wisdom that happens to be a correct generalization, namely, that serious street crime flourishes in areas in which disorderly behaviour goes unchecked.*
>
> (Wilson and Kelling, 1982, p34).

In practice, what came to be known as zero tolerance policing was the brain child of William Bratton, Police Commissioner of the NYPD, who reorganised New York policing strategies by making each precinct commander accountable for monitoring and reducing *signs of* crime, as well as crime itself, (Dennis, 1997). Primary emphasis was placed on crime prevention and disorder reduction. It was heralded as a great success, particularly in reducing the number of firearm offences and rates of murder. New York, once synonymous with urban violence, fell to the 144th most dangerous in a FBI comparison of crime in America's 189 largest cities. The precise reasons for such a decline, however, remain disputed. Many American cities witnessed a fall in their crime rates without, or prior to, the introduction of 'zero tolerance', and it was probably also part of a longer trend in the decline of violent offences associated with the trade in crack-cocaine. It certainly remains disputable that zero tolerance is a policy that 'works'.

Nevertheless, the rhetoric, if not the policy, of 'zero tolerance' has been embraced across the political divide. It is, for example, also reflected in Etzioni's, (1995, p24), communitarian appeal that 'we need to return to a society in which certain actions are viewed as beyond the pale'. In New Labour's appropriation of the term a clear moral authoritarian agenda emerges. Labour's rhetoric of community provides for the exclusionary targeting not just of identified offenders but of entire 'dangerous' underclass groups, (Hughes, 1998, p113). Notions of the 'anti-social' are just as capable of being used to restrict those engaged in minority cultural or political activities, or others who are unpopular with local councils: 'there is an obvious risk of victimisation of ex-offenders, 'weirdoes', 'loners', prostitutes, travellers, addicts or other people subject to rumour, gossip and prejudice', (Parratt, 1998, p2). The order has also been condemned for granting local agencies unlimited discretion and disproportionate powers in acting against 'undesirable behaviour', irrespective of whether it is criminal or not, (Ashworth et al., 1998). Asking the police to enforce the sustained policing of people who are 'out of place' or who are simply different in outlook and style may simply increase the possibilities for confrontation and undermine public confidence. And throughout, by institutionalising intolerance towards the 'different', the regular production of structures of exclusion, inequality, discrimination and oppression can be ignored, (Muncie, 1999b).

Preventing crime: moral authoritarianism and community safety

The principal aim of the youth justice system is to prevent offending by children and young persons and requires those involved in the youth justice system to have regard to that aim

(Home Office, 1997c, piii)

We will uphold family life as the most secure means of bringing up our children ... (Families) should teach right from wrong. They should be the first defence against anti-social behaviour.

(Tony Blair, April, 1997 cited by Cook, 1997, p2)

The exact nature of crime prevention has always been an ill-defined affair, so much so that almost any element of social policy and criminal justice can be justified on these grounds. Community safety, too, is even more of a 'free floating signifier', (Hughes, 1999). One basic distinction, however, can be made. Much of the Conservative crime deterrence policy was dominated by a *situational* 'locks, bolts and CCTV' strategy based on rational choice theory, (Clarke, 1980). This maintained that most offenders are reasoning and normal and that crime is performed by ordinary people acting under particular pressures and exposed to specific opportunities and situational inducements. In contrast, initiatives in the late 1980s loosely informed by left realism, attempted to supplement these with programmes of *social crime prevention*. Theoretically, these recognise that socio-economic inequalities, like poor housing, lack of community facilities, unfair income differentials and the institutions of socialisation such as family, school, and employment, can promote dispositions towards offending, (Young, 1994). The targets of intervention thus *potentially* include not only urban planning, but employment opportunities, education policy, family policy, health policy and policies related to recreation, leisure and culture, (Graham, 1990, pp18–9).

At first sight such an approach may seem to offer a radical alternative to that underlying conservative political ideology. However, social crime prevention has rarely been promoted as an alternative, but more as an adjunct to situational measures. In practice it has been realised through a series of programmes which seek either to remove young people from the street or to provide special skills training. Utting, (1996), cites numerous 'promising' projects (largely American) that may be effective in reducing criminality. These are directed at parents as well as 'at risk' youth and include pre-school programmes, parental skills training, holiday play schemes, truancy watch schemes and anti-bullying campaigns. Much of this is mirrored in both the Audit Commission's (1996) and the Home Office's reports on reducing offending, (Goldblatt and Lewis, 1998). Parental training and a range of behavioural and cognitive interventions are considered to be most effective. (In contrast, counselling, therapy, shock incarceration and corporal punishment are deemed not to work). In such ways the targets of social crime prevention have invariably become individualised and behavioural. Primary attention is given to responding to the symptoms, rather than the causes of young people's disaffection and dislocation. The social contexts of offending are bypassed. The disadvantages faced by young people, e.g. lack of income support, accommodation and leisure facilities, are obscured by a narrow focus on 'at risk' and troublesome behaviour, (Muncie, Coventry and Walters, 1995).

Much of this is in evidence in the 1998 Act. Despite the rhetoric of restoration it adopts a particularly narrow and draconian version of what social crime prevention and community safety entail. Parenting orders, for example, may require parents to attend counselling or child guidance sessions to ensure that their children are not absent from school. Failure to comply can lead to a fine of £1,000. Child safety orders may require children under the age of ten to abide by the conditions of a local child curfew. This imposes bans on unsupervised children being present in certain public areas between 8pm and 6am. The maximum penalty for parents who are deemed to be condoning truancy has been raised from £1,000 to £2,500. The commitment to *doli incapax* has been removed. Some of the Act's more positive measures, such as reparation orders, are based less on compliance than on coercion and in practice have in the past been easily marginalised by the courts, (Dignan, 1999). Throughout, the objective seems to be rather one of compelling parents to take 'proper' care and control of their children, whilst by the age of ten children will be held fully responsible themselves, (Goldson, 1999).

Above all, New Labour's commitment to prevention has done nothing to undermine the pivotal position of youth custody. New Labour, it seems, is only prepared to sanction inclusion as long as exclusion is retained for particular groups of young offenders. This authoritarian mood has persisted, despite compelling evidence of custody's damaging effects. The numbers sent to young offender institutions (YOIs) continues to grow – for example by eight per cent for sentenced male young offenders between 1994 and 1998, (White, 1999, p2). As numerous campaign groups have maintained, there is an expectation that this resort to custody will prevent re-offending. Yet reconviction rates are well established and if anything are worsening. Of those male young offenders released in 1995, 77 per cent were reconvicted within two years of release, (White, 1999, p3). It is also difficult to assess the value of custody as a more widespread deterrent. Certainly there is no evidence that in those areas where alternatives to custody are operating with considerable success that there is an increase in offending. Moreover, custody precludes any restitution or reparation to the victim of offences. On the contrary, it diverts considerable resources from community provision to high security institutions. It is clear that the great majority of young people sentenced to custody pose no serious risk to the community and indeed by leading to broken links with family, friends, education, work and leisure they may become a significantly greater danger on their return, (Children's Society, 1993).

Labour has tended to remain silent on the exclusionary practices of custody. Rather it has fulfilled the Conservatives' commitment to establish a new network of secure training centres for 12–14 year olds and introduced a new generic custodial sentence, the Detention and Training Order, which is only likely to blur the distinction between local authority and Home Office secure provision. Labour, it seems, is quite happy to run its logic of communitarian crime prevention through that of populist authoritarianism, (Hughes, 1996). In the field of penal custody the principles of restorative crime prevention are ignored.

The concepts of 'social crime prevention' and 'community safety', because of their ill defined and kaleidoscopic nature, can be readily co-opted and incorporated into existing criminal justice discourse. A policy of 'what works' tends to focus on the immediate problems of individual young people and their parents. Whilst this may well deliver some successes, an overemphasis on adaptation encourages the dissolution of any long-term objectives, and is reflective of a failure to impact on the broader social contexts of disadvantage and disaffection. The problems of, and facing, young people cannot be eliminated with quick-fix approaches. Radical readings of the potential of community safety ultimately require a commitment to long-term change which cannot simply be measured in reducing the costs of crime and crime control, or by managing 'risks', but by improving the quality of life for all young people, (Muncie, 1999a, p248). As currently conceived, 'social crime prevention', 'community safety' or 'risk management' strategies, may open up new spaces for a re-imagining of crime prevention, away from an exclusive focus on individual and technicist concerns and towards social democratic forms of control, but can carry no guarantee of delivering social justice. It is indicative that community safety is part of a Crime and Disorder Act rather than crime and disorder in a Community Safety Act, (Hughes, 1998; 1999). Meanwhile, the most ostensible forms of crime prevention, those firmly grounded in principles of target hardening, rational choice and privatised security, such as fortified communities and electronic surveillance, continue unabated.

Crime risk management: actuarialism and counting 'what works'

> *Monitoring progress and evaluating impact should be an automatic requirement ... It is necessary to know what works, why it works, under what conditions it works and whether it is cost-effective.*
>
> (Straw and Michael, 1996, p19)

> *Practitioners need to see the value of the multi-agency approach ... Joint training of practitioners working in the target areas can help promote shared understanding and help identify shared problems.*
>
> (Audit Commission, 1996, p104)

One of the key influences on Labour policy was the Morgan report on crime prevention, (Home Office, 1991). Dismissed by the Conservatives for giving too much power to local authorities, it had stressed that for successful outcomes to be achieved, responsibility for law and order should be devolved from a central state to a series of semi-autonomous local partnerships, voluntary agencies and priva-tised bodies. It also advocated use of the term community safety, instead of prevention, as a means of encouraging a wider participation from all sections of the community. Meanwhile, the Audit Commission, (1996), came to emphasize the need to act primarily on evidence based research which revealed 'what works' and to ignore any alternative approaches considered uneconomic and inefficient. Accordingly, a major Home Office review of the 'what works' literature advised that any promising initiative should be subject to continual monitoring and evaluation, (Goldblatt and Lewis, 1998). Such developments have been described as symptomatic of a shift from an old to a new penology: a new mode of governance based on community responsibilisation, (Garland, 1996), and the practices of actuarial justice, (Feeley and Simon, 1992).

Whereas the old penology was largely concerned with adjudicating on matters of individual guilt and innocence, actuarial justice is primarily concerned with 'techniques for identifying, classifying and managing groups assorted by levels of dangerousness', (Feeley and Simon, 1994, p171). Crime is to be avoided rather than understood. Rather than intervening to punish or rehabilitate, its purpose is 'the regulation of aggregates' in an attempt to 'manage danger' and reduce risk. 'Transformative' issues, such as individual need, diagnosis, rehabilitation, and reformation are replaced, or subsumed within a range of 'actuarial' techniques of classification, risk assessment and system management. As a result, evaluation of success or failure comes to rest on indicators of internal systems performance. It was in such a vein that the Audit Commission's major review of youth justice in 1996 recommended the establishment of forums in which all relevant local authority services participate to develop local crime audits and strategies to achieve a *measurable* impact on the management of youth crime. It is indicative that its persistent concern has been to reduce the amount of time taken between arrest and conviction, for such an initiative would be clearly amenable to quantitative data analysis, (Audit Commission, 1998)

Such actuarialism is also part of a much broader process of public sector managerialisation. This, as Clarke and Newman, (1997), have catalogued, has generally involved the re-definition of political, economic and social issues as problems to be managed rather than necessarily resolved. A neo-Taylorist vision of rationalised inputs and outputs being employed to reduce the cost of public services has become embedded in the drive to impose the three E's of economy, efficiency and effectiveness. Social issues have become depoliticised. Policy choices have become transformed into a series of managerial decisions. Evaluations of public sector performance have become dominated by notions of productivity, task remits and quantifiable outcomes. By the 1990s these 'mean and lean' and 'more for less' mentalities began to have a significant impact on criminal and youth justice policies.

The 1998 Crime and Disorder Act is the epitome of this ethos of solving problems through managerial audits, systemic partnerships and joint ownership. For example, at a local level the Act for the first time imposes a *statutory* duty and responsibility on all local authorities 'to prevent offending by young people' and requires all agencies involved with young people to have regard to that aim. All aspects of local authority work are now infused with crime prevention responsibilities. Youth Offending Teams (YOTs) are obliged by statute to include representatives from each of social services, probation, police, health and education authorities. Others, for example from the voluntary agencies, may also be included. YOTs are empowered to co-ordinate local provision to ensure each agency acts in tandem and delivers a range of interventions and programmes that will ensure that young people 'face up to the consequences of their crimes and learn to change the habits and attitudes which led them into offending and anti-social behaviour', (Home Office, 1997b, pp27–8). Such interventions include supervising community sentences, dealing with parents, organising reparation and curfews, providing school reports to the courts, providing careers advice, giving advice on drug and alcohol issues and so on. To co-ordinate this work a new managerial position of YOT manager has been created whose central skill is one of not necessarily having prior experience of young offenders, but of being able to manage effectively. But in contrast to such local empowerment, every local authority with social service and education responsibilities is required to formulate and submit its annual youth justice plan to a national Youth Justice Board for approval. Its role is to monitor the performance of youth justice nationwide and to encourage 'best practice'. It is an extremely broad and powerful remit: overseeing all aspects of the youth justice system, advising the Secretary of State on how the aim of preventing offending can be achieved, assessing how far that objective is being reached at a local level, commissioning research, awarding grants to develop good practice and acting as a central source of promotion and publishing.

Crawford, (1997), however, points out some of the dangers inherent in this gamut of management restructuring. He argues that the new multi-agency arrangements have the potential to be highly disciplinary and authoritarian forms of administration. Pragmatism, efficiency and the continual requirement to 'get results' may well come to over-ride any commitment to due process, justice and democracy. Maintaining an equity of power and influence between the agencies and overcoming problems of information sharing /confidentiality are just two of the complex issues that are unlikely to be easily resolved. The success of restorative justice must also rest on an adequate support of health, housing and social services, yet it is these very agencies that are continually subject to financial under-resourcing. What is noticeable too is that all aspects of young people's lives are now potentially open to official monitoring and scrutiny. Moreover, it is a scrutiny which not only penetrates deeper, but also broader, by targeting younger children and those below the age of criminal responsibility. As Haines and Drakeford, (1999, p238), warned, this 'repressive intent' may not only fail to prevent offending, but instead amplify and distort young peoples' misbehaviour 'by drawing them ever earlier and ever closer into a system which cannot but do more harm than good'.

In no small measure social work professionalism is being replaced by a series of organisations whose performance is amenable only to measurable/quantifiable outcomes. The practice of youth justice is being transformed into a technical process in which 'the less than heroic' objectives of reducing risk and expenditure have replaced any notion of winning the 'war on crime', (Garland, 1996, p 448). 'Success' or 'failure' becomes a statistical artefact. At one level the primary rationale for services becomes that contained within a seemingly non-ideological and apolitical logic of evaluation/re-evaluation and audit/re-audit, but at another it is driven by a moral crusade of responsibilisation and remoralisation, (McLaughlin and Muncie, 1994). Running through much of the 1998 Act is a legitimating rhetoric of restoration, reintegration and responsibility, of ensuring offenders make amends, pay their debts to society and face the consequences of their offending, (NACRO, 1997). It is made clear that these goals are best achieved in community rather than custodial settings. But, as with so many other divisive social and economic policies inherited from the Conservatives, Labour's modernising mission is quite capable of leaving authoritarian solutions firmly in place. Indeed, the abolition of *doli incapax,* the drawing of less problematic young people into an extended social control network at an earlier age and the failure to implement penal reductionism, reveals how the logic of 'rational risk management' is quite capable of carrying with it any number of irrational and contradictory interventions.

Conclusion

Numerous criminological themes can be identified in New Labour's reinterpretation and reorganisation of youth justice. Newburn, (1998), views these as managerialism, communitarianism and populist punitiveness; to which may be added the sub themes of paternalism, responsibilisation and remoralisation, (Muncie, 1999b; Goldson, 1999). Some of these are complementary, some contradictory.

Firstly, it undoes the complexities of crime by prioritising a moral debate about the nature of 'responsible' families and 'proper' parenting. This has clear resonances to a longstanding theme of neo-conservative criminology. But it also lays claim to recognising social contexts in the insistence that a broad range of its social, and particularly economic, policies are also crime preventative. In this respect it mirrors some of the concerns of left realism. This pick and mix approach allows it to contend that it has not only moved beyond conservatism but also the forces of 'debilitating welfarism'. It can lay claim to the development of a holistic analysis of youth offending. But such holistic realism removes the theoretical integrity of realist criminologies under the guise of pragmatism.

Secondly, in the formulation of policy it can be argued that the emphasis on inclusionary crime prevention marks a significant departure from punitive justice, yet it retains a commitment to an ethos of individual responsibility and penal custody that seems to actively promote exclusion. Significantly, the principles of inclusion are frequently backed by coercive powers.

Thirdly, it has initiated a radical reform of youth justice organisation by introducing the techniques of public sector managerialism into how the system should be run. Managerialism is recast as modernisation. This may be attractive to newly empowered local authorities but it is as yet unclear whether it will foreclose the traditional paradoxes of youth justice as a system designed to offer welfare, justice and punitive interventions. Some of its provisions are likely to be severely tested by European and United Nations rulings on children's rights.

This series of contradictions allow it to ward off criticism from both sides of the political spectrum. The political advantages are clear. In times of parliamentary majority the rational, managerialist and restorative elements of the Act can be stressed; when that majority is open to electorate review it can lay claim to its credentials as a promoter of populist authoritarianism. As a result, it is an all-pervasive political pragmatism that defines the 1998 Act, rather than adherence to any one clearly articulated criminological approach. It is clouded in expediency, rather than intellectual integrity. As Garland, (1996, pp461, 466), concluded, we now have 'an official criminology which is increasingly dualistic, increasingly polarised and increasingly ambivalent . . . the new penal policies have no broader agenda, no strategy for progressive social change and no concern for the overcoming of social divisions'.

References

Ashworth, A., Gardner, J., Morgan, R., Smith, A., Von Hirsch, A. and Wasik, M., (1998), 'Neighbouring on the Oppressive: The Government's Anti-Social Behaviour Order Proposals', *Criminal Justice*, vol.16, no.1, pp7–14.

Audit Commission, (1996), *Misspent Youth*, London, Audit Commission.

Audit Commission, (1998), *Misspent Youth '98*, London, Audit Commission.

Brownlee, I., (1998), 'New Labour-New Penology? Punitive Rhetoric and the Limits of Managerialism in Criminal Justice Policy', *Journal of Law and Society*, vol.25, no.3, pp313–335.

Charman, S. and Savage, S., (1999), 'The New Politics of Law and Order: Labour, Crime and Justice' in Powell, M., (Ed.), *New Labour, New Welfare State?*, London, Policy Press.

Children's Society, (1993), *A False Sense of Security: The Case Against Locking Up More Children*, London, Children's Society.

Clarke, J. and Newman, J., (1997), *The Managerial State*, London, Sage.

Clarke, R.V.G., (1980), 'Situational Crime Prevention: Theory and Practice', *British Journal of Criminology*, vol.20, no.2 pp136–47.

Cohen, S., (1988), *Against Criminology*, New Brunswick, NJ, Transaction.

Cook, D., (1997), *Poverty, Crime and Punishment*, London, CPAG.

Crawford, A., (1997), *The Local Governance of Crime*, Oxford, Clarendon.

Currie, E., (1995), *Confronting Crime,* New York, Pantheon.

Dennis, N., (Ed.), (1997) *Zero Tolerance: Policing a Free Society*, London, Institute of Economic Affairs.

Dennis, N. and Erdos, G., (1992), *Families Without Fatherhood*, London, Institute of Economic Affairs.

Dickinson, D., (1995), 'Crime and Unemployment', *New Economy*, vol.2, no.2, pp115–120.

Dignan, J., (1999), 'The Crime and Disorder Act and the Prospects for Restorative Justice', *Criminal Law Review,* January, pp 48–60.

Etzioni, A., (1995), *The Spirit of Community*, London, Fontana.

Farrington, D., (1994), 'Human Development and Criminal Careers' in Maguire, M., Morgan, R. and Reiner, R., (Eds.), *The Oxford Handbook of Criminology*, Oxford, Clarendon.

Farrington, D., (1996), *Understanding and Preventing Youth Crime*, Social Policy Research Findings, no.93, York, Joseph Rowntree Foundation.

Farrington, D. and West, D., (1990), 'The Cambridge Study in Delinquent Development' in H.J. Kerner and G. Kaiser, (Eds.), *Criminality: Personality, Behaviour and Life History*, Berlin, Springer-Verlag.

Farrington, D., Barnes, G. and Lambert, S., (1996), 'The Concentration of Offending in Families', *Legal and Criminological Psychology*, vol.1, pp 47–63.

Feeley, S. and Simon, J., (1992), 'The New Penology: Notes on the Emerging Strategy of Corrections and its Implications', *Criminology*, vol.30, no.4, pp 452–74.

Feeley, S. and Simon, J., (1994), 'Actuarial Justice: the Emerging New Criminal Law' in D. Nelken, (Ed.), *The Futures of Criminology*, London, Sage.

Field, S., (1990), *Trends in Crime and their Interpretation*, Home Office Research Study, no.119, London, HMSO.

Garland, D., (1996), 'The Limits of the Sovereign State' *British Journal of Criminology*, vol.36, no.4 pp 445–471.

Goldblatt, P. and Lewis, C., (Eds.), (1998), *Reducing Offending*, Home Office Research Study, no.187, London, HMSO.

Goldson, B., (1999), 'Youth (In)justice: Contemporary Developments in Policy and Practice' in Goldson, B., (Ed.), *Youth Justice: Contemporary Policy and Practice*, Aldershot, Ashgate.

Gottfredson, M.R. and Hirschi, T., (1990), *A General Theory of Crime*, Stanford, CA., Stanford University Press.

Graham, J., (Ed.), (1990), *Crime Prevention Strategies in Europe and America*, Helsinki, Institute for Crime Prevention and Control.

Graham, J. and Bowling, B., (1995), *Young People and Crime*, Home Office Research Study, no.145, London, Home Office.

Haines, K. and Drakeford, M., (1998), *Young People and Youth Justice*, Basingstoke, Macmillan.

Home Office, (1991), *Safer Communities: the Local Delivery of Crime Prevention Through the Partnership Approach*, (The Morgan Report), London, HMSO.

Home Office, (1997(a)), *Tackling Youth Crime: A Consultation Paper*, London, HMSO.

Home Office, (1997(b)), *No More Excuses: A New Approach to Tackling Youth Crime in England and Wales,* CM 3809, London, HMSO.

Home Office, (1997(c)), *Crime and Disorder Bill*, London, HMSO.

Hope, T., (1998), Are we Letting Social Policy off the Hook? *Criminal Justice Matters*, no.33, pp 6–7.

Hughes, G., (1996), Communitarianism and Law and Order, *Critical Social Policy*, vol.16, no.4, pp17–41.

Hughes, G., (1998), *Understanding Crime Prevention,* Buckingham, Open University Press

Hughes, G., (1999), 'In The Shadow of Crime and Disorder: The Contested Politics of Community Safety', Unpublished Paper, The Open University.

Jordan, B., (1996), *Poverty: A Theory of Social Exclusion*, Cambridge, Polity.

Lea, J. and Young, J., (1984), *What is to be Done about Law and Order?*, Harmondsworth, Penguin.

Levitas, R., (1996), The Concept of Social Exclusion and the New Durkheimian Hegemony, *Critical Social Policy*, vol.16, no.1, pp 5–20.

Mann, K., (1991), *The Making of an English 'Underclass'?*, Milton Keynes, Open University Press.

McLaughlin, E. and Muncie, J., (1994), 'Managing the Criminal Justice System' in Clarke, J., Cochrane, A. and McLaughlin, E., (Eds.), *Managing Social Policy*, London, Sage.

Muncie, J., (1999a), *Youth and Crime: A Critical Introduction*, London, Sage.

Muncie, J., (1999b), Institutionalised Intolerance: Youth Justice and the 1998 Crime and Disorder Act, *Critical Social Policy,* vol.19, no.2, pp147–175.

Muncie, J., (2000), 'Decriminalising Criminology' in Lewis, G., (Ed.), *Rethinking Social Policy,* London, Sage/Open University.

Muncie, J., Coventry, G. and Walters, R., (1995), 'The Politics of Youth Crime Prevention' in Noaks, L., Maguire, M. and Levi, M., (Eds.), *Contemporary Issues in Criminology*, Cardiff, University of Wales.

Murray, C., (1984), *Losing Ground*, New York, Basic Books.

Murray, C., (1990), *The Emerging Underclass*, London, Institute of Economic Affairs.

Murray, C., (1994), *Underclass: The Crisis Deepens,* London, Institute of Economic Affairs.

NACRO, (1997), *Responsibility, Restoration and Reintegration: A New Three R's for Young Offenders*, London, NACRO.

Newburn, T., (1998), Tackling Youth Crime and Reforming Youth Justice: the Origins and Nature of 'New Labour' Policy, *Policy Studies*, vol.19, no.3/4, pp199–211.

Parratt, L., (1998), Crime and Disorder, *Liberty*, Spring.

Pyle, D., (1998), Crime and Unemployment: What do Empirical Studies Show? *International Journal of Risk, Security and Crime Prevention*, vol.3, no.3, pp169–180.

Straw, J. and Michael, A., (1996), *Tackling the Causes of Crime: Labour's Proposals to Prevent Crime and Criminality*, London, Labour Party.

Utting, D., (1996), *Reducing Criminality Among Young People: A Sample of Relevant Programmes in the UK*, Home Office Research Study, no.161, London, HMSO.

Van den Haag, E., (1975), *Punishing Criminals*, New York, Basic Books.

White, P., (1999), The Prison Population in 1998: A Statistical Review, *Research Findings*, no.94, London, Home Office.

Wilson J.Q., (1975), *Thinking about Crime*, Vintage, New York.

Wilson, J.Q. and Herrnstein, R.J., (1985), *Crime and Human Nature*, New York, Simon and Schuster.

Wilson, J.Q. and Kelling, G., (1982), 'Broken Windows', *Atlantic Monthly*, March, pp29–38.

Young, J., (1994), Incessant Chatter: Recent Paradigms in Criminology in Maguire, M., Morgan, R. and Reiner, R., (Eds.), *The Oxford Handbook of Criminology*, Oxford, Clarendon.

Young, J., (1999), *The Exclusive Society*, London, Sage.

CHAPTER 3

Wither Diversion? Interventionism and the New Youth Justice

Barry Goldson

Out with the 'old' in with the 'new': from diversion to intervention

> *For some years now, efforts have been made to divert young people away from court.*
>
> (Gibson and Cavadino, 1995: p 41).

> *current practice is working and there appear to be few reasons to change it.*
>
> (Reid, 1997, p 7).

> *Speaking to his party conference in October 1997, the new Home Secretary, Jack Straw, characterised the sort of diversionary approach which had guided youth justice policy and practice in the post-war era as one of 'endless cautions and no action' grounded on a 'fantasy that "they will grow out of it"'.*
>
> (Brownlee, 1998: p 315)

The issuing of informal warnings and cautions, as distinct from formal prosecution, is a long-established practice in relation to children and young people in trouble. Indeed, two particularly important Home Office Circulars, (14/1985 and 59/1990), actively promoted the use of such *diversionary* measures, (Home Office, 1985 and 1990). In addition to providing a steer towards the employment of cautions the 1985 circular, as Muncie, (1999: p 272), has noted, also 'encouraged the use of informal warnings'. Such warnings not only served to divert a significant number of children and young people from the formal justice process, they also ensured that such children had no 'record'. Indeed, the Audit Commission, (1997: p 20) estimated that since the mid-1980s the available data suggests that 'around 10 per cent of young offenders identified by the police ... are now warned', and Home Office guidance provides that such informal warnings should 'not be cited in court nor recorded as a caution in the criminal statistics' (ibid: pp 20–21).

Home Office Circular 59/90 provided that the purpose of cautioning was to deal quickly and simply with less serious offenders, to divert such offenders from the criminal court, and to reduce the likelihood of re-offending. In some cases cautions were administered within hours of the commission of an offence. In others, the police would determine that further information was required, necessitating a visit to the child's home and consultation with other agencies. Indeed, inter-agency diversion panels – comprising police officers, youth justice social workers, probation officers and education professionals – were established in many areas of England and Wales. In certain areas quite sophisticated diversionary partnerships and inter-agency arrangements were developed, (Bell, Hodgson and Pragnell, 1999), which pluralised agency decision-making, and served (to some extent at least) to diffuse the power and influence of the police.

The effect of the Home Office Circulars, together with the development of strategic diversionary practice, was not insignificant. Gibson and Cavadino, (1995, p 56), note that the number of offenders cautioned doubled between 1985 and 1995, and Gelsthorpe and Morris, (1999, p 210), have observed that 'most children who offended over this period were diverted by the police: 90 per cent of boys and 97 per cent of girls in 1993'. However, a sequence of well-documented high-profile events in late 1992 and early 1993 combined to create a powerful sense of 'moral panic' in relation to the behaviour of identifiable groups of children, and juvenile crime was spectacularly re-politicised, (Goldson, 1997 and 1999). A new mood of 'toughness' consolidated, within which cautioning was conceptualised as an unacceptably lenient means of dealing with 'yobs'. It was of little surprise therefore that Home Office Circular 18/94, (Home Office, 1994), 'represented a significant departure from existing policy and practice' in relation to diversion and cautioning, (Evans and Ellis, 1997, p 1). Thus the 1994 Circular, introduced under John Major's Conservative administration, had a marked impact in undermining diversionary practice in youth justice: 'the discouragement of repeat cautions (most commonly used with this group) may account for the particularly sharp decrease in the rate of cautioning for juveniles ... there is some evidence to suggest that the 1994 circular has been successful ... in lowering the overall cautioning rate', (ibid: p 4). New Labour, elected in May, 1997, went substantially further. Cautioning was to be completely abolished, diversion fundamentally diluted and 'early intervention' trumpeted as a cornerstone of the 'new' youth justice.

Within just six months of seizing power New Labour issued a radical White Paper ominously entitled *No More Excuses*, (Home Office, 1997a).

> *The trouble with the current cautioning system is that it is too haphazard and that too often a caution does not result in any follow up action, so the opportunity is lost for early **intervention** to turn youngsters away from crime ... Inconsistent, repeated and ineffective cautioning has allowed some children and young people to feel that they can offend with impunity ... The Government feels that more radical action is now needed ... The Crime and Disorder Bill will **abolish cautioning** and replace it with a statutory police reprimand and Final Warning scheme. Within a clear statutory framework*

*the **police will decide** whether to reprimand a young offender, give a Final
Warning or bring criminal charges. When a Final Warning is given, this will
usually be followed by a community **intervention programme** ... to address
the causes of offending and so reduce the risk of further crime.*

(Home Office, 1997a: para 5. pp 10–12, my emphasis)

The government's 'consultation paper', *Tackling Youth Crime*, which was
published two months earlier, had a rather more direct tone: 'if they ignore the
Warning and offend again, they can expect a significant punishment from the
courts', (Home Office, 1997b, p 5). Cautioning, a remarkably successful diversionary policy, as we shall see later, has been swept aside and replaced by a police-
managed reprimand and (interventionist) Final Warning scheme. New Labour's
youth justice policy gaze is unequivocally fixed upon 'early intervention', to be
followed, if 'necessary', by 'significant punishment'.

Indeed, the effect of Sections 65 and 66 of the Crime and Disorder Act 1998
(which received Royal Assent in July, 1998) is to put an end to cautioning and
establish instead, on a statutory basis, the system of reprimands and Final
Warnings. The reprimand is intended for children who 'have not previously been
convicted of an offence', (S.65(1)(d)), whilst the Final Warning, a 'one-off'
disposal unless at least two years have elapsed from the date of an earlier warning,
is reserved for 'second-time' offenders, and those who are alleged to have
committed an offence which is not considered so serious that a charge must result,
(S.65(3)(b)). A Final Warning may be issued instead of a reprimand for the child's
first offence where 'the constable ... considers the offence to be so serious as to
require a warning', (S.65(4)). When a Final Warning is administered by a police
officer they are required to refer the child to the local Youth Offending Team for a
'rehabilitation programme' assessment, (S.66(1)). New Labour is investing
considerable faith in such an interventionist approach: 'by intervening early and
effectively before crime becomes a habit, we can stop today's young offenders
becoming tomorrow's career criminals', (Home Office, 1997b para. 47).
However, there are at least four sets of concerns with this.

First, whether to issue a reprimand, to administer a Final Warning, and refer the
child to a youth offending team, or to prosecute, has become a decision which is
vested exclusively with the police. NACRO, (1998, p 1), has observed that 'there
is neither provision nor expectation, either in the Act or the guidance, for the use
of multi-agency panels or other consultative processes'. In other words, the
management of the 'front end' of the youth justice system is now simply a 'matter
for the police', (Gordon, Cuddy and Black 1999, p 39). This clearly raises a fundamental concern with regard to single-agency 'colonisation' of a critically
important stage of the youth justice process, and this itself generates additional
considerations. Bell, (1999, p 200), has noted that 'there has been no suggestion to
date that persons who will make such decisions will receive special training to

enable them to do so consistently and effectively', and it is 'relevant to note that the United Nations Committee on the Rights of the Child has consistently recommended that all those involved with children in the juvenile justice system receive adequate training'. Indeed, international standards, treaties and rules are clear in this respect. Rule 12 of the United Nations Standard Minumum Rules for the Administration of Juvenile Justice, (the Beijing Rules), for example, states that 'in order to best fulfill their functions, police officers who frequently or exclusively deal with juveniles ... shall be specially instructed and trained, (United Nations, 1985). Furthermore, it will be the police who both investigate and adjudicate upon an offence, thus assuming the role of investigator, prosecutor, judge and jury under the new reprimand and Final Warning arrangements. Here, Bell raises questions of primary justice:

> *In the case of either 'diversionary' disposal the police will have to satisfy themselves that there is evidence that the child or young person has committed an offence and that there is a realistic prospect of them being convicted. As a fundamental principle of any system aspiring to deliver justice no person should be a judge in their own cause. Yet this is precisely what the new arrangements promote. In addition, the evidential test falls well short of being 'beyond reasonable doubt'.*

> (Bell, 1999, p202).

In terms of equality of outcome for all children the powers that the Crime and Disorder Act 1998 conveys upon the police are particularly problematic. Hughes, Pilkington and Leiston, (1998, pp 26–7), note that 'there is some evidence that the police may 'push' certain categories of person through such as (young) women. It is certainly a concern among some diversion workers that young women may be pushed through to formal intervention for offences which would be viewed less seriously when committed by young men'. There is certainly no shortage of research findings which confirm gendered decisions of this nature, (Worrall, 1999), and black children and young people are similarly exposed to over-zealous and unjust forms of criminalising intervention, (Goldson and Chigwada-Bailey, 1999).

Second, as already indicated, when a police officer issues a Final Warning to a child, they are then obliged to refer them to a Youth Offending Team. The recently published draft, *National Standards for Youth Justice* provide that such notification must occur 'within one working day (and) the YOT must contact all offenders who have received final warnings within five working days of the warning', (Youth Justice Board for England and Wales, 1999, paras 5.2 and 5.3). Moreover, within ten working days of the Final Warning the Youth Offending Team 'must have undertaken an assessment', (ibid, para 5.4), which 'must be informed by':

> *1. At least one interview with the offender.*
> *2. An interview with the offender's parents or primary carer.*

3. *Existing reports ... and any other information about contact with police, health and social services.*
4. *Discussion with individuals or agencies who are currently, or have recently, been involved with the offender. (ibid, para 3.2)*

If the assessment 'indicates the need for a *rehabilitation programme*' (and the presumption is that it will, Home Office 1997b, para 56), the Youth Offending Team 'must produce a programme' to include components which:

1. *Addresses the factors which contributed to the offending.*
2. *Describes the commitment the parents or primary carer can make in supporting the programme.*
3. *Describes the contact made or attempted with the victim.*
4. *Describes work planned to increase the offender's awareness of the harm caused by crime, or to make reparation. (ibid, para 5.4)*

The interventionist priorities that underpin the Final Warning, which will largely be targeted at children with no more than two minor criminal transgressions, raise serious concerns with regard to proportionality and the commensurate relation of offence and intervention. This is not to mention undue criminalisation and labelling which will be discussed later. Bell argues:

> *It is also conceivable–no inevitable–that the concept of proportionality will be stood on its head with more intrusive interventions being provided on the basis of pre-court warnings for less serious offences than those disposals that are the sole prerogative of the court. It is quite clear that the new system of reprimands and warnings (effectively a two strikes and you're in court rule) will lead to a significant increase in the number of children and young people appearing before the Youth Court in many cases for alleged minor infringements of the criminal law.*

(Bell, 1999, p 203)

Third, Section 66(5) of the Crime and Disorder Act provides that reprimands, Final Warnings and 'any report on a failure by a person to participate in a rehabilitation programme' (related to a Final Warning), 'may be cited in criminal proceedings in the same circumstances as a conviction'. The reasons for citing 'diversionary' disposals in court in this way were highlighted in the *Tackling Youth Crime* 'consultation' paper:

> *...for the Final Warning to be effective in preventing re-offending, there must be sufficient incentive for young offenders and their parents to co-operate and complete the intervention programme ... further sanctions may be required ... any unreasonable non-compliance would be recorded on the individual's criminal record ... and that record might be taken into account by a court when sentencing for any subsequent offence.*

(Home Office, 1997b, paras 65–68)

Indeed, the consequences of this are clearly designed to 'up-tariff' children, and the courts are likely to respond with heavier and more punitive forms of intervention in relation to those who re-offend whilst subject to a Final Warning, particularly if their 'rehabilitators' have reported a lack of compliance and co-operation. Again, Bell captures this problem very effectively:

> *Under current arrangements magistrates generally consider a caution as a 'ticking off'. However, how will they, over time, come to view a failure to comply with a programme of rehabilitation? Is it likely that it will come to be viewed as an unwillingness to respond to a previous disposal? How is a programme of rehabilitation to be distinguished from those sanctions available to the court; the new Action Plan Order being the most obvious example? Will prompt and recent failure to comply with a rehabilitation programme coupled with the commission of a fresh offence during its currency, lead sentencers to conclude that there would be little purpose in dealing with an offence by a Supervision or Action Plan Order? The very fact that 'diversionary' disposals have been placed on statute diminishes their diversionary value and promotes a proclivity to prosecute.*
>
> (Bell, 1999, pp 201–202)

Fourth, and closely related to the previous point, Section 66(4) of the Crime and Disorder Act 1998 provides that where a child commits an offence within two years of receiving a Final Warning, the sentencing court 'shall not make an order' for conditional discharge unless it is of the opinion that there are 'exceptional circumstances relating to the offence or the offender which justify its doing so'. The *Tackling Youth Crime* 'consultation' paper had prepared the way for this in stating that:

> *If, following a Final Warning, a young person offends again, they will know to expect quick and appropriate punishment from the courts ... there must be a penalty to pay ... a significant punishment ... as an added incentive to the young offender to stay out of trouble ... the option of conditional discharge should not be available to the courts when sentencing.*
>
> (Home Office, 1997b, p 3 and paras 54, 57 and 69)

This will produce a very substantial 'push-in' effect. The Audit Commission, (1997, p 36), found that 28 per cent of cases in the Youth Court were dealt with by way of discharges. As a result of the new interventionist approach therefore, the overwhelming majority of such cases will face the 'penalty' and 'significant punishment' to which New Labour alluded in its 'consultation' document. The precise nature of such 'punishment' is to be determined and dispensed via the new Referral Order and concomitant interventions as provided by Part 1 of the Youth Justice and Criminal Evidence Act 1999, (Goldson, 2000a). During the Bill's passage through Parliament, Paul Boateng, the Home Office Minister of

State, described the Referral Order as 'a fundamentally different way of considering how to intervene most productively and effectively in the life of a young person to stop crime and offending', (cited in Wonnacott, 1999, p 271). The *No More Excuses* White Paper had provided the earliest indications of New Labour's interventionist intentions in this regard when it proclaimed that: 'more radical action is needed to maximise the impact of the youth court on young offenders, making it as effective as possible at tackling offending behaviour, especially for young people appearing before the court for the first time', (Home Office, 1997a, para 9.20).

The Referral Order is critically examined in some detail later. For our purposes here it is suffice to note that Part 1 of the Youth Justice and Criminal Evidence Act 1999 provides that the Referral Order is intended to become the standard sentence imposed by the Youth Court, or other Magistrates Court, for children who have been convicted of an offence or offences for the *first time*. Such children will normally be referred by the Court to a Youth Offender Panel. The Panels will establish a *'programme of behaviour'* which the child will be obliged to observe. The principal aim of the programme will be the prevention of re-offending by the child, (S.8(1)). Section 8 of the Act identifies typical components of such an interventionist programme which include:

- financial or other forms of reparation to the victim/s of the offence/s;
- mediation sessions with the victim/s;
- unpaid work as a service to the community;
- conditions that require the child to be at home at specified times and attend school or work;
- specified activities to 'address offending behaviour' and/or to serve rehabilitative purposes with respect to drug and/or alcohol misuse;
- reporting conditions to persons and/or places;
- prohibition from association with specified persons and/or places;
- compliance with the supervision and recording requirements of the programme.

The terms of the programme form the basis of the 'youth offender contract', (S.8(6)) which the child will be required to sign, (S.8(5)(b). Once a 'programme of behaviour' has been established and a 'youth offender contract' has been signed, the child's 'progress' in complying with its terms will be subject to review by the Youth Offender Panel which will convene meetings for this purpose, (S.11).

New Labour has set great store by the principles of correctional early intervention, deterrence and punishment in order to prevent children's offending. Well-established diversionary priorities, policies and practices have been all but abandoned. Formal intervention, potentially quite intensive and wide-ranging, by way of 'rehabilitation programmes' attached to Final Warnings, will apply to children as young as ten, for only their second (minor) offence, and in some cases their first, contingent upon the means by which the privileged discretion which is exclusively reserved for the police is exercised. In the event of a third, or possibly even second transgression, such measures, together with reports relating to the child's standard of compliance with 'rehabilitation', will be citable in court. Discharges will not normally be available to the Courts and the child will instead face further intervention through the medium of the Referral Order. For an administration ostensibly wedded to 'evidence-based' policy formation, and informed by 'what works', such an approach is curious. Quite apart from the concerns raised above, and those discussed later in this chapter, and elsewhere in this volume, the new interventionism is at odds with established theory, research findings and practice experience.

The problematics of intervention: the effectiveness of diversion

> *One of the most recurrent themes of those who felt that the criminal justice system was in crisis was simply that there was too much of it ... As has often been remarked, however modern crime policies may have failed, they have certainly succeeded in recruiting vast numbers of people into the crime/crime control 'industry'. All this criminal justice was demonstrably ineffective at reducing crime, and the insights of labelling theory ... told us that becoming involved in official responses to crime could actually make continued career criminality more rather than less probable. The call to 'leave kids alone wherever possible' became a rallying cry of the juvenile justice movement and diversion ... became a dominant theme of reform.*

(Hudson, 1993, p 38)

Diversionary strategies are theoretically derived in interactionist, social reaction and labelling perspectives and they are informed by the relative 'normality' of juvenile crime. Put at its simplest the underpinning contention rests upon the fact that it is not uncommon for children and young people to transgress the law, and the primary difference between those who are conceptualised as 'offenders', and those who are not, is 'understood not as a difference in psychological character but as a consequence of whether or not the young person has become entangled in the criminal justice system', (Pearson, 1994, p 1186). The 'normality' of juvenile crime is evidenced in self-report studies which have consistently, and over-time, indicated that offending is not uncommon in adolescence (see, for example, Shapland, 1978 and Graham and Bowling, 1995). Interactionist, labelling and social reaction theorists, (Becker, 1963; Lemert, 1951 and 1967; Matza, 1964 and 1969) help us to understand the means by which formal interventions – particularly the processes of prosecution and court appearances – serve to apply offender labels to children and young people and thus confirm delinquent identities. Blackmore captures this particularly well:

The labelling perspective is particularly relevant ... as it focuses specifically on how the process of social control can affect delinquent behaviour. Traditionally the agencies of social control (police, schools, social services, probation and courts) were viewed as passive responders to delinquency. In other words they were seen as merely reacting to delinquent behaviour. However, labelling theorists have questioned this and instead focused attention on the ways that social control agencies react can in fact create and lead to further deviant behaviour.

(Blackmore, 1984, pp 45–6).

In a nutshell, the argument is that the application of stigmatising labels, followed by negative social reactions, is an inevitable consequence of intervention: the labels produce 'outsiders' and this then necessitates further and more concentrated forms of targeted intervention. Moreover, such interventionist processes are more likely to 'create', or at least consolidate and confirm, delinquent identities for children which, once established, tend to lead them to further offending. This led Lemert, (1967), to conclude that 'social control leads to deviance' and Matza, (1969: p 80), to comment on the 'irony' and self-defeating nature of certain professional interventions: 'the very effort to prevent, intervene, arrest and "cure" persons ... precipitate or seriously aggravate the tendency society wishes to guard against'.

In addition to theoretical developments within academic criminology, research, grounded in practice, has raised further concerns in relation to the counter-productive nature of early intervention. Perhaps most notable within this context was the work of a group of social scientists at Lancaster University in the early 1980s, (Thorpe et al., 1980). The Lancaster researchers carefully traced the processes which linked early intervention, even when it is underpinned by benign intentions, to spiralling and more intensive interventionist measures which were, in turn, characterised by increasingly punitive tendencies. Following the implementation of the Children and Young Persons Act 1969, Thorpe and his colleagues found that various professional constituencies were designing and implementing intensive interventionist programmes of 'treatment' which were spurious in nature. Moreover, such 'Intermediate Treatment' interventions had a dramatic effect in terms of 'up-tariffing' children and young people in the juvenile courts. Commenting upon the Lancaster research, Haines and Drakeford, (1998, p 42), note that: 'highly interventionist programmes of treatment often did more harm than good in systems terms because once a young person had tried and failed at treatment then punishment was the inevitable outcome of further criminal justice involvement'. The 1970s were thus witness to an enormous influx of children into residential 'treatment' environments often on their way to custodial institutions. Early intervention, often for very minor offences, or even because they were thought to be 'at risk' of offending, had the effect of catapulting children very rapidly into the formal criminal justice system.

The combination of the theoretical insights offered by labelling perspectives and the messages from research, raised serious challenges to the efficacy and legitimacy of interventionist policies and practices in relation to the significant majority of children in trouble. Indeed, it became increasingly apparent that early intervention – and the concomitant involvement of children in criminal justice proceedings – neither served the interests of the child or the public. This principle was widely, unequivocally and authoritatively endorsed throughout the 1980s, the 'decade of diversion for juveniles', (Dignan, 1992, p 433), and 'normalisation and informalism' underpinned practice, (Pitts, 1990, p 107). A Home Office consultation document recognised that:

> *...there may be positive advantages for the individual and society, particularly in the case of juveniles, in using prosecution as a final resort: delay in the entry of a juvenile to the criminal justice system may prevent his (sic) entry altogether.*

(Home Office, 1984)

Diversion was repeatedly affirmed in government documents, including circulars to the police, (Home Office, 1985 and 1990) and in the Code of Practice for prosecutors, (Crown Prosecution Service, 1986). There was little doubt that diversion had 'become the official government policy for young offenders', (Davis et al., 1989, p 221), and even the Association of Chief Police Officers statements confirmed that the most senior officers had been persuaded that diversion was effective, (Hughes et al., 1998).

Widespread endorsement of cautioning and diversion was inevitably mirrored in its increasing application. Thus the proportion of 14–16 year old boys cautioned for indictable offences increased from 34 per cent in 1980 to 69 per cent in 1990, and the corresponding figures for 10–13 year olds were 65 per cent and 90 per cent, (Gelsthorpe and Morris, 1994, p 977). In 1994, 97 per cent of 10–13 year old girls were similarly cautioned, (Gordon et al., 1999, p 36). Such diversionary practices were in line with developments elsewhere in Europe, (Ruxton, 1996, p 307) and NACRO's Juvenile Crime Committee had no hesitation in making a series of recommendations 'to build on many of the excellent developments in diversionary practice in local areas and to deal with the major outstanding problems', (NACRO, 1989, p 15). More recently, the Association of County Councils, the Association of Metropolitan Authorities, the Association of Directors of Social Services, NACRO and the Association of Chief Officers of Probation, (1996, p 25) have extolled the value of diversion from prosecution and urged the development of appropriate cautioning schemes across England and Wales.

The consensual endorsement and widespread application of diversionary practice in youth justice was neither an act of blind faith nor a simple knee-jerk reaction to the lamentable mistakes of the 1970s. Neither was it an expression of deference to the theoretical priorities of the labelling and social reaction theorists. Whilst it is true that cautioning has a particular fiscal appeal, it being substantially cheaper to administer than prosecution, (Audit Commission, 1996, p 26), the fact of the matter is that it is also 'an effective means of preventing re-offending by young people', (Reid, 1997, p 4). It would be misleading to suppose that diversionary strategies have been perfected however. Indeed, this is far from the case. Many commentators have argued that cautioning can serve to 'net-widen' and hence expand rather than limit social control, (Blagg, 1986; Cohen, 1986; Ditchfield, 1976; McMahon, 1990; Pratt, 1986; Rutherford, 1992). Others have raised concerns in relation to multi-agency practices with respect to issues of confidentiality, (Crawford, 1994), and criticism has been levelled at the degree of unaccountable discretion exercised within cautioning panels, inconsistent decision-making and the disproportionate influence of the police, (Evans and Ellis, 1997; Reid, 1997). There is ample evidence of geographical variations in diversionary practices and cautioning rates, (NACRO, 1988; Pitts, 1990). There is also clear evidence that black children and young people do not have an equal share of the benefits of diversion compared with their white counterparts, (Goldson and Chigwada-Bailey, 1999; Home Office, 1999; Landau and Nathan, 1983; NITFED, 1986), and similar forms of gendered discrimination and injustice also prevail, (NACRO, 1988; Worrall, 1999). Finally, it has been suggested that the needs of victims of crime are neglected within diversionary contexts, (Davis et al., 1989). Such critique raises a series of important issues. Notwithstanding this, there is little getting away from the effectiveness of cautioning and diversionary practices in the youth justice system and Smith observes that:

> *The latest Criminal Statistics devote some space to research on the effectiveness of cautioning. Overall, only 19 per cent of 'young offenders' cautioned in 1994 were convicted of a standard list offence in the subsequent two years ... and there is no evidence that cautions have become less effective since the mid-1980s. There is, not surprisingly, evidence that conviction rates are higher among those who have received more than one caution ... but the numbers involved are not, and never have been high ... The conclusion most people would draw from these figures (is) that cautions are effective as well as quick and economical ... The principle of diversion by cautioning thus continues to receive authoritative support.*
>
> (Smith, 1999, p 155).

As we have seen however, effectiveness and 'authoritative support' is seemingly not enough to sustain effective practice within the highly-charged politics of the 'new' youth justice.

The politics of intervention: 'nipping crime in the bud' and 'catching them early'

> *...in the inane world of corrections, nothing fails like success and succeeds like failure.*
>
> (Miller, 1991: xi)

The rc-politicisation of crime in general, and juvenile crime in particular, underpins key elements of the New Labour policy trajectory, (Goldson, 1997 and 1999; Pitts, this volume). The 1997 general election campaign evidenced the extent to which New Labour intended to 'play the crime card', and thus crime, and the fear of crime, was mobilised and exploited in 'ways quite unprecedented in its history', (Brownlee, 1998, p 313). Indeed, New Labour was not content simply to neutralise the traditional electoral advantage of the Conservatives in law and order matters, rather it aimed to establish *itself* in the public mind as the party with an unequivocally 'tough' line. In 1979 Margaret Thatcher, the incoming 'Iron Lady' Prime Minister, impatiently dismissed those who had created a 'culture of excuses' and pledged to 're-establish a code of conduct that condemns crime plainly and without exception', (cited in Riddell, 1989, p 171). In 1997 it was New Labour who were announcing that the time to 'be tough on crime' had arrived and 'no more excuses' could be tolerated, (Home Office, 1997a).

Indeed, New Labour has 'stolen back the issue of law and order from their political opponents', (Brownlee, 1998, p 315). Further to the defeat in the 1992 general election the new leadership has embraced the 'modernising project' and set about re-constructing the party, its constitution and its central policy priorities. New Labour has engaged uncritically with rhetorical constructions of populist punitiveness and is clearly determined to avoid any charge of being 'soft'. Speaking at his first party conference as Home Secretary in 1997, Jack Straw announced 'we said we would make Labour the party of law and order and we did', (cited in Brownlee, 1998, p 318). A raft of 'consultation' papers and two major pieces of legislation, the Crime and Disorder Act 1998 and the Youth Justice and Criminal Evidence Act 1999 have followed, all underpinned by a 'tough' line on law and order. There are no signs of relaxation in this regard and Straw reiterated the position at the party conference in September, 1999: 'there is no room for complacency ... the government has embarked on nothing less than a crusade against crime', (Straw, 1999).

Central to its 'crusade' is juvenile crime, and the political and ideological tide has unquestionably turned against state support for diversionary strategies. Rutherford, (1993, p 164) has noted that support for diversion, notwithstanding its effectiveness, was always 'nascent and tentative' and, as such, vulnerable within a re-politicising context. The notion that diversion is tantamount to condoning juvenile crime and cautions are an ineffectual gesture, has a particular resonance with the public. Moreover, certain policy commentators regard multi-agency diversionary schemes as 'casinos of care', (Brock, cited in Wright, 1993) and similar sentiments have been known to exist within the agencies themselves, most notably the police, (Hughes et al., 1998). The combination of these factors, harnessed and applied to shifting political priorities and a 'bastardised form of moral scolding', (Brownlee, 1998, p 328), have served to undermine diversionary strategies:

> *Insufficient attention is given to changing behaviour, to teaching the difference between right and wrong. Police and magistrates are frustrated. The public cannot understand why so many young offenders go unchecked ... far too many youngsters are holding up to ridicule the very idea that the law can be enforced ... Too little is done to change youngsters behaviour early in their offending career ... We believe that the time has come for fundamental changes to be made ... In many areas cautioning continues to be used when it patently does not work ... cautioning for many is therefore a waste of time ... too often it is not associated with effective intervention ... We have to start again ... by prioritising early intervention to nip offending in the bud.*

> (Straw and Michael, 1996: *passim*)

Early intervention, 'fast track punishment', (Juvenile Offenders Unit, 1998, p 1) and 'nipping offending in the bud' characterises the new interventionist order. 'Catching them early' was the title of a major conference organised by the Youth Justice Board for England and Wales in March, 1999 and it is symptomatic of the development of a 'pre-emptive escalation of social control', (Cohen, 1972, xxiv), which is destined to draw more and more children into the formal criminal justice system. This manifests far more about the sticky mess that is politics than it reveals in relation to the development of effective and responsible policy and practice approaches to children in trouble.

Early intervention and the referral order: 'righting' children's wrongs or 'wronging' children's rights?

> *...more radical action is needed to maximise the impact of the youth court on young offenders, making it as effective as possible at tackling offending behaviour, especially for young people appearing before the court for the first time.*

> (Home Office, 1997a: para 9.20)

In many respects the Referral Order (as outlined earlier in this chapter) is the flagship of early intervention. Part 1 of the Youth Justice and Criminal Evidence

Act 1999 provides for the Order, which represents a significant addition to the sentencing powers available to the courts and will comprise the principal means of dealing with children on *first conviction*. The Referral Order will enable the courts to refer such children to newly established 'Youth Offender Panels' which will be charged with responsibility for examining the reasons for the child's offending, and designing a 'programme of behaviour' and a 'Youth Offender Contract' to allow for action to be taken in order to 'tackle' it. The Referral Order is to be piloted from June 2000 with national implementation planned for the early part of 2002 and it raises a wide range of critical concerns, (Goldson, 2000a; Haines, this volume; Wonnacott, 1999). For the purposes here I want to focus on three primary justice issues: proportionality, legal safeguards and 'contracts', and to locate the provisions of Part 1 of the Youth Justice and Criminal Evidence Act 1999 within the broader context of international standards, treaties and rules.

First, the question of proportionality. Rule 5.1 of the United Nations Standard Minimum Rules for the Administration of Juvenile Justice, the 'Beijing Rules', states that 'the juvenile justice system … shall ensure that any reaction to juvenile offenders shall always be in proportion to the circumstances of both the offenders and the offence', (United Nations General Assembly, 1985). Similarly, rules 17.1(b) and 17.1(d) provide that 'restrictions on the personal liberty of the juvenile shall … be limited to the possible minimum', and 'the well-being of the juvenile shall be the guiding factor in her or his case', (ibid). Indeed, the concept of proportionality, usually expressed in terms of just deserts in relation to the gravity and seriousness of the offence, is a well-established legal principle which serves to offset the likelihood of over-zealous intervention and concomitant forms of injustice. In essence, this important principle, which is also enshrined in Article 40.4 of the United Nations Convention on the Rights of the Child, (United Nations General Assembly, 1989), requires no more and no less than a fair and proportional reaction in any case where a child is convicted of a criminal offence: it is sometimes referred to as the practice of minimum necessary intervention and it has substantial antecedent in criminal justice, (Von Hirsch, 1976).

By restricting the Referral Order to children who have never previously been convicted of a criminal offence however, and by exposing such children to the wide-ranging powers available to the Youth Offender Panel in setting the 'programme of behaviour' and the 'Youth Offender Contract', the principle of proportionality is at risk. It is not beyond the realms of possibility that Youth Offender Panels, in accordance with Section 8(2) of the Youth Justice and Criminal Evidence Act 1999, may impose restrictions on the child's liberty, including measures which will require them to undertake unpaid work as a service to the community; to be at home at defined times; to participate in specified activities; to report to persons and/or places; and to terminate their association with particular persons and/or places for first offences of a non-serious nature, believing that this will prevent further offending which is, after all, the stated purpose of the Referral Order. The child will be required to take responsibility for, and face the consequences of, his or her offence. Children may well be expected to engage in direct contact with victims, and in activity which is adjudged to make direct amends to the victim. There is abundant evidence to confirm that for many children in trouble, offending is but one problem amongst many which combine and interlock to form a complex network of disadvantage and difficulty, (Goldson, 2000b). Within this context such heavy emphasis on the child's individual responsibility for their behaviour and to the victim, together with the stigmatising labelling that will accompany this, and the relative absence of similar emphasis on the responsibility of others, including state agencies, to the child threatens a sense of justice and balance. This is morally and ethically problematic. Moreover, as Haines and Drakeford, (1998, pp 229–234) have noted, there is little research evidence to suggest that victim-oriented and reintegrative approaches of this particular nature actually 'work'.

Second, the question of legal safeguards. The *No More Excuses* White Paper, (Home Office, 1997a, para 9.37) states that 'there would be no legal representation at the youth panel stage ... Legal representation would put an obstacle in the way of the panel dealing directly with the defendant'. More recently, draft guidance in respect of the implementation of the Referral Order provides:

> *Young people will not be legally represented at a youth offender panel meeting as this could seriously hinder the process of the panel ... The panel should be alert to attempts to introduce a legal representative in the guise of the offender's supporter.*
>
> (Juvenile Offenders Unit, 1999, paras 3.31 and 3.32)

Thus, nowhere in Part 1 of the Act is there provision allowing for the child to be legally represented at the Youth Offender Panel and, as Wonnacott, (1999, p 284), has noted, this places the child 'in a substantially worse position than if he (sic) were being sentenced in the court'. Although guilt will have been established in the Youth Court prior to referral, there can be no guarantee that the child will have been legally represented at court. Moreover, it will presumably be important for the Youth Offender Panel to consider the degree of the child's guilt and responsibility, together with any aggravating or mitigating factors, before it establishes the 'programme of behaviour', the 'Youth Offender Contract', and determines the extent of the restrictions that are to be applied to the child's liberty. These are exactly the kind of issues that a legal representative would ordinarily address.

Section 5 of Part 1 of the Act provides for the attendance of an 'appropriate person' at the Youth Offender Panel and Section 7(3) allows for a person of the child's choice 'aged 18 or over' to attend, subject to the approval and agreement of the Panel. Notwithstanding this, neither the 'appropriate person' nor the adult identified by the child, should the panel approve of his/her attendance, is an adequate substitute for a trained legal adviser and advocate. Denying the child the right to such advice and representation conflicts with Article 3 of the United Nations Convention on the Rights of the Child, (United Nations General Assembly, 1989), which provides for the 'best interests of the child'; Article 12(2) which provides the child with the opportunity 'to be heard in any judicial and administrative proceedings ... either directly, or through a representative or appropriate body, in a manner consistent with the procedural rules of national law'; and Article 40.2(b)(ii) which allows the child 'to have legal or other appropriate assistance', (ibid). Similar tensions exist with the 'Beijing Rules' which provide, by way of rule 15.1, for the child's right 'to be represented by a legal adviser', (United Nations General Assembly, 1985), and Wonnacott, (1999, p 285) claims that 'it seems likely that the exclusion of the lawyers ... are breaches of the European Convention for the Protection of Human Rights and Fundamental Freedoms'.

Third, the question of contracts. Section 8(5) of Part 1 of the Act states that where a 'programme of behaviour' is 'agreed between the offender and the panel, the panel shall cause a written record of the programme to be produced' and once this record is signed by the child and a member of the Panel it takes effect as the terms of the 'Youth Offender Contract'.

Bearing in mind the points that have already been made with respect to the restrictions on the child's liberty which may be imposed by such 'contracts', together with practices and activities that the child may be obliged to undertake, both the ethics and justice of requiring a child, perhaps as young as ten, to sign such a contract are questionable. Furthermore, if we add to this the prohibition of legal advice and representation for the child in the process of determining the 'programme of behaviour', and the punitive consequences of the child's failure to meet the conditions of the 'contract' as provided by the Part 1 of the Act, then the issue of the child as signatory becomes even more problematic. Wonnacott observes:

> *The referral order is ... supposed to be different from other disposals available to the youth court in that it is essentially consensual; the offender and the panel are supposed to reach an agreement to be embodied in a contract. But, in substance, the referral order is likely to prove just as coercive as any other criminal disposal, because in practice the panel will be in a position to dictate terms to the offender ... Notwithstanding that the imagery is overwhelmingly consensual, in substance the contractual basis of the referral order is a sham, because all the negotiating power is in the hands of the youth offender panel ... A contract agreed under compulsion is not a contract at all, and it is dishonest to suggest otherwise ... Furthermore, notwithstanding the Government's protestations to the contrary and the general cross-party support, its provisions will almost certainly involve a breach of the European Convention on Human Rights.*
>
> (Wonnacott, 1999, p 287)

An ever-widening net: crime, criminalisation and the children of the poor

> *No doubt punitive rhetoric, replayed through the approving comment pages of new-found media allies, appeases the fears of a certain constituency of 'middle-Englanders'. But if the new government merely hides behind the rhetoric of censure and continues, as its predecessor did, to heap all the blame for social ills at the feet of 'maladjusted' individuals and 'dysfunctional' families, it will find that it merely preserves the conditions under which a growing number of people turn to crime and, as a result, managing rather than reducing the offender population will remain its priority.*
>
> (Brownlee, 1998, p 331, original emphasis)

The aetiological linkages between deprivation and juvenile delinquency are well- established in academic criminology and are vividly evidenced in seminal and defining studies both from the USA and the UK, (Merton, 1938; Shaw and McKay, 1942; Whyte, 1943; Mays, 1954; Cohen, 1955; Cloward and Ohlin, 1960; Downes, 1966; Suttles, 1968 and Parker, 1974). Such studies are characterised by different strains of theoretical interpretation and analysis and they are not beyond critique. Notwithstanding their differences and respective shortcomings however, they each reveal the relation that binds specific forms of structural disadvantage with an increased likelihood of youthful delinquency. Contemporary discourse prefers to identify 'risk-factors', invariably a scientised and sanitised code for poverty and associated forms of human misery, of which there is plenty in modern Britain. Bradshaw, (1999), has reported that child poverty has increased more in Britain since 1980 than any other Luxembourg Income Survey country for which there is data, and the prevalence of child poverty is now higher in Britain than any other country in the European Union, (see also Child Poverty Action Group, 1998; Joseph Rowntree Foundation, 1998 and 1999; Shropshire and Middleton, 1999; Gregg, Harkness and Machin, 1999). Child 'offenders' normally live at the sharp-end of such adverse socio-economic formations. This applies equally to boys and girls and it is as true for the youngest children as it is for those aged 15–17 years. Crowley, (1998), found very similar patterns of disadvantage in her sample of 12–14 year old 'offenders', drawn from Unitary Authorities in England and Wales, to those which beset older children in a Merseyside study, (Goldson, 1998). Crowley concludes her analysis of the circumstances and life experiences of her sample by highlighting their 'very sad, bereft and damaged lives', (ibid, p 25). Haines and Drakeford, (1998, pp 141–178) also survey the multiple forms of disadvantage endured by children in trouble, and Hagell and Newburn, (1994), and Bottoms, (1995), each found that family difficulties and contact with the official 'care system' prevailed amongst their respective research samples of 'young offenders'.

It is inevitably the children of the poor who will be drawn into criminalising processes and who will be 'managed' by the new interventionist measures that have been discussed above. The new interventionism is distinctive. It is not the benign welfare-oriented interventionism that characterised Intermediate Treatment in the late 1960s and throughout the decade of the 1970s. Rather it is an interventionism which appeals to correctional, punitive and deterring priorities for its legitimacy. It is an interventionism which emphasises the child's individual responsibility and accountability. It is an interventionism which seemingly gives reign to indeterminacy and erodes procedural safeguards. It is an interventionism which places children at greater risk of counter-productive intrusion and interference from 'informal' panels than they would face in the formal criminal courts. It is an interventionism which 'promotes prosecution' (Bell, 1999), violates rights, and, in the final analysis, will serve only to criminalise the most structurally vulnerable children.

It is likely that the United Nations Committee on the Rights of the Child in Geneva will take a particular interest in the new youth justice. When the Committee last considered a report from the UK government in respect of its compliance with the provisions of the United Nations Convention on the Rights of the Child and other related international standards, treaties and rules, it found that 'policy after policy had broken the terms' of the Convention, (cited in Goldson, 1997, p 142). The UN Committee was especially concerned with policies and practice responses targeted at juvenile crime. Of course at that time it was the Conservative administration that faced authoritative international critique. New Labour has recently published its report to the UN Committee, (UK Government, 1999a). The language that features in the report with regard to the government's youth justice priorities is deeply problematic. New Labour engages benign forms of expression in order to legitimise overtly coercive and interventionist practices. This is not the first time that the government has distorted meaning in this way, (Goldson, 1999, p 15). Early intervention, the erosion of legal safeguards and concomitant criminalisation, is packaged as a courtesy to the child and as such is presented as if it is necessary:

> *to ensure that, if a child had begun to offend, they are **entitled** to the earliest possible intervention to address that offending behaviour and eliminate its causes ... the changes will ... (place) all juveniles on the same footing ... and will contribute to the **right** of children ... to develop responsibility for themselves.*
>
> (UK Government, 1999a, 180, emphasis added).

Scraton has observed that:

> *The UK Government steadfastly denies the charge that its new legislation will lead inevitably to widening the net of criminalisation. Yet ... (it) effectively does criminalise, both in perception and consequence. The media,*

public, police, schools and other agencies will not suddenly and sublimi-
nally undergo a radical transformation of perception and understanding.
Offences are offences, and courts are courts. For those young children
caught up in law's ever-expanding web the words of reassurance within the
UK Government's report are rendered meaningless and cynical. They
become children with a record, children who have been before a magistrate
and labelled within their communities.

(Scraton, 1999).

There are profound and complex contradictions and tensions which underpin
New Labour policy. The Prime Minister has repeatedly stated his determination to
eradicate child poverty and the government has announced a broad programme.
£540 million is being invested in 'early years' programmes; an additional £19
billion is to be spent to raise standards in education; £500 million is committed to
reduce school exclusion; it is estimated that the Working Families Tax Credit will
provide 'extra help' to 1.5 million families; £470 million is being invested in a
National Childcare Strategy for children from birth to 14 years; £375 million is
being invested in 'Quality Protects' initiatives for children 'looked after' by local
authorities; and a range of so-called 'new deals' and 'action zones' have been
established, (UK Government, 1999b). These initiatives are not beyond critique,
but they mark, at least in part, a departure from the systematic erosion of public
services and the relentless antagonism to the welfare state that had characterised
Conservative administrations for the best part of the previous two decades. What
New Labour has singularly failed to dispense with however, is the legacy of
punishment, retribution and correctionalism. On the contrary, it has embraced the
rhetoric of 'toughness' with enthusiastic gusto, and the child's experience of state
policies and practices will not be ameliorated by deceptive packaging and
insidious 'spin'. Indeed, for as long as interventionist priorities are left to drive the
new youth justice, more and more, and younger and younger children will be
criminalised and needlessly damaged.

References

Association of County Councils, the Association of Metropolitan Authorities, the
   Association of Directors of Social Services, NACRO and the Association of Chief
   Officers of Probation, (1996), *National Protocol for Youth Justice Services: Statements
   of Principle for Local Services in England and Wales*. London, Association of
   Metropolitan Authorities.
Audit Commission, (1997), *Misspent Youth Young People and Crime*. London, The Audit
   Commission.
Becker, H., (1963), *Outsiders*. New York, Free Press.
Bell, A., Hodgson, M. and Pragnell, S., (1999), Diverting Children and Young People from
   Crime and the Criminal Justice System pp91–109 in Goldson, B., (Ed.), *Youth Justice
   Contemporary Policy and Practice*. Aldershot, Ashgate.

Bell, C., (1999). Appealing for Justice for Children and Young People: A Critical Analysis of the Crime and Disorder Bill, 1998, pp191–210 in Goldson, B., (Ed.), *Youth Justice Contemporary Policy and Practice.* Aldershot, Ashgate.

Blackmore, J., (1984), Delinquency Theory and Practice: A Link Through IT *Youth and Policy, 9.*

Blagg, H., (1986), *The Final Report on the Juvenile Liaison Bureau,* Corby, Lancaster University.

Bottoms, A., (1995), *Intensive Community Supervision of Young Offenders: Outcomes, Process and Cost.* The University of Cambridge Institute of Criminology, Cambridge.

Bradshaw, J., (1999), Children 5–16: Growing into the 21st Century Research Programme. *Economic and Social Research Council Conference 23.02.99,* Royal Horticultural Conference Centre, London.

Brownlee, I., (1998), New Labour: New Penology? Punitive Rhetoric and the Limits of Managerialism in Criminal Justice Policy. *Journal of Law and Society,* Vol. 25 No. 3 pp313–335.

Child Poverty Action Group, (1998), *Poverty: Journal of the Child Poverty Action Group,* Number 101. Child Poverty Action Group, London.

Cloward, R. A. and Ohlin, L. E., (1960), *Delinquency and Opportunity: A Theory of Delinquent Gangs.* New York, Free Press.

Cohen, A., (1955), *Delinquent Boys: The Culture of the Gang.* New York, Free Press.

Cohen, S., (1972), *Folk Devils and Moral Panics: The Creation of the Mods and Rockers.* New York, St Martins Press.

Cohen, S., (1986), *Visions of Social Control.* Cambridge, Polity Press.

Crawford, A., (1994), The Partnership Approach to Community Crime Prevention: Corporatism at the Local Level. *Social and Legal Studies,* 3, pp 497–519.

Crowley, A., (1998), *A Criminal Waste; A Study of Child Offenders Eligible for Secure Training Centres.* London, The Children's Society.

Crown Prosecution Service, (1986), *Code of Practice for Prosecutors.* London, CPS.

Davis, G., Boucherat, J. and Watson, D., (1989), Pre-court decision making in juvenile justice. *British Journal of Criminology,* Vol. 29 pp 219–35.

Dignan, J., (1992), Repairing the Damage: Can Reparation Work in the Service of Diversion? *British Journal of Criminology,* Vol. 32 pp 453–72.

Ditchfield, J., (1976), *Police Cautioning in England and Wales: Home Office Research Study No. 37.* London, HMSO.

Downes, D., (1966), *The Delinquent Solution: A Study of Subcultural Theory.* London, Routledge and Kegan Paul.

Evans, R. and Ellis, R., (1997), Police Cautioning in the 1990s. *Home Office Research and Statistics Directorate Research Findings no. 52.* London, Home Office.

Gelsthorpe, L. and Morris, A., (1994), Juvenile Justice 1945–1992 in Maguire, M.; Morgan, R. and Reiner, R. (Eds.) *The Oxford Handbook of Criminology* pp 949–93. Oxford, Clarendon Press.

Gelsthorpe, L. and Morris, A., (1999), Much Ado About Nothing: A Critical Comment on Key Provisions Relating to Children in the Crime and Disorder Act 1998. *Child and Family Law Quarterly,* Vol 11, No. 3 pp 209–221.

Gibson, B. and Cavadino, P., (1995), *Criminal Justice Process.* Winchester, Waterside Press.

Goldson, B., (1997), Children in Trouble: State Responses to Juvenile Crime pp 124–45 in Scraton, P. *'Childhood' in 'Crisis'?* London, UCL Press.

Goldson, B., (1998), *Children in Trouble: Backgrounds and Outcomes*. Liverpool, The University of Liverpool Department of Sociology, Social Policy and Social Work Studies.

Goldson, B., (1999), Youth (In)Justice: Contemporary Developments in Policy and Practice pp1–27 in Goldson, B., (Ed.), *Youth Justice: Contemporary Policy and Practice*. Aldershot, Ashgate.

Goldson, B., (2000a), Youth Justice and Criminal Evidence Bill Part 1: Referrals to Youth Offender Panels, in Payne, L., (Ed.), *Child Impact Statements 1998/99*. London, National Children's Bureau and UNICEF.

Goldson, B., (2000b), 'Children in Need' or 'Young Offenders'? Hardening Ideology, Organisational Change and New Challenges for Social Work with Children in Trouble. *Child and Family Social Work, Vol. 5 No. 3.*

Goldson, B. and Chigwada-Bailey, R., (1999), (What) Justice for Black Children and Young People? pp51–74 in Goldson, B., (Ed.), *Youth Justice: Contemporary Policy and Practice*. Aldershot, Ashgate.

Gordon, W., Cuddy, P. and Black, J., (1999), *Introduction to Youth Justice*. Winchester, Waterside Press.

Graham, J. and Bowling, B., (1995), *Young People and Crime*. Home Office Research Study 145. London, HMSO.

Gregg, P., Harkness, S. and Machin, S., (1999), *Child Development and Family Income*. Joseph Rowntree Foundation, York.

Hagell, A. and Newburn, T., (1994), *Persistent Young Offenders*. London, Policy Studies Institute.

Haines, K. and Drakeford, M., (1999), *Young People and Youth Justice*. London, Macmillan.

Home Office, (1984), *Cautioning by the Police: A Consultative Document*. London, Home Office.

Home Office, (1985), *The Cautioning of Offenders, Circular 14/1985*. London, Home Office.

Home Office, (1990), *The Cautioning of Offenders, Circular 59/90*. London, Home Office.

Home Office, (1994), *The Cautioning of Offenders, Circular 18/94*. London, Home Office.

Home Office, (1997a), *No More Excuses: A New Approach to Tackling Youth Crime in England and Wales*. London, Home Office.

Home Office, (1997b), *Tackling Youth Crime: A Consultation Paper*. London, Home Office.

Home Office, (1999), *Statistics on Race and the Criminal Justice System*. London, Home Office.

Hudson, B., (1993), *Penal Policy and Social Justice*. London, Macmillan.

Hughes, G.; Pilkington, A. and Leiston, R., (1998), Diversion in a Culture of Severity. *The Howard Journal of Criminal Justice* Vol. 37, No.1 pp16–33.

Joseph Rowntree Foundation, (1998), *'Findings' March 1998: Income and Wealth, the Latest Evidence*. Joseph Rowntree Foundation, York.

Joseph Rowntree Foundation, (1999), *'Findings' March 1999: Child Poverty and Its Consequences*. Joseph Rowntree Foundation, York.

Juvenile Offenders Unit, (1998), *On Track: Newsletter for Youth Justice Practitioners*. London, Home Office.

Juvenile Offenders Unit, (1999), *The Referral Order: Draft Guidance to Youth Offending Teams 8 November 1999*. London, Home Office.

Landau, S.F. and Nathan, G., (1983), Selecting Delinquents for Cautioning in the London Metropolitan Area, *British Journal of Criminology* 23/2 pp128–49.

Lemert, E., (1951), *Social Pathology*. New York, McGraw-Hill.

Lemert, E., (1967), *Human Deviance, Social Problems and Social Control.* Englewood Cliffs, New Jersey, Prentice Hall.

Matza, D., (1964), *Delinquency and Drift.* New York, Wiley.

Matza, D., (1969), *Becoming Deviant.* Englewood Cliffs, New Jersey, Prentice Hall.

Mays, J. B., (1954), *Growing Up in the City: A Study of Juvenile Delinquency in an Urban Neighbourhood.* Liverpool, Liverpool University Press.

McMahon, M., (1990), Net-widening: Vagaries in the use of a Concept. *British Journal of Criminology,* vol. 30 pp121–49.

Merton, R.K., (1938), Social Structure and Anomie. *American Sociological Review, 3.*

Miller, J., (1991), *Last One Over the Wall.* Ohio, Ohio State University Press.

Muncie, J., (1999), *Youth and Crime: A Critical Introduction.* London, Sage.

NACRO, (1988), *NACRO Briefing: Cautioning Juvenile Offenders.* London, NACRO.

NACRO, (1989), *Diverting Juvenile Offenders from Prosecution.* NACRO Juvenile Crime Committee Policy Paper 2. London, NACRO.

NACRO, (1998), *NACRO Briefing: The Final Warning Scheme, Summary of Home Office Draft Circular.* London, NACRO.

NITFED, (1986), *Anti-Racist Practice for Intermediate Treatment.* London, National Intermediate Treatment Federation.

Parker, H., (1974), *View from the Boys: A Sociology of Down Town Adolescents.* London, David and Charles.

Pearson, G., (1994), Youth, Crime and Society in Maguire, M.; Morgan, R. and Reiner, R., (Eds.), *The Oxford Handbook of Criminology* pp1161–1206. Oxford, Clarendon Press.

Pitts, J., (1990), *Working with Young Offenders.* London, Macmillan.

Pratt, J., (1986), Diversion from the Juvenile Court. *British Journal of Criminology*, vol 26 pp212–33.

Reid, K., (1997), The Abolition of Cautioning? Juveniles in the 'Last Chance' Saloon. *The Criminal Lawyer,* No 78 pp 4–8.

Riddell, P., (1989), *The Thatcher Effect.* Oxford, Blackwell.

Rutherford, A., (1992), *Growing Out of Crime: The New Era.* Winchester, Waterside Press.

Rutherford, A., (1993), *Criminal Justice and the Pursuit of Decency.* Oxford, Oxford University Press.

Ruxton, S., (1996), *Children in Europe.* London, NCH Action for Children.

Scraton, P., (1999), Threatening Children: Politics of Hate and Policies of Denial in Contemporary Britain. A paper presented to *Organization for the Protection of Children's Rights Fourth International Conference on the Child, Children and Violence: Our Individual, Family and Collective Responsibilities.*, Quebec 13–15 October unpublished.

Shapland, J., (1978), Self-Reported Delinquency in Boys Aged 11 to 14. *British Journal of Criminology* Vol. 18 No. 3.

Shaw, C. R. and McKay, H., (1942), *Juvenile Delinquency and Urban Areas.* Chicago, University of Chicago Press.

Shropshire, J. and Middleton, S., (1999), *Small Expectations: Learning to be Poor.* York, Joseph Rowntree Foundation.

Smith, D., (1999) Social Work with Young People in Trouble: Memory and Prospect pp148–69 in Goldson, B., (Ed.), *Youth Justice: Contemporary Policy and Practice.* Aldershot, Ashgate.

Straw, J. and Michael, A., (1996), *Tackling Youth Crime: Reforming Youth Justice.* London, Labour Party.

Straw, J., (1999), *The full text of Home Secretary Jack Straw's speech to the Labour Party Conference*, Thursday 30 September.

Suttles, G. D., (1968), *The Social Order of the Slum: Ethnicity and Territory in the Inner City.* Chicago, University of Chicago Press.

Thorpe, D., Smith, D., Green, C. and Paley, J., (1980), *Out of Care.* London, George Allen and Unwin.

UK Government, (1999a), *Convention on the Rights of the Child: Second Report to the UN Committee on the Rights of the Child by the United Kingdom.* London, The Stationery Office.

UK Government, (1999b), *Opportunity for All: Tackling Poverty and Social Exclusion.* London, The Stationery Office.

United Nations General Assembly, (1985), *The United Nations Standard Minimum Rules for the Administration of Juvenile Justice.* New York, United Nations.

United Nations General Assembly, (1989), *The United Nations Convention on the Rights of the Child.* New York, United Nations.

Von Hirsch, A., (1976), *Doing Justice: The Choice of Punishments.* New York, Hill and Wang.

Whyte, W. F., (1943), *Street Corner Society: The Social Structure of an Italian Slum.* Chicago, University of Chicago Press.

Wonnacott, C., (1999), New Legislation. The Counterfeit Contract; Reform, Pretence and Muddled Principles in the New Referral Order. *Child and Family Law Quarterly,* Vol. 11, No. 3 pp271–87.

Worrall, A., (1999), Troubled or Troublesome? Justice for Girls and Young Women pp28–50 in Goldson, B., (Ed.), *Youth Justice: Contemporary Policy and Practice.* Aldershot, Ashgate.

Wright, A., (1993), Towards an Appropriate Model of Diversion from the Criminal Court Process. *Justice of the Peace,* 20 March, pp 184–6.

Youth Justice Board for England and Wales, (1999), *Draft National Standards for Youth Justice.* London, Youth Justice Board.

CHAPTER 4

Referral Orders and Youth Offender Panels: Restorative Approaches and the New Youth Justice

Kevin Haines

Introduction

The main provisions of the Youth Justice and Criminal Evidence Act 1999 that concern young people are those which create the new sentence of a Referral Order and the establishment of Youth Offender Panels. The Referral Order is intended to replace the Conditional Discharge and, in line with the government's interventionist policy towards young people who have offended, this new measure will replace the formal 'ticking off' of the Conditional Discharge with a package of interventions.

The operation of Youth Offender Panels and the range of interventions they make possible draw heavily on restorative justice thinking. This chapter will assume a working knowledge of the relevant provisions of the Youth Justice and Criminal Evidence Act 1999, but it does not assume that policy makers, managers or practitioners will have worked through issues concerning the implementation of these measures in the light of current knowledge about restorative justice. The aim of this chapter, therefore, is to evaluate the under-lying principles and practical application of restorative justice techniques as applied to Referral Orders and Youth Offender Panels. As we shall see, this analysis gives rise to some significant concerns about these measures and their place within a system of justice. Finally, some pointers are provided which, if followed, offer a more positive approach to implementing restorative principles in the new youth justice framework.

Understanding restorative justice

A major problem in claiming to implement 'key principles of restorative justice' within the provisions concerning Youth Offender Panels is that the concept of restorative justice is poorly articulated and understood.

What is restorative justice? What are its aims? How does it work? How does it apply to *children* and the justice process? These may seem like basic questions to be asking of a concept that has such widespread popularity, but these are issues to which there are no simple or consensual answers. For a new theory about crime and the treatment of offenders to be effective it must be clearly understood by those who have responsibility for legislation and policy, management and practice; because it is these people who will give it expression in practice. At present, however, it is difficult to lay any claim to coherence or consistency in the concept of restorative justice. On the whole, if the growth in restorative justice practices are any indication, policy makers and practitioners do not appear to have been too much troubled by this problem. Some academics, however, have been more aware of the difficulties. Walgrave, (1995, p 244), for example, recognises that the boundaries of restorative justice have not yet been drawn, and proposes his own way forward based on community service. A more collective and sustained effort to clarify the central concepts of restorative justice was made by the Alliance of Non-Governmental Organisations on Crime Prevention and Criminal Justice. The Alliance formed a working party in 1995, made up of experts from around the world, with the aim of using a structured method to develop a consensual definition of restorative justice in order to give it 'a sufficiently high profile so it will be placed on the agenda of the Tenth United Nations Crime Congress in the year 2000', (McCold, 1998).

The divergence of opinion in what is meant by the term restorative justice was recognised by the working party. General agreement was reached that 'the purpose of restorative justice was to provide victims with a central role in justice and that offenders should repair the harm done by the offence as much as possible', (McCold, 1998), but significant disagreements were found concerning the place of punishment and the role of the state. Ultimately, these efforts failed to produce agreement and the working party adopted the following definition of restorative justice developed by Tony Marshall:

> *Restorative justice is a process whereby parties with a stake in a specific offence collectively resolve how to deal with the aftermath of the offence and its implications for the future.*

(Marshall, 1999).

This definition, and the process whereby the working party adopted it, are wholly unsatisfactory. The inability of the working party to reach a consensual definition does not reflect badly upon the participants, but it does point to some deep conceptual problems with the central aspects of restorative justice. In essence, the problem is not so much rooted in the diversity of practice or opinion, but in the absence of a central defining characteristic which has the utility of a philosophy or a touchstone, (or 'principles' as Marshall calls them), from which practice may be derived. This difficulty is reflected in the work of Marshall himself, who, in his work which post-dates the adoption of the above definition persists in offering alternatives:

Restorative justice is a problem-solving approach to crime which involves the parties themselves, and the community generally, in an active relationship with statutory agencies.

(Marshall, 1999).

For Marshall, it seems, the state, in the guise of statutory agencies, has an important, if not central, and hence 'active', role to play in restorative justice practice, but he also identifies the philosophical deficiency of current definitions and argues that restorative justice is 'not any particular practice, but a set of *principles* which may orient the general practice of any agency or group in relation to crime', (Marshall, 1999, *original emphasis*). Thus, according to Marshall, these principles are:

- Making room for the personal involvement of those mainly concerned (particularly the offender and the victim, but also their families and communities).
- Seeing crime problems in their social context.
- A forward-looking (or preventative) problem-solving orientation.
- Flexibility of practice (creativity).

On this view diversity of practice is not a problem for restorative justice, indeed it may be a distinct advantage. More traditional forms of treatment for juvenile offenders have been criticised where issues of 'justice by geography' have arisen, but there is also great diversity of practice within traditional approaches which is seen as both an important and necessary aspect of the individualisation of treatment. The goal in any attempt to clarify what we mean by restorative justice should not, therefore, be concerned with standardising methods or practices. It was this approach which led to the ultimate failure of the working group, discussed above, to reach common ground. What is necessary to establish the credibility of restorative justice is a test by which the diversity of practices may be measured to ascertain conformity with an overarching philosophy.

To be sure, restorative justice practice is, and it must be, characterised by certain activities, including; the problem-solving approach and the family group conference milieu. What is important, however, is how these characteristics and activities are applied in practice. In other words, what their purpose is, and what the motivation of those responsible for delivering them is. One of the main deficiencies, therefore, of restorative justice, on a global and local scale, is to be found in this area.

It is not surprising, therefore, to find this weakness of definition, poorly articulated methods and a tenuous link between the range of interventions and stated purpose in the provisions concerning Youth Offender Panels. One cannot lay claim to a restorative justice foundation simply because features of a new system borrow from restorative justice. The use of a panel, some members of which may be drawn from the local community, and the involvement of victims does not make something restorative justice. There must also be a link between the range of measures that may be applied to a young person and the stated intention of the system. It is far from clear how, for example, financial or other forms of reparation, unpaid work in the community, or a curfew are related to achieving re-integration of the young person into a law-abiding community, or making the young person take more responsibility for their behaviour. This lack of a robust link between types of intervention and the intended outcomes is a serious problem. How can one hope to achieve one's intended outcomes if the chosen methods do not directly lead to these outcomes?

The stated objectives of Youth Offender Panels, however, go beyond re-integration and increasing the responsibility felt by children. The Act requires Panels to ensure that any measures taken in respect of a young person are directed towards reducing further offending. The same problem persists with this objective to the extent that the range of measures envisioned in the Act as forming part of the Youth Offender Contract are, at best, only tenuously linked to the risk or protective factors associated with offending behaviour. It will be essential, under the Panel system, for managers and practitioners to develop more robust links between purpose and method. In order to do this, however, a clearer definition of the purpose of the Panel and the intentions of Panel members will need to be articulated. Talk of developing a philosophy of restorative justice is explicitly intended to fill this gap; it is concerned with developing a touchstone from which practice may be derived and measured.

It is this activity which led Marshall in the direction he has taken and to the adumbration of his 'principles', but they are not sufficiently prescriptive to offer a test of restorative justice practices, nor do they possess the characteristics necessary of a philosophy. The 'principles' offered by Marshall are all features or aspects of a restorative justice approach, but they do not constitute a philosophy. Moreover, what is needed is a single philosophical statement from which all other actions and intentions can be derived, since a set of statements creates room for a hierarchy or debate about alternatives which is destined to be ultimately confusing.

It is possible to argue that a philosophical statement already exists, which possesses sufficient support to lay claim to being a touchstone for restorative justice, and that is that 'restorative justice seeks to repair the harm done by a crime', (see McCold, 1998). This statement has the advantage of being clear and readily understood, although sometimes difficult to operationalise it leads to a definitive set of actions and it may be tested against practice. Thus, repairing the harm done by a crime may be a sufficiently robust philosophy for restorative justice, but questions remain as to whether it is sufficient in terms of the justice process. Actions which seek to ameliorate the conditions of the victim, the family and the community are all possible within such a philosophy, as are actions in line with Marshall's principles. So too, actions which seek to meet the needs of the offender are possible, but if repairing the harm done by the crime is the aim, then the extent to which meeting the needs of the offender is given sufficient attention is diminished, if the offence is put before the offender, and there is nothing to guarantee that such actions are taken.

Whatever philosophy is adopted to guide and shape restorative justice practice it is absolutely essential that the best interests of the offender are secured and protected. In making this statement it is necessary to remember that the offenders in this context are children under the age of 18 years and thus protected by the principles set out in a range of international agreements. Restorative justice as a concept and as a diverse set of practices has not been fully tested against these international protocols.

International texts concerning the special treatment which should be afforded to children, including juvenile offenders, have a long history. The Geneva Declaration of the Rights of the Child, (1924), stated that particular care must be extended to children. This sentiment has been echoed in a series of international conventions, including: The UN Declaration of the Rights of the Child, (1959); the Universal Declaration of Human Rights; the International Covenant on Civil and Political Rights; the International Covenant on Economic, Social and Cultural Rights; the United Nations Standard Minimum Rules for the Administration of Juvenile Justice, (The Beijing Rules, 1985); the United Nations Guidelines for the Prevention of Juvenile Delinquency, (1990); and the European Convention for the Protection of Human Rights and Fundamental Freedoms, (1970). The importance of these documents continues to grow and develop as courts make further judgements on individual cases which have wider implications for the justice system in particular countries. The basic principles laid down in these international agreements, however, have a continuing and robust relevance. The United Nations Convention on the Rights of the Child, (1989), stated, in Article 3, that:

> *In all actions concerning children, whether undertaken by public or private social welfare institutions, courts of law, administrative authorities or legislative bodies, the best interests of the child shall be a primary consideration.*

In the UK the wording 'a primary consideration' has been used to argue that there are other considerations which are also 'primary' and may be in conflict or competition with the rights of the child. In fact this term is a mis-translation of the original French in which the Convention was drafted. In the original French text the wording of Article 3 was the same as the wording of Article 21 which stated that the best interests of the child shall be the *paramount* consideration, and it was this meaning which the Convention sought to establish. This principle is further strengthened in the United Nations Standard Minimum Rules for the Administration of Juvenile Justice, (The Beijing Rules, 1985), which states that, as a fundamental principle, the aim of the juvenile justice system *should* be the promotion of the well-being of the juvenile and that criminal proceedings, of any kind, *should* be conducted in the best interests of the juvenile.

These international conventions firmly establish the principle that in any action taken as a result of an offence committed by a juvenile, primary consideration must be given to the best interests of the child. Advocates of restorative justice, (see, for example, Wright, 1996), who persist in placing the victim, or the family or the community, at the centre of their arguments or practices must grapple with this point. It is significant that one of the main things missing from definitions of restorative justice, and from practice, is any statement or recognition of the rights or needs or best interests of the child. At best, the child in restorative justice theory and practice is replaced by the offence, and its resolution, whilst at worst the victim is given a central position. This ordering of priorities must be addressed and if, it is argued, the child is placed at the centre, then action which promotes the best interests of the child can operate as a defining principle or philosophy of restorative justice.

The UN Convention does not seek to preclude or diminish practices that may be identified with restorative justice. Indeed, Article 40 promotes such activity, provided 'that human rights and legal safeguards are fully respected'. This does not mean that consideration of victims should be excluded from criminal proceedings although victims generally may not be best served by an approach which relies solely on this method, (see Haines, 1998), but it does mean that victims issues may only be actively pursued where any such actions do not contravene the principle of the best interests of the child. Of course, one may argue that this is a fine distinction to make and that the operationalisation of a 'children first' philosophy, (see Haines and Drakeford, 1998), is dogged by the same problems as articulating a preventative philosophy, but it is nevertheless the case that we all share a responsibility to work towards putting the best interests of the child first.

In 1998 the British government enacted the Human Rights Act which enshrined the European Convention on Human Rights within domestic legislation. While it was previously possible for a UK citizen to bring a case of alleged human rights abuse before the European Court of Human Rights, the enactment of this domestic legislation means that courts and, inter alia, those responsible for carrying out court orders, must ensure that their actions do not contravene this Act. Importantly, in interpreting alleged cases of human rights abuse the European Court, and henceforth domestic appellate courts, may draw on a range of international conventions, for example, the United Nations Convention on the Rights of the Child, and the Beijing Rules. It is thus not only a moral obligation to work within such conventions, but a legal imperative.

One might be forgiven for thinking that those responsible for drafting the Youth Justice and Criminal Evidence Act 1999, and particularly those provisions relating to Referral Orders and Youth Offender Panels, had not read the Human

Rights Act 1998. The Youth Justice and Criminal Evidence Act confers general rights on the community, to receive reparation, and particular rights to victims, to have their views heard and to attend panels and not to be compelled to participate in any measure. The Act does not confer, nor does it appear to even recognise, that children have rights and that these are protected in law. Indeed, the Act establishes only that children have responsibilities. There is a prima facie case, therefore, that the Youth Justice and Criminal Evidence Act 1999 gives expression to neither the intention nor the provisions of the Human Rights Act 1998. The challenge is to rectify this omission in developing practice which is not only sensitive, but aggressive in its pursuit of international standards.

Responsibilities of the state

In arguing that the best interests of the child should be the primary consideration which informs our actions and interventions in working with young people, it is essential to recognise that the state has responsibilities towards children. The influential documentary film maker and criminologist, Roger Graef, addressing the annual conference of the National Association for Youth Justice in Shropshire, England in September, 1999, spoke warmly about restorative justice and its ability to make children take responsibility for their behaviour; 'and that is what we all want', he said, 'to make juveniles take more responsibility for what they do'. Although it remains to be established that restorative justice actually makes children take more responsibility for their behaviour, the belief in this capacity is at the root of its appeal. It makes sense, after all, for children to be more responsible. Not only is this a good thing in its own right, but if children are more responsible then they will commit fewer offences!

It is this common sense notion that underpins the provisions for Youth Offender Contracts which emphasise the responsibilities of the child and which fail to recognise the responsibilities that others have towards the child. Yet children are prevented from accessing the full rights of citizenship, and they are protected in international and domestic laws from bearing the full responsibility of adulthood. Thus it is more correct to argue that overriding the responsibility that young people may have to others is the responsibility that others and especially the State has towards them. The problem, however, goes much deeper than this.

Part of the process whereby young people may be encouraged to take their responsibilities more seriously involves re-integrating them within law-abiding communities. Indeed, the government has stated that it wishes to see local communities strengthened and empowered, through directly elected Mayors and Community Councils, which are more locally accountable and responsive. The problem, however, at the root of this process is a general theoretical weakness of thinking about restorative justice and in particular a poorly adumbrated concept of community and an underdeveloped analysis of the role of the state. In fact, restorative justice practice is rooted in individualism and the strongest features of this approach are: the individual offender, their family, the individual victim and significant individuals from the local community. Thus individuals are key components of restorative justice thinking and practice, and even where use of the term community is common this is typically taken, in practice, to mean specific individuals from the community.

This tendency is not surprising given the origins and major developments in restorative justice around the world. The roots of restorative justice are imbedded deep within the past in tribal communities where the roles of all individuals in the life of the community were paramount and where there is no formal administrative state or its associated mechanisms. It is not just that the formal administrative state did not exist in these earlier times that is important, but that within these types of 'community' organisation the individual and the community were indivisible. Thus thinking in terms of individuals is deeply rooted in restorative justice.

The political agenda of right-wing thinkers, epitomised by the Reagan and Thatcher administrations, dominated the USA and the UK throughout the 1980s. It is no accident or anomaly that restorative justice appealed to the politics of the right. It enjoyed the quality of promoting the interests of victims of crime and it promised a visible form of punishment as individual victims or communities received an apology, compensation or restitution from the offender. Such qualities touch central concerns within right-wing thinking, notably diminishing the role of the state and the promotion of individual responsibility.

Lash and Urry, (1987), have characterised the results of the dynamic between increasingly globalised capitalism and national governments in terms of the 'hollowing of the State' thesis. According to this thesis the role and power of national governments is diminished, or 'hollowed', from both 'above' and 'below'. The 'hollowing' from above arises out of the increasing role and power of supra-national, globalised, structures: globalised economic/financial markets, globally unregulated trading, and supra-national governmental structures. National governments are 'hollowed' from below by the process of shifting 'state' provision into 'arms length' agencies, and non-governmental organisations or the private sector. Intimately bound up with this 'hollowing' process is an economic belief in the importance of shifting taxation from income to expenditure, as governments seek to levy fewer direct taxes and as individuals are exhorted to resort to the private sector to make provision for health services and pensions. In many countries this recourse to the private sector has expanded to include areas of criminal justice provision, not just in terms of private prisons, but also in areas of personal safety and policing.

Thus the 'hollowed state' is a diminished or impoverished structure which seeks to exert less control over the lives of individuals and possesses fewer resources to do so. The product of these trends is a system of governance where governments themselves are weakened – politically and economically. Governments have progressively diminished the extent to which they directly provide or control the range of services or structures within which citizens live out their lives, although paradoxically, the general 'hollowing of the State' has been accompanied by increased efforts on the part of national governments to exert more control over the remaining activities of State agencies through an increasing and pervasive 'managerialism', (Farnham and Horton, 1993). These developments have not been accidental, but the product of a deliberate and planned strategy. The result, of course, is that the role of government is diminished and the provision of state sponsored public services has been massively reduced, or cut altogether. Consequently, the role of individuals has risen, in both rhetoric and reality, to fill the void, and individualised models of thinking have dominated theory and practice.

This analysis illustrates that theorising and thinking about the role of the state in the development of restorative justice has been underdeveloped, and that the globally dominant models of restorative justice have been significantly influenced by individualised thinking. It is important to remember, however, that restorative justice occupies a social position within the criminal justice system as one of a number of social systems that states use to regulate the lives of citizens. One cannot, therefore, insulate or divorce thinking about restorative justice from wider concerns about social justice, notions of citizenship, and the administrative structures of the state. Crime is not just a problem for the criminal justice system. The aetiology of crime has its roots in a plethora of social factors, (Stewart and Stewart, 1993; Sampson and Laub, 1993; Farrington, 1994; Graham and Bowling, 1995; Goldson, 1998; Haines and Drakeford, 1998; Haines, 1999). The response to crime cannot be, nor generally is it, left only to the agencies of the criminal justice system. Such an approach inevitably leads down the sterile and austere road of ever increasing punitive responses to those who have committed offences.

The stark social inequalities of this approach are drawn into sharp relief. The political and social consequences of right-wing policies is an escalation in social and financial inequality, which itself has correlates in the broader areas of health, housing, education, and leisure. Moreover, the consequences of right-wing thinking for those who have committed offences are extreme and typically manifest in terms of ever increasing and repressive forms of policing, increasingly punitive and intrusive criminal justice sanctions, and in England and Wales they have led to the growth in a range of public order offences which have attracted severe consequences for those brought within their provisions, some of which have been directly targeted at children, for example, Anti-Social Behaviour Orders. The exacerbated social injustices typical of modern nation states, (Hutton, 1995; Davies, 1997), cannot be divorced from the nature of these modern states, and, we must remember, the state remains the primary structure which has the responsibility for the criminal justice system and its operation.

The shadows of right-wing social and economic policies have been cast over Western Europe and it is very much the case that we have felt the pains of increasing individual responsibility and diminished state provision, (Eekelaar, 1991; Haines, 1997 and 1999). Nevertheless, in most Western European countries the role of the state in providing criminal justice and a range of other social provisions is still significant and greater than in many other countries around the world. Much of this state provision will be subject to national legislation and the policies of national governments, but for most of us, although the national context remains important, the majority of these services are not provided directly by the national governments but through local agencies accountable to local structures of government. Education, including provision for special needs, housing, social services and some criminal justice services are provided through locally accountable structures. Even organisations who are primarily answerable to central government, such as health, probation, and police, are often intimately linked into locally accountable structures of inter-agency working and thus in operational terms have strong local links, although these agencies tend to experience a degree of tension between central control and local affiliations. Thus local structures play a significant role in shaping the local community. They constitute a major social structure within which we all live.

Further development of restorative justice must be made in a manner which places crime, those who have committed offences, and the response to crime and offenders in the broader social structural context of the state and its responsibilities. It is not socially or morally acceptable to simply punish a young person, without placing them and their actions in their social context. Many restorative justice projects are often guilty of such action, as videos of the Thames Valley experiment testify. The mere act of encouraging a young person to make an apology to a victim, when that young person may themselves be a victim of vast social inequality, while the 'victim' may be a relatively wealthy beneficiary of recent social and economic policies, is morally and ethically unacceptable. It is not acceptable to punish the young shoplifter when the state has abrogated its responsibilities to provide effective full-time education for that child. Beyond the individual, the state, and particularly the local state, has a crucial role to play in social and criminal justice.

Developing practices in Youth Offending Teams

Although Youth Offending Teams are presently in their infancy, most areas in England and Wales are in the process of implementing new structures and measures. As Youth Offending Teams (YOTs) are taking shape, two distinct models are beginning to emerge. The first is an independent model, where the YOT is conceived as a stand alone service which, as the 'empire' grows, will directly provide more and more services to more and more children, largely without reference to other local agencies. The second is a more integrated model where, as the YOT takes shape, it is increasingly integrated with a whole range of

Local Authority departments, schools, other agencies and private or voluntary sector organisations. In this model the YOT provides specialist youth justice services, but it links to the service delivery responsibilities of a wide range of other organisations which seek to meet the holistic needs of young people.

The first of these models is a mistake. It is a mistake of management, although its greater simplicity is attractive, and it is a mistake in terms of practice. The new youth justice carries considerable extra (financial) costs leading to higher resource demands on YOTs in the new system. YOTs are required to work more intensively with larger numbers of children than was previously the case, and any 'stand alone' team will have great difficulty in meeting these needs and expectations. A team member drawn from another agency, in a stand alone YOT, will not be a guarantee of access to the resources of others.

In practice terms, while research has shown that in work with older, 'heavy end' offenders, a clearly identifiable project with a strong pro-social philosophy is an important factor in reducing recidivism, (Haines and Drakeford, 1998), such an approach is less effective with children who are younger and who have committed fewer, less serious offences (Goldson, this volume). The weight of research evidence also suggests that a more normalising approach to service provision is more effective, (Haines and Drakeford, 1998), for all young offenders. This is especially so with younger children and those who have committed less serious offences, that is, those with whom YOTs will be increasingly working as the new system takes hold. There is thus a fundamental question of approach here and it applies to YOTs themselves and to the new measures they are implementing, including Youth Offender Panels.

This point is not new in the criminological literature. It was first made in the 1970s following research into the Massachusetts de-institutionalisation experiment, (Coates, 1980). In the 1970s Massachusetts took the radical measure of closing all its residential institutions for juvenile offenders and invested the money in newly developed community programmes. Research into these new programmes tended to show that they were characterised by one of two approaches. Firstly, there were those programmes which operated on a closed groupwork model, where the juveniles were brought together over a period of time for a planned and structured series of interventions that were contained within the group. Secondly, there were those programmes which also worked with a group of juveniles in a structured and planned manner, but the interventions were not restricted to the closed groupwork model. In this second case the nature and content of the activities undertaken with the juveniles were more thoroughly integrated with broader community-based activities and services.

This second model was much more in keeping with the philosophy of the de-institutionalisation experiment, and research demonstrated that these programmes had significantly better re-conviction results than the closed programmes. The researchers, (Coates, 1980) concluded that it was possible to effectively replicate the characteristics of institutionalised forms of treatment in community-based projects and that such an organisational form had no better impact on future behaviour than the institutions themselves. In contrast, the researchers also concluded that it was possible to develop and deliver genuinely community-based programmes and that the closer these programmes were to the community, the greater the extent of the linkages between the programme participants and normalised community activities, and the higher the probability of securing a positive longer term outcome became. Further research, in a different context, has also produced findings which support this conclusion, (Bottoms and McClintock, 1973).

These findings have important implications for the manner in which Youth Offender Panels are conducted. The majority of restorative justice practices with juveniles involve various forms of the family group conference. These conferences are usually chaired by a trained convenor or facilitator and attended by the young person, their family, or a family representative, the victim, and possibly a representative, and, in some cases, other significant individuals or representatives of the community. Typically, in examples of best practice, conferences will not seek to apportion blame, but they will be problem-solving oriented with the aim of finding a solution to the problem of repairing the harm done by the crime, (Jackson, 1999). If, however, the conference operates with an individualised model then the solution to the problem of repairing the harm done by the crime can only come from within the room, and in such circumstances it is really only the offender who can take such actions. At the very least, an individualised approach leads to the build up of increasing pressures on the offender to initiate and carry through some reparative action. Put into the context where the offender is a child, in a room full of adults, then this dynamic raises ethical questions about the morality of treating children in such a manner, it raises questions about the degree to which such practices implement the provisions of international conventions on the treatment of children, and it raises questions about the likelihood of success based on the limited ability of a non-adult to make decisions and take actions in a free and informed manner.

Braithwaite and Mugford, (1994), have articulated the 'conditions of successful re-integration ceremonies', which amounts to a process through which the conference must work sequentially to the point of achieving closure, where the young person, once censured for their actions, is finally re-integrated symbolically back into the community. Notwithstanding the assumptions this model makes about the nature of the community and the utility of re-integration as a conforming influence, there is a very real possibility that the process described by Braithwaite and Mugford actually serves to further marginalise and exclude the young person. Successful re-integration ceremonies must be complete and closure of the process must take place, but if closure does not take place then the young person is stuck at the point in the process where their behaviour, and by implication the young person, is being censured. This, in itself, is likely to exacerbate marginalisation and exclusion of the young person.

Closure can only be achieved if the young person is engaged by the process. The pressure placed on the young person in an individualised model to make the necessary reparative actions leaves the young person in a position of responsibility generally denied to children. Moreover, it fails to recognise the role of adults in taking their responsibilities towards children seriously, as well as failing to place the behaviour of the child in its social context and failing to articulate and act on the responsibilities of a range of social agencies towards children. Thus the more individualised the nature of the proceedings the less likely it is that the re-integration part of the process will be achieved. Research has shown how children tend to acquiesce to the demands made of them during conferences, but to respond to their perceptions of injustice in the proceedings by way of a variety of adaptive mechanisms to distance themselves from the experience, (Blagg, 1985; Pratt and Grimshaw, 1985). This is clearly an undesirable outcome to the conference and may constitute a failure of the process, especially if further offending is the adaptive result of perceived injustice.

During research conducted in Swansea, (Haines, Jones and Isles, 1999) young people were invited to describe how a system of sanctions for misbehaviour in school should operate. A very strong theme to emerge from these exercises was the concern of young people, that, whatever the sanctions, there must be a sense of justice and fairness in their application, and, of particular significance, the children said that in all cases there must be a 'way back' for the young person concerned. In other words, young people did not wish to see themselves or others placed in a position of exclusion as the final result of a sanction and they expected the adults involved to provide a mechanism whereby the young person was not left in such a situation. Not only was this experience significant in itself, but it illustrated how the children did not feel as if they were in a position to control the system of sanctions or their outcomes; this was an adult responsibility. Thus children need to be offered a way back following censure for their misbehaviour. It is not reasonable or realistic to expect them to create such routes, they possess neither the intellectual maturity, nor the physical means to do so. The individualisation inherent in much restorative justice practice does not offer the young person a way back which is in balance with their sense of justice or fairness. Individualisation places too much responsibility on the young person, responsibilities which they are not equipped to fulfil, and it does not place sufficient responsibility on the adults concerned. Putting the responsibility on the young person is too easy and it does not test adults' capabilities to a sufficient extent.

These problems, therefore, arise from an approach to restorative justice which is rooted in individualism and within which the role of the community is poorly articulated. The community in this context means those adults who have responsibility towards children and, more importantly, those adults who work in state agencies with responsibilities towards children.

Much current practice within restorative justice is not rooted within existing criminological knowledge about the effectiveness of interventions, but stands alone in the claim to represent a paradigm shift. This claim, however, is unsubstantiated and there is much that we can learn from previous research. We know, for example, that punitive responses to juvenile offending are largely unsuccessful in reducing criminal behaviour, (Lipsey, 1992 and 1995; Haines and Drakeford, 1998), and may actually have an amplificatory effect, (Mackenzie et al., 1995); and despite claims to the contrary, young people experience sanctions for their behaviour, even if applied in restorative justice settings and even if the sanctions are presented in a positive manner, as punishment, although the claims of an amplificatory effect of punitive sanctions is probably overstated and is more likely to arise where the young person considers the sanction to be unjust or unfairly applied. Research has also shown the importance of reducing risk factors, whilst simultaneously increasing protective factors which diminish the likelihood of further offending and that many of these factors are social in nature, (Sampson and Laub, 1993). A negative focus on risk and criminogenic need is not only ineffective, it misses the point. Risk and protective factors often have a janus quality, increasing protective factors thereby reduces risk factors. The importance of engaging with these protective factors is often missing from restorative justice practice which is based on an individualised, closed model.

In the distance, off to the right, an echo is growing louder and louder; 'but these young people have done wrong, they must be punished (or else they will do it again with impunity)'. The first response to this is to repeat the injunction made earlier that in line with international conventions on the treatment of children, we must recognise the special status accorded to children and the presumption that interventions taken are predicated on the best interests of the child. Proper adherence to these principles necessarily limits and shapes our responses to juvenile misconduct. This does not mean, however, that the 'incident' or the offence is not dealt with. Children need to have boundaries placed around their behaviour if they are to learn the difference between right and wrong and if they are to be helped to become productive members of society. Sometimes these boundaries need to be reinforced with a sanction, sometimes censuring is important, but at all times sanctions and censures must be applied justly and fairly, and in the case of children this means that the social context of their behaviour must be understood and taken full account of and that the responsibilities of others must be acted upon. Thus, in all interventions with children and particularly in restorative justice practice, including Youth Offender Panels, it is important to deal effectively with the behaviour of young people, but this must be done appropriately with due regard to issues such as justice and fairness and where there is a proper articulation of how the state, particularly the local state, exercises its responsibilities towards children. Youth Offender Contracts that fail to clearly articulate and place a proper emphasis on the responsibilities of adults and other agencies to provide services for children are likely to fail.

In this context it is not surprising that the philosophy or purpose of Youth Offender Panels is muddled and confused. If the goal of Youth Offender Panels was to meet the needs of children, in full recognition that meeting these needs will have a beneficial impact on their wider life as well as specific aspects of their behaviour, then one would expect to find a clear statement to this effect and a set of measures which were designed to promote this aim. Instead, we find the rhetoric of restorative justice and a package of interventions which give primacy to the victim and the community, and which seek to confer only responsibilities onto the very young. Interventions designed to meet the needs of young people would include measures which protect them from harm, and promote their well-being and development. Instead, amongst the package of interventions listed in the Act, we find financial and other reparative penalties, community service, curfews and other restrictive orders. Any attempt to promote the well-being of the child and to encourage positive behaviour would be contained within a flexible package of measures designed to be appropriate for the age and stage of development of the young person. Instead, we find a set of bureaucratic and administrative regulations which bind the child into a complex and inflexible arrangement which carries severe penalties for default.

In fact there is very little, if anything, in the measures available to Panels, as listed in the Act, which draw in any meaningful way on restorative justice. It is difficult to escape the conclusion, therefore, that Referral Orders and Youth Offender Panels are essentially about retribution and punishment; more concerned with political objectives than the rights of children. Furthermore, with few exceptions, there is very little in any of these measures which research has shown to be of any benefit in reducing re-offending or preventing crime. Nor is it possible to claim significant benefits for individual victims from involvement in the criminal justice process, and it is to this issue that we now turn.

Restorative practices, Youth Offender Panels and victims

There is not much evidence to suggest that victims actually get very much out of being involved in restorative practices. Launay, (1985), points out that there is only one British study which confirms that victims wish to meet 'their' offender – that of Shapland, (1984) – and there is only qualified support for such meetings from other research, (Lee, 1996), although there is evidence of wider support amongst victims and the general public for reparative measures such as compensation or community service over punitive penalties, (Hough and Moxon, 1985; Walker and Hough, 1988). When victims do meet 'their' offenders there is little evidence from the research that they receive meaningful reparation or restitution, (Maxwell and Morris, 1996; Davis et al., 1988 and 1989; Marshall and Merry, 1990). It appears that victims can feel 're-victimised' by unsatisfactory attempts at mediation and there are generally higher reports of victim satisfaction from schemes which do not bring victim and offender together, but take other forms of action to support victims, (Launay, 1985).

These are difficult results for those who favour the victim's perspective, but they should not come as a surprise. How can an offender make sufficient reparation or restitution to the victim in any way that approaches the harm done or loss experienced as a result of a crime? In simple monetary terms most offenders simply do not possess the means to make amends. If one considers any physical injury or the emotional upset caused by a crime, even quite a minor crime, the equations become impossible to quantify, but whatever the 'amounts' are, they greatly exceed the ability of offenders to match. This is so for adult offenders, but in the case of juveniles the hopelessness of this strategy is particularly exposed. It may be argued that achieving some kind of parity or equity in these matters is so ridiculous as not to merit serious consideration. This is not borne out by the evidence which shows that victims expect more than mere tokenism, and schemes have to cope with demands from victims for excessive penalties or measures which may belittle or ridicule offenders, (Dignan, 1992). Where such behaviour has occurred, Dignan, (1992), reports that it was 'resolved' by removing the victim, and the offender, from the scheme, but it is difficult to see how such action can be regarded as a successful outcome and this will not be possible in Youth Offender Panels. It is also important to consider, in this respect, whether any decisions which cause a young person to make reparative actions of any kind to the victim are in the best interests of the child. Human rights principles and those established in international conventions apply, thus it must be shown that direct offender-victim reparation is in the child's best interests before such activity may be required.

Action which is in the best interests of the child does not necessarily mean that victims do not also benefit. What most victims want is not to repeat the experience of being a victim and any action which reduces the likelihood of re-offending is in the best interests of victims and the wider community. It is common for American studies of restorative justice projects to report very high victim satisfaction rates, but transposing these results into a different cultural context is fraught with assumptions and danger. North American culture is much more litigious and individualistic than British society, and it is prepared to exact greater penalties against the young than generally tolerated or supported here. There is a tendency within the restorative justice literature to assume that because restorative justice is a global movement the findings from one place are readily transferable to another. There is no evidence to support this view. If restorative justice practices work because they tap into the resources and culture of local communities, then it is essential to take local culture seriously in both designing and implementing local projects. One cannot simply say, therefore, that victims should be involved in the criminal justice process and that this is a good thing without first obtaining local evidence to support this view.

Being a victim of a crime frequently involves loss of some kind, it is at best annoying, often distressing and sometimes devastating. There is no question that the criminal justice system appropriates the crime, (Christie, 1977), and does little if anything to give regard to the victim in the process. Undoubtedly more should be done for victims of crime, both directly and indirectly, but to believe that this should be done by the criminal justice system is misplaced. Too few offenders are ever prosecuted, (97 per cent of offences do not result in an identified offender being cautioned or convicted), to pretend that the formal criminal justice system is an effective mechanism for dealing with victimisation. There is insufficient evidence to show that bringing victims into the criminal justice system results in positive outcomes for victims. And in an adversarial system it can only ever lead to calls for harsher and more negative forms of punishment.

Only harm can come from greater penetration of victims issues and victims themselves into the criminal justice system. This statement is determining as far as pre-court, pre-sentence and sentencing processes are concerned, although there are instances where the criminal justice system can have a greater sensitivity to victims, as for example, in notifying victims of violent or distressing crimes that the offender is about to be released from prison. Work that is done to support victims or ameliorate their situation should, however, be carried out by agencies outside the formal criminal justice system. Such agencies should not work directly with offenders, but have specific victim centred responsibilities.

A concluding comment about effectiveness and restorative justice

A number of issues concerning the effectiveness of Youth Offender Panels and the likely methods of intervention have already been raised in this chapter. Questions have been asked about the merit and validity of individualised modes of operation, and the failure to theoretically and empirically operationalise the concept of community in a manner which properly articulates the responsibilities of adults and the state towards young people. The way in which Panels may mirror institutional forms of treatment which, in other settings, have been shown to be ineffective or counter-productive has been discussed. The way in which many of the envisioned interventions fail to take account of and effectively operationalise existing knowledge about the effective methods of working with young people has been argued. Indeed this chapter has been centrally concerned with issues of effectiveness throughout. Yet some key issues concerning effectiveness remain to be discussed.

Much of the restorative justice-related research referred to in this chapter has been concerned with processes and procedures. Information about the effectiveness of different methods of working with young people who have offended is drawn from research into a variety of interventions, none of which are explicitly restorative. The key question which remains, therefore is: is restorative justice effective in reducing further offending? This is, in practice, a difficult question to answer as there is very little evidence on which to base any conclusions. In fact there is only one major study which has involved a long-term follow-up of re-offending patterns following a restorative justice intervention. This research has been conducted in New Zealand by Maxwell and Morris, (1999), who reached three 'important' conclusions:

The first is that almost half of the young people felt that things had gone well for them over the last five years; a quarter felt that things had gone very well. Only just over a tenth felt that things had gone poorly ...

The second important finding is that, some six years after their family group conference in 1990/91, more than two fifths of the young people were not reconvicted or were convicted once only and not much more than a quarter were classified as being persistently reconvicted. These reconviction rates cannot be directly compared with those in other jurisdictions but, ... they are certainly no worse and may be better in some respects than the closest comparisons available to us from within New Zealand and Australia.

The most important finding, however, is that family group conferences can contribute to lessening the chance of reoffending even when other important factors identified by the literature on offending ... and when other events which may be more related to chance are taken into account ...

Life events since the family group conference, although they are, to a considerable extent, predictable from the past, also had an influence on the ultimate outcomes measured here ... . The particular events identified in this study indicative of reintegration into the community were: gaining educational qualifications and vocational skills, developing close and positive relationships with family, friends and partners, and settling into a stable life style. In brief, they point to the importance of strategies to effect social inclusion.

(Maxwell and Morris, 1999, p 68).

These results show moderately positive effects for the impact of family group conferences on re-offending and highlight the importance of social factors for positive behaviour. The question remains, however, whether it is possible to transpose these findings into the British context and the particular provisions for Youth Offender Panels. As far as the impact on re-offending is concerned, the answer to this question is almost certainly no. Not only is the cultural context of New Zealand different from that in England and Wales, but the nature of the system of family group conferences in that country, and the range of measures applied to children who participate in that process, are quite different from those that apply in the UK jurisdiction, (Jackson, 1999). We cannot expect the same impact on re-offending to result from Youth Offender Panels simply because of a broad similarity of structure. There is good research evidence, however, as discussed earlier in this chapter, to support the findings of Maxwell and Morris, (1999), that factors associated with re-integration into the community are relevant to future behaviour and further offending. As noted previously, however, although the provisions relating to Referral Orders and Youth Offender Panels talk about community integration there is little in the actual measures that may be applied to juveniles, as listed in the Youth Justice and Criminal Evidence Act, which promote this activity or outcome. Quite the reverse, the Act lists measures which are expressly punitive, controlling and retributive, and which are likely to produce the opposite effect. How then, can restorative approaches and the provisions for Youth Offending Panels be made more positive?

A positive approach to Youth Offender Panels

It will not be possible for Youth Offending Teams to correct some of the features of Youth Offender Panels. The Youth Justice and Criminal Evidence Act requires courts to make Referral Orders when certain conditions are met, and Youth Offending Teams must comply with the Act in establishing and running Panels. There is sufficient scope, however, to implement these Panels, and a range of measures or interventions, in a manner which is more consistent with human rights legislation, international conventions and what research has shown to be more effective in working with young people who have offended. The following principles should be applied to the management of Youth Offender Panels:

- The best interests of the child should be the defining principle of the aim of Panels, in full recognition that in so doing measures to promote the prevention of re-offending will be maximised.
- Panels should not be known as Youth Offender Panels, but by another name, such as Young Person's Panel, or simply Panel Hearings.
- YOTs should make use of section 7(4)(b) of the Youth Justice and Criminal Evidence Act 1999 allowing participation in the Panel of 'any person who may be capable of having a good influence on the young person', to appoint a member of the YOT, or other independent person, whose primary role is to safeguard the best interests of the child.
- Representation on Panels should include agencies and organisations who have general and specific responsibilities to protect and provide services to children. Panels should be managed in such a way to ensure these agencies' responsibilities are properly discharged.
- Youth Offender Contracts should be entitled 'Young Person's Contract' and should include the responsibilities that others have towards the young person, and it should be the responsibility of the appointed person, (under s.7(4)(b) above), to monitor the delivery of these services.

- The discharge of the responsibilities of others should be taken into account in making assessments concerning the extent of a young person's compliance with the terms of the Contract.
- The measures applied to young persons under the Contract should reflect the age and maturity of the young person, their degree of culpability and the seriousness of the offence.
- In general, punitive measures should be avoided. Fines, community service, and curfews are negative and retributive, and should not be used unless it can be demonstrated that to do so is in the best interests of the child.
- Particularly for young and minor offenders, overly intrusive measures which focus on criminogenic need are inappropriate and should be replaced by interventions which seek to promote positive behaviour.
- Contracts should not contain punitive or retributive measures relating to the needs of young people derived from poor social circumstances or broader social inequality.
- Panels should avoid the routine inclusion in contracts of standard measures, for example, written letters of apology to victims. Contracts should be individualised documents tailored to each young person.
- It should not become routine to involve victims in Panel Hearings unless there are good and specific reasons for believing this to be of particular value in an individual case.
- Panels should ensure that any actions which are implied in a Young Person's Contract are not left to the young person to discharge unaided or unassisted. Young people must not be made responsible, by virtue of the content of a contract, for actions or behaviour which they have little or no ability to control.

Conclusion

The Audit Commission, (1996), believed the conditional discharge was a valued and useful sentence of the court. This measure has been swept away in a political drive to re-shape and re-articulate the values of the juvenile justice system, (Goldson, this volume). The analysis presented in this chapter shows that some of the thinking behind Referral Orders and Youth Offender Panels has been flawed. The desire to prevent crime is laudable and widely shared, but it must be implemented in a manner which is consistent with what we know about children and the effectiveness of different types and intensities of intervention. These new provisions flaunt this knowledge and seek to replace it with a new paradigm, that of restorative justice. As this chapter has shown, however, current restorative justice thinking and practice do not deliver what we need in terms of processes or outcomes.

At the core of this fallibility are two central failings; the lack of recognition and understanding that the people we are dealing with are children, and a poorly articulated concept of community and the role of the state in shaping how the needs of the community are met. Only when full recognition of the importance of international conventions for the treatment of children in trouble is placed at the centre of practice can restorative justice hope to provide a paradigm that may make a success of Referral Orders and Youth Offender Panels.

References

Audit Commission, (1996), *Misspent Youth: Young People and Crime*, London: Audit Commission.

Blagg, H., (1985), Reparation and Justice for Juveniles, *British Journal of Criminology*, Vol.25 No.7 pp267–79.

Bottoms, A. and McClintock, F., (1973), *Criminals Coming of Age,* London: Heinemann.

Braithwaite, J. and Mugford, S., (1994), Conditions of Successful Reintegration Ceremonies: Dealing with Juvenile Offenders, *British Journal of Criminology,* Vol. 34 pp139–71.

Christie, N., (1977), Conflicts as Property, *British Journal of Criminology*, Vol.17 pp1–15.

Coates, (1980), Community-Based Services for Juvenile Delinquents: Concept and Implications for Practice, *Journal of Social Issues*, Vol. 37 No. 3 pp 87–101.

Davies, N., (1997), *Dark Heart: The Shocking Truth About Hidden Britain*, London, Chatto and Windus.

Davis, G. Boucherat, J. and Watson, D., (1988), Reparation in the Service of Diversion: The Subordination of a Good Idea, *The Howard Journal*, Vol.27 No.2 pp127–34.

Davis, G. Boucherat, J. and Watson, D., (1989), Pre-Court Decision-Making in Juvenile Justice, *British Journal of Criminology*, Vol.29 pp219–35.

Dignan, J., (1992), Repairing the Damage: Can Reparation be Made to Work in the Service of Diversion? *British Journal of Criminology*, Vol.32 No.4 pp 453–72.

Eekelaar, J., (1991), Parental Responsibility: State of Nature or Nature of the State? *Journal of Social Welfare and Family Law* Vol. 37 pp37–50.

Farrington, D., (1994), Human Development and Criminal Careers, in: Maguire, M. Morgan, R. and Reiner, R., (Eds.), *The Oxford Handbook of Criminology*, Oxford, Clarendon Press.

Farnham and Horton, (1993), *Managing the New Public Services*, London, Macmillan.

Giddens, A., (1990), *The Consequences of Modernity*, Cambridg, Polity Press.

Goldson, B., (1998), *Children in Trouble: Backgrounds and Outcomes*, University of Liverpool: Department of Sociology, Social Policy and Social Work Studies.

Graham, J. and Bowling, B., (1995), *Young People and Crime*, HORS 145, London, Home Office.

Haines, K., (1997), Young Offenders and Family Support Services: An European Perspective, *International Journal of Child and Family Welfare*, Volume 2 No.1 pp 61–73.

Haines, K., (1998), Some Principled Objections to a Restorative Justice Approach to Juvenile Offenders, in: Walgrave, L., (Ed.), *Restorative Justice for Juveniles*, Belgium, University of Leuven Press.

Haines, K. and Drakeford, M., (1998), *Young People and Youth Justice*, Basingstoke: Macmillan.

Haines, K., (1999), Crime is a Social Problem, *European Journal on Criminal Policy and Research*, Vol. 7 pp 263–75.

Haines, K. Jones, R. and Isles, E., (1999), *Promoting Positive Behaviour in Schools*, Report submitted to the Wales Office of Research and Development.

Hough, M. and Moxon, D., (1985), Dealing with Offenders: Popular Opinion and the Views of Victims. *The Howard Journal*, Vol.24 No.3 pp160–75.

Hutton, W., (1995), *The State We're In*, London: Vintage.

Jackson, S., (1999), Family Group Conferences and Youth Justice: The New Panacea? in: Goldson, B., (Ed.), *Youth Justice: Contemporary Policy and Practice*, Aldershot, Ashgate.

Lash, S. and Urry, J., (1987), *The End of Organized Capitalism*, Cambridge: Polity Press.

Launay, G., (1985), Bringing Victims and Offenders Together: A Comparison of Two Models, *The Howard Journal*, Vo.24 No.3 pp 200–12.

Lee, A., (1996), Public Attitudes Towards Restorative Justice, in: Galaway, B. and Hudson, J., (Eds.), *Restorative Justice: International Perspectives*, Amsterdam, Kugler.

Lipsey, M., (1992), Juvenile Delinquency Treatment: A Meta-Analytic Inquiry into the Variability of Effects, in: Cook, T. et al., (Eds.), *Meta-Analysis for Explanation*, New York: Russell Sage.

Lipsey, M., (1995), 'What do we Learn from 400 Research Studies on the Effectiveness of Treatments with Juvenile Delinquents?', in: McGuire, J., (Ed.), *What Works: Reducing Reoffending*, John Wiley and Sons.

Mackenzie, D, Brame, R. McDowell, D. and Souryal, C., (1995), Boot Camp Prisons and Recidivism in Eight States, *Criminology*, Vol. 33 No. 4(2) pp110–6.

Marshall, T., (1999), *Restorative Justice*, London: Home Office.

Marshall, T. and Merry, S., (1990), Crime and Accountability: Victim/Offender Mediation in Practice, London: HMSO.

Maxwell, G. and Morris, A., (1996), Research on Family Group Conferences with Young Offenders in New Zealand, in: Hudson, J. Morris, A. Maxwell, G. and Galaway, B., (Eds.), *Family Group Conferences: Perspectives on Policy and Practice*, Leichhardt, The Federation Press.

Maxwell, G. and Morris, A., (1999). *Understanding Reoffending*, Wellington, Victoria University of Wellington.

McCold, P., (1998), Restorative Justice: Variations on a Theme, in: Walgrave, L., (Ed.), *Restorative Justice for Juveniles*, Belgium, University of Leuven Press.

Pratt, J. and Grimshaw, R., (1985), A Juvenile Justice Pre-Court Tribunal at Work, *The Howard Journal*, Vol.24 No.3 pp 213–28.

Sampson, R. and Laub, J., (1993), *Crime in the Making: Pathways and Turning points Through Life*, Cambridge: Harvard University Press.

Shapland, J., (1984), Victims, the Criminal Justice System and Compensation, *British Journal of Criminology*, Vol. 24 pp131–49.

Stewart, G. and Stewart, J., (1993), *Social Circumstances of Young Offenders Under Supervision*, London: Association of Chief Officers of Probation.

Walgrave, L. (1995), Restorative Justice for Juveniles: Just a Technique or a Fully Fledged Alternative? *The Howard Journal*, Vol. 34 pp 228–49.

Walker, N. and Hough, M., (1988), Public Attitudes to Sentencing: Surveys from Five Countries, Aldershot, Gower.

Wright, M. and Galaway, B., (1989), *Mediation and Criminal Justice: Victims, Offenders and Community*, London, Sage.

Wright, M., (1996), *Justice for Victims and Offenders: A Restorative Response to Crime*, Winchester: Waterside Press.

CHAPTER 5

Children, Responsibility and the New Youth Justice

Sue Bandalli

From protection to responsibility

The 1990s has been a decade during which the responses of the criminal justice system to children have significantly changed, engaging them at a younger and younger age in ever more determined ways. Between 1993 and 1999, legislation systematically eroded much of the 'special status' of childhood in criminal law and produced a matrix of provisions to facilitate and increase the criminalisation of children; the Sexual Offences Act 1993, Criminal Justice and Public Order Act 1994, Crime (Sentences) Act 1997, Crime and Disorder Act 1998 and Youth Justice and Criminal Evidence Act 1999 all contain such provisions. The recently abolished presumption of *doli incapax* which results in an untrammelled age of criminal responsibility (ten years) in England and Wales will be closely examined to illustrate the means by which the child has been 'responsibilised' in criminal law.

Two statements of government policy, appearing in documents at the beginning and end of the decade demonstrate a significant change in attitudes towards children who offend:

> *The criminal law is based on the principle that people understand the difference between right and wrong. Very young children cannot easily tell this difference, and the law takes account of this. The age of criminal responsibility, below which no child can be prosecuted, is 10 years; and between the ages of 10 and 13 a child may only be convicted of a criminal offence if the prosecution can show that he knew what he did was seriously wrong. The Government does not intend to change these arrangements which make proper allowance for the fact that children's understanding, knowledge and ability to reason are still developing.*
>
> (Home Office,1990, para.8.4).

> *It is ... important to emphasise that the abolition of the presumption of doli incapax does not affect the age of criminal responsibility in England and Wales, which remains at 10 years ... if children aged 10 or older start to*

*behave in a criminal or anti-social way, the Government considers that we
do them no favours to overlook this behaviour. It is in the interests of
children ... themselves to recognise and accept responsibility.*

(UK Government, 1999, para.10.31).

A person returning to England after being away for some years might be
forgiven for expecting the first statement to have emanated from a Labour
Government and the second from the Conservatives, whereas the reverse is the
case. It is not the behaviour of children that has changed across the 1990s, rather
populist discourse and the political priorities of New Labour. Such policy change
has shifted from the *protection of children* from the criminalising effects of the
formal justice system in the 1960s, (Home Office, 1965; Home Office, 1968 and
the Children and Young Persons Act 1969) to the increasing *'responsibilisation'* of
children towards the end of the 1990s. Responsibility and protection are incon-
gruous concepts and it is protection which has been jettisoned through the
abolition of the presumption of *doli incapax*. As Gelsthorpe and Morris, (1998, p
213), indicate, '(the) importance of the presumption lay in its symbolism: it was a
statement about the nature of childhood, the vulnerability of children and the
appropriateness of criminal justice sanctions for children.' Its abolition at the end
of the twentieth century, after many hundreds of years existence, is a telling
statement about all three.

The presumption of *doli incapax* – a principle with a history

The age of criminal responsibility in England and Wales was seven years at the
beginning of the twentieth century. It was raised to eight and then to ten by the
Children and Young Persons Acts of 1933 and 1963 respectively. It remains at ten
years to this day, endorsed in 1993 by the Home Affairs Select Committee. The
age of criminal responsibility has a longer history than this however. At the
beginning of the second millennium, criminal responsibility seems to have been
strict: those causing harm were liable, irrespective of culpability. After the twelfth
century, with the growing insistence on moral blameworthiness as a foundation
for criminal responsibility, there developed aspects of *mens rea*, that is, requirements that the harm was caused with a proscribed state of mind. Here, the origins
of 'special treatment' for children can be discerned: children might be prosecuted
and convicted but would generally be pardoned, (Sayre, 1932, p 988). Forfeiture
of goods followed pardons and as children had none, it became a pointless
exercise: by the fifteenth century judges invariably dismissed cases against young
children. Whilst some children were simply too young to be punished and cases of
exempted seven year olds can be found as early as 1302, others, at the 'sub-
adolescent period', were liable to punishment only if malice could be proved,
identified as an ability to discern between good and evil, (Kean, 1937, pp
366–367). At a time when a defendant accused of a felony was not allowed to give

evidence at their trial, determination of capacity and discretion were sought in legal presumptions. Towards the end of the seventeenth century when Hale wrote *Pleas of the Crown, (1682)*, these presumptions were well established: children under seven were irrebuttably presumed to be *doli incapax*, those between seven and fourteen were presumed to be *doli incapax* and could only be convicted if it appeared to the court that they were able to discern between good and evil at the time they committed the offence.

So for hundreds of years, probably dating back to before the time of Edward III, there existed a special measure which applied to children over the age of criminal responsibility but under fourteen years: they benefited from the presumption of *doli incapax* used to protect them from the detrimental effects of the enforcement of the criminal law. This presumption applied until the Crime and Disorder Act 1998, although with the rise of the secular society, it was modified from children's capacity to discern good from evil to knowledge that what they was doing was wrong, in the sense of gravely and seriously wrong, (*Gorrie*, 1919, 83 JP 136). The modern presumption, therefore, was that children from aged ten to fourteen years were presumed to be *incapable of crime* unless and until the prosecution adduced evidence which proved *beyond reasonable doubt* not only that the child defendant committed the offence with the mental element required by the criminal law, but also that when so doing, they knew what they were doing was *seriously wrong*, as distinct from naughty or mischievous (C v. DPP, 1996, AC 1). The presumption had been reinstated by the House of Lords in March, 1995, after a 12 month abolition by the Divisional Court, (Bandalli, 1997; Cavadino, 1997; Fionda, 1998).

Lord Lowry, who delivered the main judgement of the House of Lords in C v. DPP, carefully considered the authorities and the history of the presumption before declaring that it was still part of the law of England. He examined the reasons given in the Divisional Court by Mr Justice Laws for his decision to abolish it and produced reasoned arguments for taking a less definitive and more protective stance towards 'offending children'. Lord Lowry commented at the close:

> *There is a need to study other systems, including that which holds sway in Scotland ... Whatever change is made, it should come only after collating and considering the evidence and after taking account of the effect which change would have on the whole law relating to children's anti-social behaviour.*
> (C v DPP, 1996, AC, 40).

It is clear from comments by the Law Lords that any changes were to be set within the context of a better system of justice for children, possibly with the Youth Court having jurisdiction over all anti-social and offending behaviour by children; raising the age of criminal responsibility and using only civil measures for the younger group, (Lord Lowry, ibid, p. 40). Lord Jauncy expressed the hope that Parliament would look at the presumption perhaps as part of a larger review of the appropriate methods in a modern society of dealing with youthful offenders and referred to the system of children's hearings in Scotland, where he observed that although the age of criminal responsibility was lower, at eight years, many children were effectively dealt with outside of the formal criminal courts, (ibid, 20–21). It was noted that abolition of the presumption of *doli incapax* without a corresponding increase in the age of criminal responsibility, could expose children to the full criminal process at an earlier age than in most European countries. Their Lordships did not call for its abolition but indicated that a wide-ranging review of the wider issues of social policy respecting the treatment of delinquency in this group would be appropriate, (Lord Bridge, ibid, 21). At the end of his judgement, as Lord Lowry astutely observed, it was not so much a legal as a social problem, with a dash of politics thrown in, (ibid, 40). Very soon it was to be politics that would drive the agenda.

New Labour: new youth justice

Even before the New Labour government was elected in May, 1997, indications of the future direction of responses to children, premised on responsibility and embedded in the criminal justice system were evident. A Labour party pre-election manifesto statement, observed that although:

> ...*the younger the offender, the less developed may be their sense of respon-sibility a young person caught committing a crime must be challenged and a sanction must be applied to develop their sense of right and wrong and the consequences which follow from offending.*
>
> (Labour Party Media Office, 1996, p9).

The statement proceeded:

> *Ultimately, the welfare needs of the individual young offender cannot outweigh the needs of the community to be protected from the adverse consequences of his or her offending behaviour ... in our view most young people aged 10–13 are plainly capable of differentiating between right and wrong, especially where the issue is one of theft or criminal damage'.*
>
> (ibid, pp 9–11).

This mis-statement of the presumption as being able to tell the difference between right and wrong, rather than naughty and seriously wrong, continued until the White Paper in 1997.

The next document within which New Labour addressed this issue was *Tackling Youth Crime: a Consultation Paper*, in which a proposal was made to modernise the archaic rule of *doli incapax* in order to ensure that children face the consequences and take responsibility for their actions, (Home Office 1997a, 2). Views were sought on the Government's preferred option of abolishing – rather than reversing – the presumption of *doli incapax*. Reversal of the burden of proof would align the defence with the structure of others in the criminal law, where the offender would have the evidential burden of establishing the defence on the *balance of probabilities,* which the prosecution would then have to disprove *beyond reasonable doubt.* These were not entirely new debates. (see Williams, 1954). New Labour proposed that abolition would be the simplest course and would send a signal that, in general, children of ten or over should be held accountable for their own actions, (Home Office, 1997a, para 15). It would also solve practical difficulties in securing the prosecution and convictions of children under 14 ... (and) ensure that justice in such a case was made simpler, speedier and clearer, (ibid, para 18). The subsequent White Paper, *No More Excuses – A New Approach to Tackling Youth Crime in England and Wales,* (Home Office, 1997b), took, as its title indicates, a more entrenched approach, based on the position that to presume that children aged 10–14 years old do not know the difference between *naughtiness* and *serious wrongdoing* was contrary to common sense. Moreover, New Labour expressed concern about the practical difficulties of rebutting the presumption, which was preventing the prosecution of some children who should be prosecuted and punished, (ibid, para 4.4).

To place any emphasis on the obstructive nature of the presumption of *doli incapax* with regard to legitimate prosecution is clearly disingenuous. Indeed, in practice, the presumption was often ignored and easily rebutted in the few tried cases where it became an issue. Almost invariably, the child's statement at initial interview under police caution is such that the presumption of *doli incapax* is very readily rebutted. Further, given that the only protection a child has in interview with the police is the appropriate adult, often either passive or actively assisting the police, the childs' tendency to confess very early on in the interview, along with the high level of guilty pleas and the low level of provision of legal advice, it is difficult to take seriously any suggestion of prosecutorial difficulties, (Brown, 1997; Audit Commission, 1996).

Notwithstanding these points, many people involved in the everyday operation of the criminal law with regard to children advocated the retention of the presumption. It may have served to protect some children by requiring the police and the Crown Prosecution Service to acknowledge the childhood status of the alleged 'offender' and possibly make decisions other than prosecution or official caution. The *doli incapax* rule has the merit of making the police, prosecutors, and the judiciary stop and think, however briefly in some cases, about the degree of responsibility of each individual child, (Cavadino, 1997, p 170).

Equally, earlier proposals to abolish the presumption of *doli incapax* have usually been accompanied by parallel proposals to raise the age of criminal responsibility, (Home Office, 1960; Home Office, 1965). The Law Commission, in drafting the revised criminal code in 1989, reversed its previous position and recommended retention of the presumption, declaring itself loath to recommend an isolated change in the law that might be interpreted as encouraging greater use of the criminal process as a means of dealing with children, (Law Commission,1989, para.10.28). As noted above, the House of Lords, in C v DPP was also mindful of the wider implications, but despite all of this the presumption was jettisoned without further ado by Section 34 of the Crime and Disorder Act 1998.

A compelling legal argument has been proposed by Walker, (1999, p 64) who suggests that although the presumption of *doli incapax* may have been abolished, the defence of *doli incapax* still remains: it is hardly logical to suggest that the presumption is about a non-existent defence. Walker argues that the effect of section 34 of the Crime and Disorder Act 1998 is only to place the evidential burden of producing evidence that the child did not know what they were doing was seriously wrong on to the defence. Furthermore, Walker notes that this is what the Solicitor-General reported during the second reading of the Bill:

> *The possibility is not ruled out, where there is a child who has genuine learning difficulties and who is genuinely at sea on the question of right and wrong, of seeking to run this as a specific defence. All that provision does is remove the presumption.*
>
> (House of Lords, Hansard, 16 December, 1997, col. 596).

Walker's argument is intriguing, and one can only hope that it comes to be tested in the appeal courts. However, Walker's analysis was certainly not the intention of New Labour. The Government's unequivocal intention is that children who do not know the seriousness of what they are doing should be prosecuted, irrespective of their immaturity and lack of understanding. The Home Office admitted that no research had been undertaken to substantiate any of the alleged problems, (House of Commons, Hansard, 12 January 1998, col.67). There has been no research undertaken to indicate either that the presumption was a problem for prosecutors or witnesses, or that children 'grow up' quicker and have developed a more sophisticated understanding of degrees of wrongdoing, (Curtis, 1999). Or, indeed, that early exposure to the criminal justice system might become a beneficial or an effective crime-reduction strategy for children. There has been no reconsideration of the social policy surrounding offending children as envisaged by the House of Lords in their concluding comments in C v DPP. At some point, early intervention through the criminal justice system has become spuriously reconstructed as both the *entitlement* of children and an *appropriate response*. If for some reason a child is lacking in this most basic moral under-standing, it is all the more imperative that appropriate intervention and rehabili-tation should begin as soon as possible, (UK Government, 1999, paras 10.30.1 and 10.30.2). Such reconstruction is ultimately premised upon personal responsibility: 'as they develop, children must bear an increasing responsibility for their actions', (Home Office, 1997b, para.4.1). However, 'development' is no longer a signif-icant variable in ascribing responsibility. Indeed, the approach now to all children over the age of ten years is one of holding them unequivocally responsible and accountable for choices made and harm caused, and there is no longer a filter to assess levels of responsibility which recognises immaturity or lesser understanding as an intrinsic consequence of non-adulthood.

The criminal law and children: ever increasing responsibility

Government rhetoric and political priorities in relation to children and crime have focused on responsibility and response, without any serious consideration of the complexities of such concepts in criminal law. To be convicted of a crime there needs to be the *actus reus* (prohibited action or omission) together with the requisite *mens rea* for the offence charged and the absence of a defence. There is often too little concern about ensuring that children are given dynamic defence, to guarantee that every case is processed and proved in accordance with the legal requirements of the specific offence. The criminal law is an overtly adult context into which the child does not easily fit.

In criminal law, the *moral agency* of the offender is reflected in the *mens rea* requirement, the mental element which, in explanations of the principles of criminal liability, normally accompanies the *actus reus*, the conduct element. *Mens rea* is normally based on a subjective test regarding the state of mind of the individual offender. The majority of offences for which children are prosecuted, theft, are offences of subjective liability, so that intentionality and knowledge needs to be established to secure a conviction. Here, there is clearly ample opportunity, in principle at least, to take account of the child's limited liability and responsibility, contingent upon the status of 'child'.

The definition of theft is provided by legislation: a person is guilty of theft if they dishonestly appropriate property belonging to another with the intention of permanently depriving the other of it, (Section s1(1), Theft Act 1968). The concept of 'dishonesty' does not have a statutory definition but working principles emerged from the Court of Appeal in Ghosh, 1982, QB 1053, in the form of two questions. Was what was done dishonest according to the ordinary standards of reasonable people? If so, did the defendant realise that reasonable and honest people would regard what they did as dishonest? The second question is the subjective one that would need to be asked of the child, and, should the child answer it in the negative, they would be acquitted. The concept of intention to permanently deprive, further expanded in Section 6 of the Theft Act 1968, 'sprouts obscurities at every phrase', (Spencer, 1997), and is by no means an easy concept. This would be particularly so with regard to children who have a very flexible approach to ownership of (other people's) property and the concept of 'borrowing'. In fact, theft is a highly complex offence, generating weighty academic tomes and numerous appeal cases every year, and particular care should be taken in the cases of children who should be on the very margins of its provisions. The unashamed criminality of nursery rhymes and the appealing alternative morality of the characters in children's stories, Robin Hood providing a perfect example, should be enough to raise questions about the *mens rea* of children on theft charges. It is unlikely that the average police constable, (see R v. Commissioner of Police for the Metropolis ex p. P, 1995, 160 J.P.367), or for that matter the average Youth Court clerk or magistrate, will be conversant with the finer points of the law of theft when applied to children.

There are other offences where concern in relation to issues of children's responsibility should prevail for different reasons, particularly where liability can be imposed based not on subjectivity but objectivity, reflecting a level of understanding that could be expected of a reasonable adult. Criminal damage has such objective elements, (Metropolitan Police Commissioner v. Caldwell, 1982, AC 341), and the courts have steadfastly refused to modify judgements and assessments of the foresight required to that which could reasonably be expected of a child. Reckless damage to property may be committed where there is an obvious risk of damage, obvious that is, to the reasonable adult, but where the child has not thought about it and where no reasonable child of the same age could have been expected to think about it. In 1983 this made some judges distinctly uncomfortable, (Lord Goff in Elliot v C, 1983, 1WLR 939). By 1995 however, the judiciary seemed less troubled and such complexities were rejected, (Hobhouse L.J. in Coles, 1995, 1 Cr App R 157).

The age of criminal responsibility is only the beginning of the process by which children are charged, prosecuted and convicted of crimes in the criminal courts. Most children are processed before magistrates in the Youth Court, but an increasing minority are tried in adult Crown Court. The Criminal Justice and Public Order Act 1994, (Section 16(3)), reduced the minimum age for Crown Court trial in cases of serious crimes from thirteen to ten, so more and more younger children can be tried as 'adults' in open court. Recently, this issue has come under critical review in the European Court of Human Rights which ruled (inter alia) that Thompson and Venables, the two boys aged eleven when convicted in adult Crown Court of the murder of James Bulger, were too young to understand the proceedings in which they were tried and convicted of murder, and had therefore not received a fair trial as required by Article 6 of the European Convention on Human Rights. Such injustice was thought to have prevailed even though the boys were represented by skilled and experienced lawyers and other minor concessions made in relation to court room procedure, (V. v. The United Kingdom and T. v. The United Kingdom, 16th December 1999; http: //www.dhcour.coe.fr/hudoc./V, para 90). Notwithstanding this very significant judgement, procedural protections for children appearing in criminal cases (already minimal) are being further eroded. The right of silence of a child questioned and charged was removed by the Criminal Justice and Public Order Act 1994, (Section 34), which meant that adverse inferences could be drawn by a jury from a child's silence or failure to mention 'relevant matters' when interviewed by the police. Hitherto, similar inferences from a child, who was under fourteen years old and was reluctant to give evidence at trial could not be drawn. However, such protection and legal safeguard was swept away in a last-minute amendment to the Crime and Disorder Act 1998, (Section 35), which equates the position of children aged 10–14 years old not only with older juveniles, but with adults too. Children aged 10–14 now risk adverse inferences being drawn if they do not enter the dock or answer questions during cross-examination. The abolition of the presumption of *doli incapax* and the right of silence in the dock are declared by the Government to have the same purpose:

> *...to ensure that, if a child has begun to offend, they are entitled to the earliest possible intervention to address that offending behaviour and eliminate its causes. The changes will also have the result of putting all juveniles on the same footing as far as courts are concerned, and will contribute to the right of children appearing there to develop responsibility for themselves.*
>
> (U.K. Government. 1999, para. 10.30.2)

The wording of this statement is profoundly disingenuous and distorted. The increasing extent to which legal safeguards are being removed and children are being held responsible in criminal law is presented here as a courtesy to children's rights, child development and justice. However, the 'responsibilised child' is someone who can be tried in adult Crown Court, but not by a jury of their peers since jury members have to be 18, (Juries Act 1974, (Section 1)); they belong to the only category of citizen who cannot elect trial by jury, once thought to be every 'Englishman's right'. They may not be competent to instruct a lawyer, but one may act for them under the general duty to act in any client's best interests, (Venton et al., 1996, Practice Rule 1.01), although it has been suggested that in such a case, serious consideration should be given to arguing that the child is unfit to plead, (Ashford and Chard, 1997, p 3).

Even in the Youth Court, where the majority of children charged with criminal offences are processed, there are aspects of criminal procedure which raise serious questions in relation to the extent to which children are held responsible in criminal law. This is particularly conspicuous when compared with the protective measures employed in family proceedings. Where the child is involved in public law proceedings, such as applications for care or supervision orders by the local authority under Section 31 Children Act 1989, for example, the court has a positive duty to appoint a *guardian ad litem* unless satisfied that it is not necessary to do so in order to safeguard the child's interests, (Section 41(1) Children Act 1989). The *guardian ad litem* has a central role in advising the court on the child's understanding in matters where their consent may be required, and files reports on the child's interests and considers the options available and their suitability for the child, (Family Proceedings Rules 1991). The *guardian ad litem* is a qualified social worker who specialises in child care issues and in cases where a guardian is appointed, a solicitor who is a specialist in child law and a member of a local child care panel will also be instructed to represent the child. The Children Act 1989, (Section 1(1) and (3)(a)), also provides that the welfare of the child should be the court's 'paramount consideration', and that the 'wishes and feelings' of the child should be ascertained, making specific reference to the child's 'age and under-standing'. This is in stark contrast to criminal proceedings and contradicts the urge to criminalise and 'responsibilise' the child as discussed above.

The age of criminal responsibility – the international context

The age of criminal responsibility is a significant indicator of perceptions of childhood, (Goldson, 1999, pp 17–20). In a European context the age of ten which applies in England and Wales is low, other countries absolve their children from criminal responsibility until a much later age. Belgium and Luxembourg have an age of criminal responsibility of 18, Spain and Portugal of 16, Germany and Austria 14, Netherlands and Greece 12. Children in countries with a higher age of criminal responsibility are no less mature than those in England and Wales, but the response chosen to deal with them is quite different. Some countries, like Scotland, have a lower age of criminal responsibility but then process the majority of their 'offending' children through non-adversarial administrative tribunals as opposed to criminal courts, (McGhee et al., 1996).

The majority opinion in the European Court of Human Rights case of Thompson and Venables did not consider that the low age of criminal responsi-bility in itself violated Article 3 of the European Convention of Human Rights, (referring to inhuman and degrading treatment). The majority opinion was that there was no clear common standard amongst the signatories of the European Convention and ten was not so young as to differ disproportionately from the age followed in other European States. The partly dissenting joint opinion of Judges Pastor Ridruejo, Ress, Makarczyk, Tulkens and Butkevych differed however. With only four contracting states having an age of criminal responsibility as low as, or lower than, England and Wales, they submitted:

> *We have no doubt that there is a general standard among the member states of the Council of Europe under which there is a system of relative criminal responsibility beginning at the age of thirteen or fourteen – with special court procedures for juveniles – and providing for full criminal responsi-bility at the age of eighteen or above.*
>
> (V. v The United Kingdom and T. v. The United Kingdom, 16th December 1999, http: //www.dhcour.coe.fr/hudoc/V
> Partly dissenting joint opinion: para 1).

They were particularly struck by the paradox that children who were deemed to have sufficient discrimination to engage their criminal responsibility, had a play area made available to them during adjournments.

The low age of criminal responsibility in England and Wales has been the subject of concern elsewhere. The Committee on the United Nations Convention on the Rights of the Child, even at a time when the presumption of *doli incapax* was still in existence, has raised such concern, for example, (Committee on the Rights of the Child 1995, para 17). The United Kingdom ratified the Convention in 1991 and undertook to comply with a raft of principles which set out international obligations towards children, (Goldson, 1997). The United Nations Standard Minimum Rules for the Administration of Juvenile Justice, (the Beijing Rules), cited in the Convention, indicate that the age of criminal responsibility should not be too low bearing in mind the facts of emotional, mental and intellectual maturity, (Rule 4.1). The commentary in the Beijing Rules states that:

> *The minimum age of criminal responsibility differs widely owing to history and culture. The modern approach would be to consider whether a child can live up to the moral and psychological components of criminal responsibility; that is, whether a child, by virtue of her or his individual discernment and understanding, can be held responsible for essentially anti-social behaviour. If the age of criminal responsibility is fixed too low ... the notion of responsibility would become meaningless. In general, there is a close relationship between the notion of responsibility for delinquent behaviour and other social rights and responsibilities (such as marital status and civil majority).*
>
> (United Nations, 1985).

Law and the legal capacity of the child

In law, childhood begins at the moment of independent existence of the mother and adulthood begins at midnight eighteen years later, (Family Law Reform Act 1969, Section 9). Children as a group therefore can be legally defined as those under the age of 18, and childhood extends from infancy at the beginning through to adolescence at the end. Clearly, the capacity of the infant is decidedly less than that of the adolescent on the brink of adulthood and the law has had to reflect this. In many areas legal capacity is triggered automatically by the attainment of a certain age. For example, the age of majority was lowered from 21 to 18 in the Family Law Reform Act 1969 and this is the age at which many legal consequences of adulthood become effective in law, particularly those relating to property and money. Eighteen is the age at which complete contractual capacity is acquired, together with the capacity to hold and sell legal interests in property, apply for a loan and write a will. In some situations, whilst there is no legal designation of incapacity, childhood is recognised. For instance, there are special provisions for children taking oaths and giving evidence in court. In other areas, capacity may be conceded on the basis of maturity and understanding before actually attaining the required chronological age, (Hamilton, 1999). There has been a movement since the 1980s in favour of giving minors increased rights and responsibilities for making decisions in their lives contingent upon the child's 'sufficient understanding'. However, decisions in cases which have come before the courts invariably indicate that the child's 'maturity' and 'understanding' is often quite limited.

The Children Act 1989 incorporates the right of mature minors to make some decisions. These include the right to seek the court's permission to initiate legal proceedings in certain family matters, but the court will only grant permission if it considers the child is of 'sufficient understanding'. Even the statutory provision of consent to psychiatric or medical examination, or other assessment made with an interim care order, emergency protection order or child assessment order, can be overridden by the Courts if this is deemed to be in the interests of the child's welfare. Legal capacity in this area only really enables a child to align themselves with the wishes of one adult rather than another: these rights and responsibilities are located within a broader 'protective' context as the processes are so closely circumscribed and scrutinised by adults. In this way, the civil law approach to the responsibility of mature children empowers them to make choices about their own lives, whilst protecting them from the damaging effects of court room procedures and litigious involvement. Civil law aims to provide autonomy and responsibility within a system geared to protection. In criminal law, autonomy and responsibility are increasingly imposed within a system where even the pretence of protection is being jettisoned.

Control and criminalisation: but what about children and childhood?

The criminal law is a method of social control. It prohibits certain conduct and defines states of mind and capacities which are required for securing liability. It is, however, only one method of social control. For children there are many alternative methods, both outside the legal system and including parents, families, schools, communities, peer groups and within it, such as local authority provision of personal and family social services. It is quite proper to avoid the enforcement of criminal law wherever possible:

> *Criminal processes such as arrest, police custody and interrogation are highly intrusive and in themselves involve stigma and humiliation. Accordingly, one should not use the criminal law to control conduct that can be effectively regulated by other areas of the law ... In any society that values liberty, the criminal law ought only to be involved as a last resort method of social control when absolutely necessary.*

(Clarkson, 1995, p 202).

Policy changes during the 1990s have increasingly selected children as an appropriate target for the stigmatising intervention of the criminal law at ever younger ages, (Goldson, 1999). Whilst the declared emphasis is not on criminalising children but on helping them to recognise and accept responsibility, enabling them to receive help to change their offending behaviour, (UK Government 1999, para 10.30.3), fundamental questions remain: what is criminal processing if it is not criminalisation? There are many aspects of this expansionist programme which would cause a criminal lawyer considerable consternation. In the Crime and Disorder Act 1998, (Section 14), and under the auspices of 'protection', children under the age of ten can be made subject to local curfews even though they have not been convicted of any offence, where the local authority considers it necessary to keep them off the streets at night to maintain public order. A child safety order under section 11 of the same Act can be granted by the civil magistrates court; the conditions include that the child has committed an act which, if they had been aged ten or over, would have constituted an offence, or to prevent them from doing so in the future. This sanctions judicial intervention in a child's life in a way which effectively lowers the age of criminal responsibility and allows pre-emptive action to be taken. The fact that this takes place in a civil court, ostensibly concerned with the child's welfare as the paramount consideration, as distinct from punishment, is a subtlety unlikely to be comprehended by the child: even children in family hearings believe if they are involved in court proceedings, they must be 'criminal', (Masson and Oakley, 1999, p 114).

The rule of law is complex and beset with difficulty. Criminal law is an arm of public law and as such is concerned with regulating the relationship between the State and its citizens. In the majority of offences, the State's position is to redress harm caused to an individual or the wider community by another individual. Such a response towards children is full of contradictions: a child's experiences from birth are controlled by others who have responsibilities towards them. The predictive factors for likely future involvement in crime including poverty, bad housing, high crime environment, low educational provision and poor parenting are not conditions for which the child is directly responsible. The position of the state holding the child responsible in criminal law is particularly questionable in this sense. Moreover, local authorities have a statutory duty to provide services to 'children in need' and are under a duty to encourage children within their area not to commit criminal offences, (Children Act 1989, Part 111, and Schedule 2, 7(b)). The life histories of children embroiled in the criminal justice system often show that they are either well-known to social services or have been in care, (Hagell and Newburn, 1994; Goldson, 1998), and it seems fair to assume that the local authority has been unable to fulfil these responsibilities.

The Crime and Disorder Act 1998 places a duty on local authorities with education and social services responsibilities, in partnership with the police, probation service, and health authority, to establish a multi-agency youth offending team in the area, to include input as appropriate from other agencies and voluntary organisations. The declared aim of the youth justice system is to prevent offending as provided by Section 37 of the 1998 Act. However, the local authority already has a similar duty imposed under the Children Act 1989 but this duty was never accompanied by the appropriate level of resources. Government initiatives and investment in education, health, employment and tackling poverty, homelessness, teenage pregnancy, school exclusions, truancy and providing a range of family support services are all measures to be applauded. In the meantime however, those whose lives and opportunities have not yet been improved will be held responsible and enmeshed at an ever younger age in the current expansion of the criminal justice system with little concern either for their rights or for the principles of criminal law. The abolition of the presumption of *doli incapax,* combined with the opposition to raising the age of criminal responsibility, the removal of special safeguards for children, and the prioritising of the responsibility of the child are all symbolic of the state's limited vision in understanding children, the nature of childhood, or the true meaning of an appropriate criminal law response.

References

Ashford, M. and Chard, A., (1997), *Defending Young People in the Criminal Justice System.* London, LAG Education and Service Trust Limited.

Audit Commission, (1996), *Misspent Youth...Young People and Crime.* London: Audit Commission Publications.

Bandalli, S., (1997), Abolition of the Presumption of *Doli Incapax* and the Criminalisation of Children. *The Howard Journal of Criminal Justice* 37(2), pp114–23.

Brown, D., (1997), PACE – Ten Years On: A Review of the Research, *Home Office Research Study 155,* London, HMSO.

Cavadino, P., (1997), Goodbye doli, Must we Leave You? *Child and Family Law Quarterly* 9(2) pp165–71.

Clarkson, C.M.V., (1995), *Understanding Criminal Law.* Second edition. London, Fontana Press.

Committee on the Convention on the Rights of the Child, (1995), (8th Session) Consideration of Reports Submitted by States Parties Under Article 44 United Nations Convention on the Rights of the Child, CRC/C/15/Add.34.

Curtis, S., (1999), *Children Who Break the Law or Everybody Does It.* Winchester, Waterside Press.

Fionda, J., (1998), The Age of Innocence? The Concept of Childhood in the Punishment of Young Offenders. *Child and Family Law Quarterly* 10(1), pp77–87.

Gelsthorpe, L. and Morris A., (1999), Much Ado About Nothing: A Critical Comment on Key Provisions Relating to Children in the Crime and Disorder Act 1998, *Child and Family Law Quarterly,* 11 (3), pp209–21.

Goldson, B., (1997), Children in Trouble: State Responses to Juvenile Crime in *'Childhood' in 'Crisis'?,* Scraton P., (Ed.), pp124–45. London, UCL Press.

Goldson, B., (1998), *Children in Trouble: Backgrounds and Outcomes.* Liverpool, Department of Sociology, Social Policy and Social Work Studies, The University of Liverpool.

Goldson, B., (1999), Youth (In) Justice: Contemporary Developments in Policy and Practice in Goldson, B., (Ed.), *Youth Justice: Contemporary Policy and Practice.* Aldershot, Ashgate.

Hagel, A. and Newburn T., (1994), *Persistent Young Offenders*. London: Policy Studies Institute.

Hamilton, C., (1999), At What Age Can I? *Childright* 157, pp 9–17.

Home Affairs Select Committee, (1993), *Juvenile Offenders*, Sixth report of the Session. London, HMSO.

Home Office, (1960), *Report of the Committee on Children and Young Persons,* Cmd.1191. London, HMSO.

Home Office, (1965), *The Child, The Family and the Young Offender*, Cmnd.2742. London, HMSO.

Home Office, (1968), *Children in Trouble* Cmnd.3601. London, HMSO.

Home Office, (1990), *Crime, Justice and Protecting the Public*, Cm.965. London, HMSO.

Home Office, (1997a), *Tackling Youth Crime: A Consultation Paper.*

Home Office, (1997b), *No More Excuses: A New Approach to Tackling Youth Crime in England and Wales*, Cm 3809. London, HMSO.

Kean, A.W.G., (1937), The History of the Criminal Liability of Children. *Law Quarterly Review* 53, pp364–70.

Labour Party Media Office, (1996), *Tackling Youth Crime, Reforming Youth Justice; A Consultation Paper on an Agenda for Change*. London.

Law Commission, (1989), *Criminal Law. A Criminal Code for England and Wales*, Law Com.No.177. London, HMSO.

Masson, J. and. Oakley, M.W., (1999), *Out of Hearing, Representing Children in Care Proceedings*. Chichester, John Wiley & Sons.

McGhee, J. Waterhouse, L. and Whyte, B., (1996), Children's Hearings and Children in Trouble in Asquith, S., (Ed.), *Children and Young People in Conflict with the Law*. London, Jessica Kingsley.

Sayre, F.B., (1932), Mens Rea. *Harvard Law Review* 45, pp 974–1026.

Spencer, J. R., (1977), The Metamorphosis of s6 of the Theft Act 1968. *Criminal Law Review* pp 653–60.

UK Government, (1999), *Convention on the Rights of the Child: Second Report to the UN Committee on the Rights of the Child by the United Kingdom*. London, The Stationery Office.

United Nations, (1985), *The United Nations Standard Minimum Rules for the Administration of Juvenile Justice*. New York, United Nations.

Venton, P., Verdin, P.A., Hughes, C.W. and Bullough, J., (1996), (Eds.). *The Guide to the Professional Conduct of Solicitors* (7th edn.). London, The Law Society,

Walker, N., (1999), The End of an Old Song? *New Law Journal* 149(6871), p 64.

Williams, G., (1954), The Criminal Responsibility of Children. *Criminal Law Review* pp 493–500.

CHAPTER 6

Parents, Responsibility and the New Youth Justice

Mark Drakeford and Kerry McCarthy

Introduction

The boundary between the private responsibilities of parents within families, and the role of the state in shaping and enforcing these responsibilities, has long been controversial. However, in the final decade of the twentieth century a decisive shift seems to have taken place, most particularly in relation to the parents of young people who appear before the criminal courts. The Crime and Disorder Act 1998 represents the most recent legislative embodiment of this shift. It states that the principal aim for youth justice services is to 'prevent offending by children and young persons', (s.37(1)). The same Act introduces a new sanction, the Parenting Order, designed, according to Government, to prevent offending by ensuring that parents face up to their responsibilities for exercising proper control over their children. This chapter investigates this shift, exploring the nature of thinking which lies behind it and the practical consequences which may follow from it. If state-enforced parenting standards are to play a major part in the drive to prevent offending by children and young persons, then the intellectual and practical basis of such a strategy, including its consequences for youth justice services, deserves close examination.

The contention that young people commit crimes due to family disruption or inadequate parenting has been an abiding feature of the debates on juvenile offending, (Pearson, 1994; Brown, 1998). As Newburn, (1997), suggests, the family is regarded as a key factor in the production of delinquency in many theoretical approaches, including psychoanalysis, social control theories and social learning theories. This preoccupation with the family as being at the root of delinquent behaviour has always found recognition in juvenile and youth justice policy. What has changed is the extent to which the tone of legislation has been dominated by the state's willingness to insist and punish, rather than advise and ameliorate. The discussion which follows traces the changing approach to parental responsibility, beginning with the landmark Acts of the 1960s and ending with the Criminal Justice Act of 1991. The central portion of the chapter then turns to the most recent manifestation of Government intentions in this area, in particular, the Parenting Order as provided by the Crime and Disorder Act 1998. This section sets out the detail of the requirements under the new Order and reports the results of an inquiry into current Pre-Sentence Report practice in relation to parents of young people in trouble. The chapter ends with some conclusions concerning the theoretical and practical worth of the new Order, and an attempt to place it within the broader context of New Labour policy making.

The parents of children in trouble

The 1963 Children and Young Persons Act was the first substantial piece of legislation in the field of post-war juvenile justice. It aimed to encourage the development of parental responsibility through the provision of family advice centres which were located in high crime areas. Such centres were designed to teach parents how to discipline effectively and develop law abiding attitudes in their children, (Pitts, 1996). There was also an emphasis on early intervention by Local Authorities for children deemed to be 'at risk'. The tone was welfarist and the argument suggested that the capacity to alter behaviour lay in changing the environment in which that behaviour was learned and reinforced. Such ideas were particularly evident in the Children and Young Persons Act 1969 which promoted early intervention on the basis that by treating individual deprivation, depravity would be 'cured', (Haines and Drakeford, 1998; Newburn, 1997). The unintended and harmful consequences of such policies have been extensively traced (see, for example, Thorpe et al., 1980; Pitts, 1988). With regard to parenting, the immediate legacy of the discrediting of the 1969 Act was a distrust of overzealous intervention in family life and a sharpened theoretical and practical understanding of the effectiveness of changing systems, rather than individuals in producing a reduction in juvenile offending. The result was a fortuitous convergence in attitudes between those working with young people in trouble on a daily basis and the political spirit of the age. The justice model, increasingly embraced by practitioners, argued for sentencing to be offence based, with a limit on interventions into family life, (Pitts, 1996). Rolling back the frontiers of the state, as a political ambition, then combined with youth justice practitioners' desire to roll back the rising tide of custodial sentencing for which the welfarist policies of the 1969 Act were thought to be responsible (for a fuller account see, for example, Goldson, 1997a and 1997b). The result was an agenda based upon maximum diversion, minimum intervention and systems management, (Cavadino and Dignan, 1997).

While the notion of leaving kids and their families alone, (Schur, 1973) possessed a clear radical and libertarian dimension it was also capable of a rather different emphasis. For those who believed that the state had accepted too much responsibility for the lives of its citizens, leaving them alone could mean transferring new obligations to individuals in general and parents in particular. The 1980 White Paper, '*Young Offenders*', (Home Office, 1980) asserted the distinction to be made between delinquency and deprivation in the criminal justice system, (Morris and Giller, 1987). The subsequent Criminal Justice Act 1982 embodied this approach, with families in youth justice regarded as a source of parental responsibility to control children and not as an area for treatment or rehabilitation, (Gelsthorpe and Morris, 1994). In the years which have followed, youth justice policies have increasingly retreated from welfare, in favour of a law and order punitiveness. For parents, as Brown, (1998), suggests, the result has been an ever-increasing emphasis upon their role in controlling and disciplining young people. By the time of the Criminal Justice Act 1991, a set of specific measures were introduced which allowed the enforcement of parental responsibility when crimes were committed by children. Parents were required to attend the court appearances of their child and the existing powers to make parents responsible for the payment of fines and compensation were strengthened, (Haines and Drakeford, 1998). The White Paper, (Home Office, 1990) also encouraged parental involvement in Supervision Orders and urged Local Authorities to provide advice and guidance to parents attending court.

The Criminal Justice Act 1991: binding-over and the politics of parenting

The most significant aspect of the 1991 Act in this respect was the introduction of the power for courts to bind over the parents of a young person 'to take proper care and exercise proper control over the child', (s.58 Criminal Justice Act 1991). Failure to meet the terms of the bind over could result in the Court's imposing a fine of up to £1000. The Criminal Justice and Public Order Act 1994 extended this power to include parents having to ensure their child's compliance with the requirements of a community sentence. Moreover, the roots of the 1998 Parenting Order itself are to be found in the parental bind over of 1991. Both sanctions are made without any legal representation for the parents and both require those parents targeted to control behaviour which is not specified, by means which are equally unspecific. With both Orders there exists the potential for a criminal sanction, in terms of a fine, should parents fail to 'take responsibility' for their children, (Penal Affairs Consortium, 1995). Drakeford, (1996), and the Penal Affairs Consortium, (1995), record the opposition to the bind over from magistrates and other youth justice practitioners. It was felt that, while parental influence might be central in preventing young people offending, the bind over could only serve to damage what could already be strained family relationships. Drakeford's (1996) research found that parents felt the bind over was an unfair punishment based on unrealistic expectations of their ability to control their children. These findings were mirrored in the Penal Affairs Consortium, (1995), research which also identified the potential for increased conflict within families.

The two studies produced broadly similar findings and concluded that the bind over is ineffective and even potentially damaging in its ability to enforce parental responsibility. More generally, there has been a recognition across the spectrum of criminal justice opinion that such measures can have an unhelpful and debilitating impact upon those for whom the raising of children is already problematic and located within disadvantaged circumstances. The Lord Chief Justice, Lord Bingham, commenting on proposals – including curfews – raised by Michael Howard, the last Conservative Home Secretary, to penalise parents for their children's behaviour, stated: 'We would be dealing with parents of the most unpromising kind and whether they would change their ways as a result of these court orders is doubtful … We need to try to prevent children getting into the courts in the first place', (*Guardian* 7.3.97). The clear consensus of academic and practitioner opinion, (as reported, for example, in Allan, 1996) has been that the targeting of parents was the product not of any confidence in the practical efficiency of such measures but, rather, their political effectiveness. The Magistrates' Association rejection of the contention that 'parents can be coerced into assuming the sort of responsibility that would result in a reduction of crime' (*The Magistrate*, 1990), holds good across the actions of political parties and across a decade of attempts to portray parents as recklessly indifferent to the conduct of their children.

The reawakening of intervention into family life in youth justice policy occurred in a context of wider social policy developments. Newburn, (1997), notes the way in which, during the 1980s, attention became concentrated upon particular groups of parents, as concerns were voiced over the rising divorce rate and number of lone parent families. Pitts, (1996), recognises how attitudes, influenced by underclass theorists such as Charles Murray, (1990), combined with the demonization of young people as rioting joyriders, ram raiders and persistent offenders to create a climate of retribution, (see also Muncie, 1999; Brown, 1998; Newburn, 1997). The death of Jamie Bulger in 1993 sparked a competition between the two main political parties as to who could appear the most 'tough on crime', (Goldson, 1999a). The attitude towards parents was not based on help and support to improve the welfare of their children. Instead a climate of blame prevailed with an insistence that parents, in particular those branded as the 'underclass', made more effort to control and discipline their children or face being held accountable in the courts. The call for a return to traditional 'family values' in the 'back to basics' campaign of 1996 provided the Government with a popular scapegoat, in the form of parents, against whom to focus the fight against crime. This approach allowed more politically complicated, structural issues of economic deprivation and social marginalization to be bypassed when searching for a solution to the crime problem.

Parenting and New Labour

Such attitudes, however, were not confined to one political party. While still in opposition, the New Labour approach to parenting was expressed through a

'Discussion Paper'. It stated that 'a wider acceptance is needed that having a child is not a totally private act but one that has significance for the whole community ...' (Straw and Anderson, 1996). In Government, an early White Paper, (Home Office, 1997b), highlighted this move away from the non-interventionist approach of the 1980s, asserting that it is the Government's role to intervene in family life to ensure that parents fulfil their responsibilities. While the White Paper explicitly states that the Youth Court should have regard to the wider social circumstances of a young offender, the emphasis within the legislation remains firmly upon individual and parental responsibilities and the extent to which they can prevent offending. The legislation which followed explicitly limits the information which a Court must consider before making a Parenting Order to 'the person's family circumstances and the likely effect of the Order on those circumstances', (section 9 (2)). Wider socio-economic and structural factors, in terms of the welfare of young people, are thus excluded from the remit. More generally, within youth justice as a whole, Home Office Minister Alun Michael, (Card and Ward, 1998), explicitly stated that welfare is not the prime concern of the youth justice system except in how far it is achieved through the principal aim of preventing young people offending. This stance is in direct conflict with the principles in the Children Act 1989, which established that intervention in young peoples' lives should be based on 'welfare checklists' and 'working in partnership' with parents in a non-adversarial manner, (Muncie, 1999).

The Discussion, Consultation and White Papers, (Straw and Anderson, 1996; Home Office, 1997a; Home Office, 1997b), which preceded the Crime and Disorder Act 1998 all refer to research findings which link inadequate parenting to higher risks of criminality in young people. Graham and Bowling's, (1995) study, for example, identified how children under weak parental supervision were twice as likely to offend than those who were closely supervised and that parental supervision was the factor most closely correlated with criminality in young people. These findings are cited by the Government as evidence of the need for a sanction to further instil in parents the seriousness of their responsibility to exercise control over the behaviour of their children, (see Home Office, 1997a). The same studies often emphasise the role that socio-economic deprivation can play in leading to increased criminality in young people by compounding existing problems, such as a lack of parenting skills. There is, however, far less evidence of reference to these politically complex findings in the Government literature. Research by Utting et al., (1993), and NACRO, (1997), indicate that stress caused by unemployment, poverty and ill-health can determine how effectively parents are able to fulfil their responsibility to control their children. While this research recognised the need to promote courses offering skills, support and information to parents it also indicated that such measures could only have a limited impact on youth offending while wider social and economic problems remained unaddressed.

Parents and the Crime and Disorder Act 1998

Labour's flagship Crime and Disorder Act contains a series of measures through which the terms of trade between parents, children and the state are fundamentally altered. The Anti-Social Behaviour Order, (ASBO), set out in Section 1 of the Act, for example, can be placed on children as young as ten. The Order itself will be available on the basis of a civil standard of proof, but breach of an ASBO will be a criminal offence, potentially punishable with a term of imprisonment of up to two years. Families of children caught up in such circumstances are likely to face further consequences, when local authority departments move to eviction notices on the basis of demonstrated anti-social conduct. Child curfews, contained in Sections 14 and 15, which may be imposed upon children under the age of ten between the hours of 8.00 p.m. and 6 a.m. are also introduced in the Act. Asked for the rationale behind the measure, the Prime Minister was reported as saying, 'Some have called it a curfew. I call it child protection', (in Drakeford and Butler, 1999). In other words, children out at night are the victim of neglect, the product of a society divided into poor, single parent households (where lone parents fail to fulfil their obligations) or rich, two parent households (where both partners are working too hard and too long to exercise their responsibilities). Child curfews, in the Blairite formulation, are the product of parental deficits which the law must make good. Such interventionism is to be applied to individual young children, in addition to under tens as a whole class. Under Sections 11–13 of the Act, a Child Safety Order will be available for children under ten, in order to prevent them from becoming involved in behaviour of a criminal or anti-social kind. The guidance prepared by the Home Office to accompany implementation of the Act specifically draws attention to the need for a social services department applying for a Child Safety Order 'to investigate the merits of a recommendation for a Parenting Order' at the same time, (NACRO, 1998).

Turning, then, to the Parenting Order itself, the Act sets out the following four circumstances in which such an Order can be made: where the child has been made the subject of a Child Safety Order or a Sex Offender Order, (s.8(1)(a) and 8(1)(b)); in relation to the parents of a convicted young offender, (s.8(1)(c)); and where parents have been convicted of failing to send their child to school, (s.8(1)(d)). There is no obligation to make a Parenting Order but there is a statutory presumption in favour of an Order in the circumstances of a young person under 16 being convicted of an offence, (s.9(1)). The Order is made up of two primary parts: a requirement that the parent attend counselling or guidance sessions no more than once a week and for no longer than three months, (s.8(4)(b)); and the imposition, for up to one year, of additional requirements which the court believes to be necessary, for example ensuring that their child attends school or is home by a certain time, (s.8(4)(a)). Failure by parents to comply with any aspect of the Order is a summary offence punishable by a fine up to £1000, (s.9(7)). Failure to pay any fine is, of course, potentially punishable by imprisonment.

Positive support?

The Parenting Order does contain a new element which, it is claimed, provides a potentially positive dimension to sanctions against parents in the youth justice system. Unlike the power to bind over parents under the Criminal Justice Act 1991, the new Order intends to provide 'help' and 'support' to parents to enable them to control the behaviour of their children more effectively. While there are issues to be considered as to how far an involuntary criminal sanction can go in achieving more effective parenting, (see Goldson, 1999b for a discussion of the more general debate between support and control measures in youth justice), it is arguably a more positive approach for a court order to offer support and guidance than simply to rely on the threat of a fine, (Card and Ward, 1998). The Discussion, (Straw and Anderson, 1996), Consultation, (Home Office, 1997a) and White Papers, (Home Office, 1997b) all contain passages which emphasise the role of the Parenting Order as being a means of offering increased help, support and guidance to the parents of young offenders.

Negative control?

Against these positive prospects, a number of more negative possibilities have been raised. Haines and Drakeford, (1998), suggest that while the new legislation marks a return to the interventionist policies of the 1960s and 1970s it does so with a totally different tone, one which is repressive, coercive and has no regard to how wider social contexts impinge on the lives of parents. Muncie, (1999), and Brown, (1998), state that the Parenting Order is a continuation of the criminalization of 'inadequate parenting', developing the earlier provisions requiring parents to attend court, pay fines and be bound over. Goldson, (1999), argues that the Crime and Disorder Act 1998 is a continuation of a new political consensus in youth justice policy. This consensus is based on punishment, retribution and remoralisation with a particular emphasis on the responsibilities of parents. The tone is summed up in John Major's proclamation in 1993 which called for a 'need to condemn a little more and understand a little less'. In practice, a series of writers have identified difficulties which Parenting Orders are likely to create. Barnados and the Children's Society believe that compulsory attendance to guidance and counselling sessions is not only less effective in terms of improving parenting but may actually lead to a worsening of relationships between children and their parents, (Card and Ward, 1998). It is unlikely that parents who have already refused advice and support of a voluntary nature will be more receptive to such information when it is provided under the threat of a criminal sanction, (Card and

Ward, 1998). A more effective approach would be to make widely available community programmes to improve parenting skills in a manner which is perceived as sympathetic and non-condemnatory, (Haines and Drakeford, 1998).

An additional problem with intervention in parenting, even when based on notions of help and support, is the potentially stigmatizing and criminalizing effect it can have. Muncie, (1999), argues that such interventions mark a return to the negative aspects of the approach to youth justice in the 1960s and 70s. The danger lies, as it did under the interventionist policies of the welfare model, in failure by parents to respond to 'help' leading to an escalation in penalties, as suggested earlier. It is unclear from the legislation who would be responsible for the breach of an Order. Were it to be the Responsible Officer working with the family, this would have implications for the likelihood of effective work being done with the family in the future.

The new structure to youth justice, in the form of multi-agency Youth Offending Teams, will involve the representatives of a series of services relevant to the life of a young offender working together in a criminal justice setting. The positive advantages of this approach, in terms of co-ordination and cohesion, have been much advanced by Government. Far less attention has been paid to the potential difficulties in what Muncie, (1999), has called a 'criminalizing of social policy'. Multi-agency working, while offering a number of important advantages, may have the effect of prioritising the 'offender' label which is attached to a young person in all their other dealings. As has been argued elsewhere, for example Haines and Drakeford, (1998), getting into trouble is only a fractional part of the range of behaviours which are characteristic of any young person. The youth justice system operates in a way which seizes upon that aspect and magnifies it, as though this were the whole, rather than only a part, of what is important about that individual. While justice and welfare systems have been kept apart, there has been at least the chance that a child in school would be regarded primarily as a pupil and that a young person in need of health service help with a drug or alcohol problem would be regarded essentially as a patient. The danger of the new multi-disciplinary approach is that a young person in trouble will become an 'offender' first and foremost. When this approach is generalised still further to include parents as well as children within its ambit, the checks and balances through which any citizen ought to be protected from the unmediated power of the state are eroded to the point of impotence.

Crouch and Marquand, (1995), have written persuasively about the role of 'intermediate institutions', such as local authorities, in mediating between the enormous powers of the central state and the individual citizen. Young people, we would argue, are even more in need of a diffusion, rather than a concentration of that power which adults, and adult institutions, impose over their lives. The 'partnerships' which are so favoured in the New Labour approach to policy-implementation turn out, on examination, to be most often partnerships of the powerful in

pursuit of imposing their values and beliefs in the form of behavioural requirements upon the less powerful. As argued in the final section of this chapter, the
approach is based upon 'assimilation', rather than inclusion, in its insistence that
the benefits of citizenship are tied to officially sanctioned and approved conduct.
In the case of youth justice, the new Youth Offending Teams do not have to
become part of this majoritarian and conservative communitarianism. The traditional values of youth justice work should provide a bulwark against regarding
young people and their families as simply fodder to be bullied into line by a united
front of social subjudication. The dangers, however, are very present. When the
boundary is eroded between the criminal justice system and mainstream services
such as education, housing and health, then for whole families the dangers of
labelling and deviancy amplification may be acute.

Current practice

At the time of writing this chapter, the Parenting Order is being introduced
through nine pilot schemes, prior to its more widespread application across Wales
and England in April 2000. In what follows we shall consider the extent to which
current practice casts light upon the issues which the new Order will have to
address. It needs to be emphasised at the outset that, under the Crime and Disorder
Act provisions, there is no obligation for a Court to obtain a Pre-Sentence Report
prior to the making of a Parenting Order. Indeed, there appears to be no obligation
for parents themselves to be in Court at all. In a piece of research, (McCarthy
1999), allied to that reported below, however, a range of professional workers
involved in the Youth Court, were of the view that sentencers would be highly
likely to rely upon Reports for the information needed in deciding whether or not
to impose the new Orders. While current practice, as set out below, should not
therefore be read as translating easily or straightforwardly into the new circumstances, there are undoubtedly important lessons which can be gleaned from
present performance.

The discussion draws on a sample of 34 Pre-Sentence Reports (PSRs) prepared
for a large South Wales Youth Court during a 16 month period in 1998 and 1999.
A majority of the Reports concerned young men, the offender was female in only
five cases. Ages ranged from eleven to sixteen, the most common being young
people aged fourteen or fifteen. Where the involvement of a parent was reported in
the production of a PSR that parent was always the child's mother.

The first and most striking finding was that only 50 per cent of the sample of
young people were living at home with their parents. Fourteen young people had
been placed in the care of the local authority at an earlier stage in their lives and
lived either in a residential unit or with foster parents. The three remaining young
people were in the informal care of extended family or friends. Similar living
patterns have been reported in earlier studies, such as those of Hagell and

Newburn, (1994); Bottoms, (1995); Crowley, (1998) and Goldson, (1998). While s.8(2) of the Crime and Disorder Act 1998 allows Parenting Orders to be placed on any individual considered to be the 'guardian' of the young person, the clear implication of Ministers' speeches and official pronouncements has been that the Order was intended for young people residing at home. The Draft Guidance issued by the Home Office, (Home Office, 1998: 3.2), for example, emphasises that Courts considering a Parenting Order in other circumstances should only do so 'with care' and after proper consideration of the 'particular factors' arising in such circumstances. How, then, will the Parenting Order work in practice if a significant number of young offenders it intends to target are not residing with their parents? Neither the legislation nor the documents which preceded it provide an explanation of the practical role for Parenting Orders when parents do not have day-to-day responsibility for their children. Rather, the Home Office guidance suggests that Courts should only impose Parenting Orders where the child is in care or accommodated by the local authority when it believes that obligations placed upon the birth parents themselves might assist in bringing about improvement. Notwithstanding such advice, however, the same guidance also suggests that 'in exceptional circumstances' a Parenting Order might be used to impose specific requirements on the local authority or on foster carers, although the guidance maintains a notable silence as to what such obligations might be, or for what purposes they might be imposed. Against this problematic background, PSRs were examined in order to obtain an insight into four main factors: the extent of parental involvement in the compilation of Reports; the extent to which involvement led to the inclusion of parental views within Reports; the nature of judgements made by Report authors concerning parental responsibility and culpability and the post-sentence role for parents suggested in Reports. However, it is also important to consider a primary question of justice: why should a PSR prepared in specific relation to a child have any bearing upon a Court's adjudication in relation to that child's parents? The practical consequences which flow from confusing the purpose of the document in this way emerge in the discussion which follows. The principle which is violated in the process, however, is more fundamental and involves the right of any individual to be made subject to a criminal justice sanction only in relation to their own conduct and level of responsibility, rather than any other.

Parental involvement

The existing procedure for the compilation of PSRs is governed by National Standards, (Home Office, 1995) and should involve the parents of the young person in three ways. First, parents should be present during the initial interview with the young person. Second, parents should be consulted during the follow up interview. Finally, a completed copy of the Report should be made available to the parents. It has been impossible to determine the extent of parental involvement in stages two and three as there was no mention of either stage in any of the Reports analysed. One tentative suggestion is that these stages are not completed. This is based on the fact that contact with any individual connected to the young person, no matter how informal, appears to be recorded. It would therefore seem unlikely that more formal involvement from parents would not be recorded in the Reports.

It was possible, however, to record how often parents were involved in the first stage, during the initial interview with the young person. In only 41 per cent (14) of the Reports analysed was a parent present during the interview with the young person. A further six Reports contain comments on the parenting of the young person and other aspects of family life drawn from the report authors' long term involvement with the family, or access to the family social worker. Of course, any comment in the Reports based on information obtained this way will not have been informed directly from the opinions of parents at that particular time. To continue to rely on information on parenting from these sources could lead to future PSRs failing to record recent, significant events or changes in circumstance which would be relevant when assessing the suitability of a Parenting Order.

In five Reports the voices of significant others in the young person's life were heard in place of parents. These included grandparents, foster carers or members of staff from residential units. However, in an additional five Reports, the fact of the young person not residing with his parents did not prevent the involvement of the mother in the interview. The Report was still able to contain a picture of family relationships and a parent's perspective on their relevance to the young person's offending. Some Reports in this second group went on to highlight the importance of parental involvement in reducing the likelihood of further offending. This is an example of a problem which could arise when young people are not living with their parents. It is unclear which individual would be the focus of an Order, the 'guardian' or the parent, and who should therefore be consulted during the process of preparing the PSR.

Parental views

The second set of results are concerned with the extent to which PSRs contain an expression of parents' views and the issues that parents raise as being relevant in explaining their children's' offending.

A parental voice is heard in a total of 13 of the 34 Reports analysed and in just over half of these such a contribution represented a major voice. In two Reports the parental voice is the only source of comment, in two others it is included only in a passing reference. In a further two cases, parental views were cited on the basis of the Report writer's previous contact with them, rather than through direct comment on the particular matter before the court. Issues of equity clearly arise in such circumstances, with widely varying opportunity for parental views to be heard.

More striking still is the finding that 21 of the Reports analysed do not contain a parental voice at all. This may indicate parents' reluctance to speak frankly about how they are coping, especially given the wider child welfare remit of the Social Services Departments by whom PSR writers are employed. The introduction of Parenting Orders will change the nature of the relationship between Report writers and parents. The content of Reports will have greater implications for those parents who are judged to be irresponsible or unable to cope, as sanctions upon them may follow. This in turn seems both more likely to make parents feel ill-at-ease and less likely to speak frankly during the PSR process. Indeed, in justice terms, it may be straightforwardly in parents' interests to have a guarded approach in their dealings with Report writers and to avoid the revelation of factors which could lead to the imposition of a Parenting Order. It is difficult to see how the PSR process used in this way could be reconciled with detailed, honest accounts of family relationships and circumstances. These may, of course, be highly important elements in relation to one of the primary purposes of any Report; the adequate consideration and conveyal to the Court of the needs of the *young person* upon whom it is being written.

Within the Reports considered here there was no consistent relationship between a young person residing at home with his or her parents and the strength of the parental voice in the Report. There are instances where the young person is in residential care and the mother's comments are the only voice in the Report and instances where a young person lives at home but the Report contains no expression of the parents' views. Issues of inequity and inconsistency once again arise.

Where views are expressed by parents, especially when they focus upon those factors which parents believe to be relevant to their child's offending, then such views are clearly important to the assessment of any role which a Parenting Order might play. In the Reports cited here the influence of an offending peer group was repeatedly cited by parents as the cause of their child's offending. Many mothers appeared to have good relationships with their children and described them as well behaved within the home but recognised the powerful, negative influence that young people can have on each other. Penalising parents seems an unlikely method of strengthening their hand in dealing with forces which already appear outside their control or influence. Indeed, when the same issue has been discussed directly with young people, (see Goldson, 1998), almost all respond by stating that parents, and wider family members, had repeatedly attempted, through advice and practical sanctions, to prevent further offending.

When parents referred directly to relationships between themselves and the young person as a cause of offending behaviour it was often the mother referring to the child's volatile or non-existent relationship with his father. It is doubtful how suitable the placement of a Parenting Order would be in such circumstances. One parent cannot justifiably be held responsible for the failings of another. In such a situation a Parenting Order may only serve to jeopardise the more positive relationship with the mother. In one Report the mother could link her son's offending to specific life events. These were the violence in the home perpetuated by the stepfather, her own suicide attempt and the rejection the young person faced from his natural father. Once again, it is very difficult to see how a Parenting Order would go any way towards helping the young person work through such complex issues.

Parental culpability

In 29 per cent (10) of the Reports the tone and comment of the authors indicate that the parents were viewed as behaving responsibly and having some success in aiding a potential reduction in offending behaviour. In all these cases the parental voice provided a direct contribution to the Report. It is possible that the relatively high level of involvement from parents during the writing of these Reports may have led to them being perceived as more responsible. These Reports describe the parents as concerned, supportive and making positive efforts to prevent the child from offending. It is difficult to see how in cases such as this a Parenting Order would be justified on the grounds that parents had been wilfully negligent in controlling their children, or that they need further help and support.

Six of the Reports assess parents as trying to prevent their children from offending, but needing additional forms of support to have any success. The tone of these Reports is far from condemnatory towards the parents involved, instead they provide a recognition of how other pressures impinge on their relationships with their children. For this group, the danger of being 'sentenced to help' through a Parenting Order appear large, with all the attendant difficulties which are known to accompany such courses of action. More generally, the economic disadvantages faced by many single parent mothers forms a regular theme in Reports. Over a quarter (nine) of the Pre-Sentence Reports analysed linked pressures from poverty, housing, ill-health and the burden of child care falling on one parent to problems in effective parenting. The 'welfare' aspect of the Parenting Order, however, is limited to improving parental responsibility and thereby preventing offending by young people, (Card and Ward, 1998). In terms of improving the socio-economic and structural factors which put pressure on parents the Order offers no solution. Until such widespread, fundamental social problems are addressed it is difficult to see how support through a Parenting Order, in the form of coerced attendance at a weekly parenting class, will offer any significant amount of help to these parents.

Eleven of the Reports analysed held parents to be in some way responsible for their children's offending behaviour. Once again, the tone used is not directly condemnatory, but parents are still clearly assessed as contributing to their child's offending. Three sub-groups within this category can be identified. In the first, long term disruption and stress within family relationships was described as contributing to a young person's offending. Feelings of neglect or of being unwanted by a parent are cited as leading to extremely strained parent/child relationships. In the second group, parents are cited as contributing towards offending as a result of neglect and insufficient supervision over their children's lives. The third group of Reports which hold parents responsible to some degree refer to a range of social, structural, economic and health problems which limit their ability to parent effectively. There is, of course, a long and dishonourable tradition of Report-writer-as-character-assassin. Research at the Watton Detention Centre, the largest in England and Wales, suggested that, during the early 1980s, 21 per cent of Reports written by Social Services staff positively recommended custody and a further seven per cent implied a custodial sentence. An additional 13 per cent provided no recommendation whatsoever, in a spirit which implied that the young person concerned was beyond the help of the Report writer. Thus fully 40 per cent of young people at the Detention Centre had been subjects of Reports which actively assisted their passage into custody. Something of the same spirit may still be at work in some of the Reports considered here and, in that sense, the assessments recorded may tell us more about the Report writer, and the prevailing occupational culture within which that person operates, than the parent. Such opinions are, nevertheless, conveyed in Reports as 'objective' or unproblematic. Given the receptivity of the Courts to bad news rather than good, (Allan, 1990), moreover, such views are also likely to be influential.

It is particularly noteworthy that, in those Reports which hold parents responsible for the behaviour of their children, the proportion of young people in Local Authority care rises to over 70 per cent (9). It is when parents are perceived as not taking responsibility for their children that the Parenting Order is intended to have a role, (Home Office, 1997a and 1997b). It is therefore likely that the complex situation will regularly arise when a Parenting Order might be considered appropriate, in terms of the parent not behaving responsibly, but the child is legally in the care of the Local Authority. The confusion contained in the Home Office's own guidance on this matter was noted earlier.

Of the eleven parents who were held as in some way responsible for their children's offending, nine did not have their voice heard in the PSRs. It may, of course, be that when parents contribute to the PSR process they are assessed more positively. Alternatively, it could be that when Report writers have no person-to-person contact with parents they find it easier to be critical. A final issue concerns whether the tone of the Reports would alter if Report writers knew that parents would see a copy of the Report. The existing National Standards, (Home Office, 1995) stipulate that parents should receive a copy of any Report written. If these guidelines are more vigorously enforced after the introduction of Parenting Orders, in recognition of the greater impact sentence proposals could have on parents, the assessments of parents contained within them may also become less blaming. In terms of the practicalities of working effectively with families it may be that a more positive tone, when describing parents and parenting, becomes necessary if relationships between families and workers are to survive and make any progress.

In 21 per cent (7) of all Reports analysed no assessment of parents was made. This is a further indication that the existing procedure for compiling PSRs would not consistently provide sufficient information on parents once the Parenting Order becomes a sanction for the court to consider.

Parents post-sentence

Only 15 per cent (5) of the Reports suggest a central role for the parents after the sentencing of the young person. One Report suggests that the young person's offending would be curbed by his returning to live with his mother and thereby reducing the negative influences of his present peer group. Two Reports recommend that support continue to be provided through social services teams and the family centre already working with the parents. The Reports express the view that by helping the parents and young people improve their relationships, offending would be reduced. The other major role proposed for parents is a continuation of the anti-offending measures already in place, particularly parentally imposed curfews. In all of these cases the parents have been assessed as already meeting their responsibility to try and curb offending behaviour and as likely to have some future success. Support is already being provided by the voluntary involvement of parents, a process recognised as more beneficial to all parties than through coerced compliance, (Card and Ward, 1998; Haines and Drakeford, 1998).

Parents are briefly mentioned in a further three Report proposals, the writers emphasising that any sentence should allow the young person to maintain links with his family. In the majority of Reports, 26 out of 34, parents are not mentioned as having any role in the different sentencing options proposed. This may indicate a belief that further parental involvement was unnecessary, or that no suitable sentence existed to act as a vehicle to give parents a role. It may also be indicative of a limited significance which current practitioners and sentencers attach to future parental conduct in dealing with the young people before them.

In overall terms, this analysis of existing PSR practice suggests that current provision of information will be inadequate once Parenting Orders are introduced as a sentencing option. This sample of Reports also suggest that, despite the National Standards prevailing at the point of their production, and other central-ising measures, Report writing remains idiosyncratic in nature.

Conclusion

The Government has presented the Parenting Order as a rational response to a primary cause of youth offending. The White Paper, (Home Office, 1997b) preceding the Crime and Disorder Act 1998 cites the 'single most important factor in explaining criminality' as 'the quality of a young person's home life, including parental supervision'. The information contained in this chapter suggests, in trans-lating ideology into practice, that this assertion has been stretched to promulgate a fundamental untruth: that problematic parenting lies at the root of youth crime. Ineffective parenting, we suggest, in most cases, is a symptom of more fundamental problems and pressures, including poverty, social exclusion and structural inequalities. The legacy which the New Labour government inherited in relation to deepening poverty and widening inequality has been extensively documented, (see, for example, Dean and Melrose, 1999). The response which has subsequently been developed does mark some important boundaries between the Blairite present and the neo-liberal past, (see Drakeford and Vanstone, forthcoming). The establishment of the Social Exclusion Unit and a number of the initiatives which have followed from its Reports, for example, suggests a belief in the positive powers of government, and a willingness to use these powers, which is quite different to the 'rolling-back-the-state' ambitions of the Thatcher years. Yet, as Rogaly et al., (1999, p 10) suggest, there is a fundamental difference between an inclusiveness which is based upon an assimilationist model, in which the 'emphasis is on inclusion in some kind of cultural mainstream' and an approach which aims to provide excluded citizens with new powers and abilities to take control over their own lives and circumstances, and to take part in the redefinition of the rules of what it means to be a citizen. New Labour's approach to structural reform seems predicated far more firmly on the former than the latter model. Those individuals who, as the Prime Minister put it, 'play by the rules', (Blair, 1997), will find themselves brought within the circles of contentment. Changing the rules – by a redistribution of power, money and wealth for example – rather than playing by them has been defined beyond the agenda.

As in the case of the previous Conservative administration, the conclusion has to be drawn that, for New Labour, parents are more important as a convenient political scapegoat than for any practical gains which might be brought about through focusing upon them. As well as being bereft of actual advantage, however, the 'low-flying authoritarianism' which Hall, (1998, p 13) describes as characteristic of New Labour's policy making poses real dangers. The vocabulary of New Labour, as Fitzpatrick, (1998, p 18) suggests, is 'conformist and prescriptive in its adherence to a moralistic conservatism'. For parents of young people in trouble, the thread which links the different elements of the 1998 Crime and Disorder Act is the belief that criminal justice agencies are the more appropriate response to essentially social difficulties. In imposing the one-sided moral transactions of the Parenting Order, the responsibilities which should really lie with government – the provision of decent housing, a worthwhile education and an income sufficient to ensure 'decency' – are side-stepped and removed from the social policy to the criminal justice sphere. Once one set of social problems appear capable of being 'solved' in this way, then others follow. At the 1999 Labour Party Conference it was announced that the maximum fine for parents of truanting children would be increased to £10,000. In the New Labour world, equality of responsibility and equality of opportunity are said to go hand-in-hand.

This is the background against which the repercussions of the punitive strand to Parenting Orders can only succeed in compounding the problems of parents and young people who are most in need of supportive intervention. This is likely to occur through an aggravation of already strained family relationships, by putting the welfare of young people at increased risk, by stigmatizing those who already feel on the margins of society and by adding to the financial pressures many parents cope with. Any beneficial effects of intervention in parenting through the Order will be harder to achieve for having to evade or tackle these new problems as they arise. In this way the Parenting Order seems destined to add to the original problem as opposed to solving it, creating rather than solving difficulties for some of the most troubled and disadvantaged families in England and Wales.

References

Allan, R., (1990), Punishment in the Community, in *Social Work and Social Welfare Yearbook*, vol. 2 pp29–41, Buckingham, Open University Press.

Allan, R., (1996), *Children and Crime: Taking Responsibility*, London, Institute for Public Policy Research.

Blair, T., (1997), 'The Will to Win', speech at Aylesbury Estate, Southwark, 2 June. London, Cabinet Office.

Bottoms, A., (1995), *Intensive Community Supervision of Young Offenders: Outcomes, Process and Cost,* Cambridge, University of Cambridge Institute of Criminology.

Brown, S., (1998), *Understanding Youth and Crime: Listening to Youth?* Buckingham, Open University Press.

Card, R. and Ward, R., (1998), *The Crime and Disorder Act 1998: A Practitioner's Guide,* Bristol, Jordan.

Cavadino, M. and Dignan, J., (1997), *The Penal System*, London, Sage, second edn.

Crowley, A., (1998), *A Criminal Waste: A study of Child Offenders Eligible for Secure Training Centres*, London, The Children's Society.

Crouch, C. and Marquand, D., (1995), (Eds.) *Reinventing Collective Action: From the Global to the Local,* Oxford, Blackwell.

Dean, H. and Melrose, M., (1999), *Poverty, Riches and Social Citizenship*, Basingstoke, Macmillan.

Drakeford, M., (1996), Parents of Young People in Trouble. *The Howard Journal of Criminal Justice*, 35(3) pp242–55.

Drakeford, M. and Butler, I., (1999), Curfews for Children: testing a policy proposal in practice, *Youth and Policy,* 62, pp1–14.

Drakeford, M. and Vanstone, M., (forthcoming) Social Exclusion and the Politics of Criminal Justice: A Tale of Two Administrations, in *Howard Journal of Criminal Justice.*

Fitzpatrick, T., (1998), The Rise of Market Collectivism, in *Social Policy Review,* 10, Brunsdon, E., Dean H., and Woods, R., (Eds.), London: Social Policy Association, pp13–33.

Gelsthorpe, L. and Morris, A., (1994), Juvenile Justice 1945–1992, in Maguire, M., Morgan, R. and Reiner, R. (Eds.) *The Oxford Handbook of Criminology*, Oxford, Clarendon Press.

Goldson, B., (1997a), Children in Trouble: State Responses to Juvenile Crime, in Scraton, P., (Ed.), *'Childhood' in 'Crisis'?*, London, UCL, pp124–145.

Goldson, B., (1997b), Children, Crime, Policy and Practice: Neither Welfare Nor Justice, *Children and Society*, 11: 2, pp77–88.

Goldson, B., (1998), *Children in Trouble: Backgrounds and Outcomes*, Liverpool, University of Liverpool Department of Sociology, Social Policy and Social Work Studies.

Goldson, B., (1999a), Punishing Times for Children in Trouble: Recent Policy Developments and the Crime and Disorder Act 1998. *Representing Children* 11(4) pp 274–88.

Goldson, B., (Ed.), (1999b), *Youth Justice: Contemporary Policy and Practice*, Aldershot, Ashgate.

Graham, J. and Bowling, B., (1995), *Young People and Crime.* Home Office Research Study No.145. London: HMSO.

Hagell, A. and Newburn, T., (1994), *Persistent Young Offenders*, London, Policy Studies Institute.

Hall, S., (1998), The Great Moving Nowhere Show, *Marxism Today*, November/December, pp 9–14.

Haines, K. and Drakeford, M., (1998), *Young People and Youth Justice,* London, Macmillan.

Home Office, (1980), *Young Offenders.* London, HMSO.

Home Office, (1990), *Crime, Justice and Protecting the Public,* Cmnd 956. London, HMSO.

Home Office, (1995), *National Standards for the Supervision of Offenders in the Community.* London, HMSO.

Home Office, (1997a), *Preventing Children Offending: A Consultation Document,* Cmnd 3566. London, HMSO.

Home Office, (1997b), *No More Excuses: A New Approach to Tackling Youth Crime in England and Wales,* Cmnd 3809. London, HMSO.

Home Office, (1998), *The Crime and Disorder Act: Draft guidance document: Parenting Order,* London, Home Office.

McCarthy, K., (1999), *Parenting Orders From Policy to Practice: An Exploratory Study*, unpublished thesis, University of Wales, Cardiff.

Morris, A. and Giller, H., (1987), *Understanding Juvenile Justice*, London, Croom Helm.

Muncie, J., (1999), *Youth and Crime: A Critical Introduction,* London: Sage.

Murray, C., (1990), *The Emerging Underclass,* London, Institute of Economic Affairs.

NACRO, (1997), *Families and Crime,* London: NACRO.

NACRO, (1998), Youth Crime Section Briefing Paper, The Parenting Order: A Summary of Draft Guidance (First Edn.), London: NACRO.

Newburn, T., (1997), Youth, Crime and Justice, in Maguire, M., Morgan, R. and Reiner, R., (Eds.), *The Oxford Handbook of Criminology,* Oxford, Oxford University Press. Second edn.

Pearson, G., (1994), Youth, Crime and Society, in. Maguire, M., Morgan, R. and Reiner, R., (Eds.), *The Oxford Handbook of Criminology*, Oxford, Clarendon Press.

Penal Affairs Consortium, (1995), *Parental Responsibility, Youth Crime and the Criminal Law,* London, Penal Affairs Consortium.

Pitts, J., (1988), *The Politics of Juvenile Crime*, London, Sage.

Pitts, J., (1996), The Politics and Practice of Youth Justice, in Mclaughlin, E. and Muncie, J., (Eds.), *Controlling Crime,* London, Sage.

Rogaly, B., Fisher, T. and Mayo, E., (1999), *Poverty, Social Exclusion and MicroFinance in Britain*, Oxford, Oxfam.

Schur, E.M., (1973), *Radical Non-Intervention: Re-Thinking the Delinquency Problem*, Englewood Cliffs, Prentice-Hall.

Straw, J. and Anderson, (1996), *Parenting: A Discussion Paper,* London, Labour Party.

The Magistrate, (1990), *Editorial*, 41: 11, p203.

Thorpe, D.H., Green, C. and Smith, D., (1980), *Punishment and Welfare: Case Studies of the Workings of the 1969 Children and Young Persons Act,* Lancaster Centre of Youth, Crime and Community, University of Lancaster.

Utting, D., Bright, J. and Henricson, C., (1993), *Crime and the Family: Improving Child-rearing and Preventing Delinquency,* London, Family Policy Studies Centre.

CHAPTER 7

Child Incarceration and the New Youth Justice

Sharon Moore

Recent trends in child incarceration

Between the early 1980s and the beginning of the 1990s the impact of successive legislation designed to limit the use of custody for children and young people (to all but the most serious of cases) had made a significant impact upon the juvenile prison population, (Littlechild, 1997). Building upon the effective practice developed by juvenile justice practitioners, and subsequently endorsed by the Government in the form of legislation and guidance, these measures promoted diversion from prosecution and decarceration as the most effective and least damaging responses to children and young people in conflict with the law, (Goldson, 1999a, pp 4–7). In addition, resources were being made available via the Department of Health to fund the development of schemes such as Intermediate Treatment that provided for intensive activity-based community supervision programmes. Overall, these developments led to a reduction in the numbers of prosecutions against children and young people by two-thirds and the number of custodial sentences fell by almost three-quarters in the period 1981 to 1991, (Children's Rights Development Unit, 1994, pp 204–207).

In 1988 Virginia Bottomley, MP, Cabinet Minister and chair of The Children's Society Advisory Committee on Juvenile Custody and its Alternatives stated that, if anything, she had become firmer in her belief that penal custody remained a profoundly unsatisfactory outcome for children, (The Children's Society, 1988). Such governmental endorsement for decarcerative policy and practice was vital and it continued into the early 1990s with Kenneth Clark, then Conservative Home Secretary, speaking on 2 March, 1993:

> *In recent years, local authorities social services, the probation service and many voluntary organisations have shown that sensible and constructive schemes for supervising young offenders in the community can be successful in preventing crime and diverting young people from the penal system. It is important that this policy should continue ...*

> (The Children's Society, 1993, p 13)

This approach underpinned developing legislation and guidance which emphasised the use of diversionary and community-based measures. The 1988 Green

Paper *Punishment, Custody and the Community,* (Home Office, 1988), followed in 1990 by the White Paper *Crime, Justice and Protecting the Public*, (Home Office, 1990), both proposed alternatives to custodial responses for young offenders on the basis that incarceration is likely to confirm them in criminal careers. The 1990 White Paper led to the 1991 Criminal Justice Act and was of particular significance in that it abolished the use of custodial remands and sentences for fourteen year old children; further limited the use of custodial remands and sentences for older children; and promised to end the use of custodial remands entirely for children under 17 years of age, (see Sections 1 (2)(a), 60 (5), 62 and 63 (2)(a) Criminal Justice Act 1991). Only the inadequate provision of secure accommodation, it was argued at the time, prevented custodial remands from being immediately abolished for those under 17 years of age. These were significant policy developments and properly reflected the Government's obligations under the terms of the United Nations Convention on the Rights of the Child which it had signed in 1991, (Children's Rights Development Unit, 1994). Indeed, in the early 1990s it was not inconceivable to suppose that the wholesale imprisonment of children might be abolished before the end of the century.

In 1993 evidence of political dissent began to emerge however. A view developed, encouraged by certain sections of the media and supported by some senior police officers, members of the judiciary and politicians, that large numbers of 'persistent' young offenders were out of control and that the courts and police were powerless to act, (Hagell and Newburn, 1994; Goldson, 1997). The Home Secretary, Kenneth Clark, soon developed a new approach to the subject opining that courts should have more powers to lock-up children who he described as 'really persistent nasty little juveniles'. The language employed by the media in their reports did nothing to discourage the public vilification and de-humanisation of children and young people whose lives were contemptuously scrutinised in the public arena. The focus of public dissatisfaction became centred upon the tragic death of James Bulger and the two children who were charged with his murder, (Davis and Bourhill, 1997). The recent tabloid response to the European Court ruling that the two child defendants had been treated unfairly was a reflection of the enduring strength of feeling aroused at the time which, encouraged by the media, exposed the perpetrators, along with other young offenders, to enormous anger and hostility, (Ferguson, 1999).

Lord Bingham in his *Prison Reform Trust Annual Lecture*, (1997), acknowledged that the successes of the youth justice system in the 1980s had been fundamentally challenged by the media and summarised the public view by commenting:

> *Whatever the figures might show, the perception of the public, fed by lurid media coverage of certain high profile crimes committed by the young, was that juvenile crime was a significant and growing problem with young offenders committing ever more serious crimes at ever younger ages.*

(Lord Bingham, 1997, p 5)

Similarly, Moxon, (1998), points out that the increasing severity of sentencing policy has been driven by political pressure and the perceived public demand for tougher sentences and that:

> *...to a large extent, therefore, the pressure on sentencers to treat offenders more severely is driven by misconceptions as to what they actually do.*
>
> (Moxon, 1998, p 7)

It is indicative that the recent third report of the Home Affairs Select Committee into *Alternatives to Prison Sentencing*, (1998), recommended that the media should 'act responsibly' in their depiction of community sentencing, and although this may have come rather too late to assist many children and young people who have suffered as a direct result of irresponsible and inaccurate reporting, it is an explicit recognition of the damage that can be caused by sensationalist populist journalism.

As a direct result of the increased public and political pressure to harden youth justice policies, the 1993 Criminal Justice Act was hastily produced by a Conservative Government that was intent on reclaiming a tough line on law and order issues. For most of its time in government from 1979 the Conservatives had been quietly and incrementally limiting the use of custodial sentencing; now they dramatically attempted to demonstrate 'toughness' by dismantling some of the more progressive elements of the 1991 Criminal Justice Act. The 'prison works' speech delivered by Michael Howard at the Conservative Party Conference in October 1993 fuelled the already escalating use of prison custody illustrated by the following graph:

Prison Population (1)
Policy Interventions 1987 – 1997

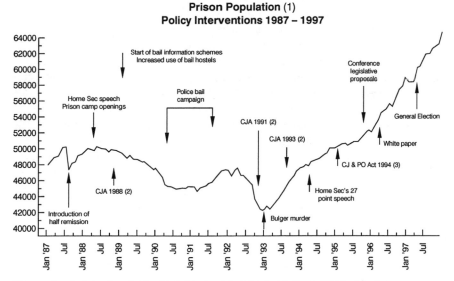

1 Seasonally adjusted series   2 CJA=Criminal Justice Act   3 Criminal Justice And Public Order Act

Source: White and Woodbridge (1998, p 20).

This reversal of youth justice policy, and the clear endorsement of prison as a primary response to the problem of youth crime, led directly to the prison population of sentenced young offenders, those under 21 years of age, increasing by 30 per cent between June 1993 and June 1996. The sentenced child prison population, under 18 years, rose by 34 per cent in just one year between 1995 and 1996 when the punitive rhetoric of Michael Howard and Jack Straw hit new heights, or depths, (White and Woodbridge, 1998). The Home Office has reported that the main factors influencing the escalating custody rate were the increasing imposition of custodial sentences by the courts and the extended length of those sentences, and that it was *not* the case that more young offenders were appearing before the courts during this period, (White, 1999). Between 1997 and 1998 the number of female young prisoners beginning custodial sentences increased by 39 per cent, an alarming trend that has continued to rise, (White and Woodbridge, 1998).

The 1994 Criminal Justice and Public Order Act was the pinnacle of the Conservative government's new approach, focussing as it did on custodial responses and creating new and harsher penalties for the youngest child offenders. The Act served to extend the availability of long-term sentences under Section 53 of the Children and Young Person Act 1933 to 10–13 year olds for offences such as dwelling house burglary. The 1994 legislation also increased the maximum sentence for 15–17 year olds from 12 to 24 months in a Young Offenders' Institution as well as strengthening the sentencing powers of magistrates in the Youth Court. Moreover, the 1994 Criminal Justice and Public Order Act extended provisions to lock up children and young people, introducing secure remands for 12–14 year old children and creating a Secure Training Order, the harshest measure of all, creating as it did the re-introduction of custodial detention for children as young as twelve, (Goldson, 1999a).

The concluding stages of Conservative youth justice policy represented a complete change in direction from the practices of diversion and the promotion of community-based programmes to an increasingly heavy emphasis on incarcerating more and ever younger children. The United Nations Children's Committee expressed particular concern in relation to the 1994 Act, especially the Secure Training Order and the continuing detention of children on remand in prisons. The Committee was certainly not alone in its condemnation of the measures, and the Secure Training Centres were described in the Times as having 'all the hallmarks of a policy both created and implemented in panic', (*Times Educational Supplement*, 3 March, 1993). Equally, an editorial in *The Magistrate*, the journal of the Magistrates' Association, in February, 1993 pointed out:

> *Removing children from home, as a measure for reforming the individual, is a discredited policy. It does not reform: nor does it succeed in educational terms. It is horrendously expensive and wasteful of funds better spent elsewhere in the juvenile justice system.*

> (NACRO, 1993, p 7)

The (in)effectiveness of custody

The ineffectiveness of incarceration as a solution to the problem of youth crime is well documented. The Prison Reform Trust paper, *Does Prison Work?*, (1993), cites Lord Justice Woolf's considered observation:

> *There are people who have to be locked up but it has to be made clear to the public that all the experience shows imprisonment is not a cure ... such talk is short-sighted and irresponsible. The easy option, which has a miserable record of failure, is to send more and more people to prison, regardless of the consequences, including the shocking waste of resources which could be spent elsewhere.*
>
> (Prison Reform Trust, 1993, pp 1–2)

To put the issue of resourcing child incarceration into some perspective, NACRO, (1993), claims that keeping juveniles in prisons costs £190 million per annum and the Howard League, (Crowley, 1998), has estimated that secure training centres cost between £4,000 and £5,000 per week. Furthermore, in the 1990 White Paper, *Crime, Justice and Protecting the Public*, (Home Office, 1990), the Government had firmly rejected the view that prison has a *rehabilitative effect*:

> *It was once believed that prison, properly used, could encourage a high proportion of offenders to start an honest life on their release. Nobody now regards imprisonment, in itself, as an effective means of reform for most prisoners ... The prospect for reforming offenders are usually much better if they stay in the community, provided the public is properly protected,*
>
> (cited in Prison Reform Trust, 1993, p 3).

Equally, the notion that prison has a *deterrent effect* is unconvincing, and fails to take into account that many offences are opportunistic, utterly unpremeditated and are committed by children and young people without reference to the weighty thought that they may be arrested or even imprisoned as a result. In addition, the reconviction rate for juveniles leaving custody has exceeded 70 per cent, indicating that only a small proportion of children and young people discharged from custody are deterred from re-offending, (NACRO, 1993).

The use of prison to *incapacitate offenders* and therefore protect the public was examined by Tarling, (1993), who concluded that to reduce the crime rate by one per cent it would require a 25 per cent increase in the use of custody, the cost of which could not be borne. Thus, in relation to rehabilitation, deterrence and the protection of the public, custodial responses to youth crime are, at best, rather ineffective and extraordinarily costly. But this is not all. Added to the heavy fiscal costs of child incarceration are the immeasurable human costs.

Indeed, what is not regularly acknowledged is the amount of crime and abuse that occurs *within* the prison system and the extent to which children and young people become victims within that system. Drugs offences, physical and sexual assaults, theft, robbery, extortion, emotional and psychological abuse are often experienced by children and young people within custodial settings, (Howard League for Penal Reform, 1995; The Children's Society 1998/9). Prison also reinforces the difficulties and problems children and young people bring with them into custody as a consequence of the barren environment that further isolates and damages them. The recent report of HM Chief Inspector of Prisons into Her Majesty's Young Offender Institution and Remand Centre, Feltham, described the conditions in which children were held as 'unacceptable in a civilised society', (Daily Mail, Friday, March 26, 1999). In the *Thematic Review: Young Prisoners*, HM Chief Inspector of Prisons, (1997), wrote:

> *I do not believe that children under eighteen should be held in prison ... The prison service is essentially an organisation for adults, neither structured nor equipped to deal with children. It is the plight of children that alarms us most, not least because of the conditions in which they are held in Prison Service establishments. These are the only conditions which the Prison Service is resourced to provide, but, in many cases they are far below the minimum conditions in Social Services Department secure units required by the Children Act 1989 and the UN Convention on the Rights of the Child. Indeed I can find no evidence that the Prison Service has acknowledged the Children Act 1989 as having any relevance to children held in Prison Service Establishments. More damage is done to immature adolescents than to any other type of prisoner, by current conditions.*
>
> (HM Inspectorate of Prisons, 1997, p 6)

Similarly, when Sir William Utting, a previous Chief Inspector of Social Services, was commissioned to investigate the issue of 'safeguards' for the protection of children living away from home, prison was described thus:

> *Prison is not a safe environment ... The Review was particularly concerned by the prevalence of bullying, ranging from physical brutality to verbal intimidation, in spite of Prison Service strategies for countering it.*
>
> (Department of Health, 1997, p 3)

It went on:

> *Prison is no place for children, especially for unconvicted children. It is almost impossible to meet the continuing needs of children there.*
>
> (Department of Health, 1997, paragraph 5.10)

Sir William Utting's report highlighted the dangers to children from malfunctioning systems and institutions which 'permanently damage prospects of successful and happy adult lives' and emphasised the deficiencies of the prison system in meeting the educational, health care, social skills and employment and training needs of young people. This has been further evidenced by HM Chief Inspector of Prisons, Sir David Ramsbotham, who has reported that amongst young remand prisoners 50 per cent have mental health needs and 39 per cent have a disability or serious health problems, (HM Inspectorate of Prisons, 1997). Moreover, the Department of Health has reported that under 21 year olds made up a fifth of the prison population but represented half of those who self-harm and the number of known suicides amongst the under 21 year old population increased from 60 in 1995 to 83 in 1998, (*Prison Service Suicide Awareness Support Unit*, August, 1999). As a consequence, the Prison Service is now under pressure from the Youth Justice Board for England and Wales, (Scott and Black, 1999), and has started to take steps to address the way in which children are treated. Whether the creation and maintenance of a 'well-designed', 'properly resourced', 'child-focused' prison sector is either achievable or appropriate is, however, a completely different matter. Indeed, the question might be should the imprisonment of children be 'modernised' or abolished?

The new youth justice

Many of those who observed the electioneering processes leading up to the 1997 General Election, whilst alarmed at the tone of the law and order rhetoric, felt confident that a newly-elected government would adopt a more constructive approach to youth crime and publicly distance itself from an ever-increasing reliance upon custodial options. To-date there is little evidence of any such retraction, and the 'tough' stance adopted during the run up to the general election in 1997 has been maintained by the new Government, (Toynbee, 1999). The approach is clearly expressed by the Home Secretary's opening statement to the 1997 White Paper, *No More Excuses – a new approach to tackling youth crime in England and Wales*:

> An excuse culture has developed within the youth justice system. It excuses itself for its inefficiency, and too often excuses the young offenders before it, implying that they cannot help their behaviour because of their social circumstances ... The system allows them to go on wrecking their own lives as well as disrupting their families and communities.

> (Home Office 1997, p 2)

The Crime and Disorder Act 1998 has established an aim for the youth justice system of preventing offending by children and young people, and has listed six objectives which emphasise the themes of punishment, reparation and responsibility, (Youth Justice Board for England and Wales, 1999). In addition, after a period of 'careful consideration' Jack Straw went one step further than his predecessor, Michael Howard, and opened the first Secure Training Centre in April, 1998, with a commitment to uphold the previous Government's plans to introduce a further four Centres, despite his party's vehement protests in opposition, (Goldson, 1999a). The difficulties and tensions involved in containing such large numbers of children in this manner were immediately apparent, with numerous incidents occurring following the opening of Medway, including the controversial involvement of the police in one distur- bance, and concluding with a highly critical Social Services Inspectorate Report, (Goldson, 1999b; Social Services Inspectorate, 1999). The Home Office accepted all thirty-eight recommendations within the Report and acknowledged that Medway was facing a 'crisis'. Since April, however, two further Secure Training Centres have opened, and two more are planned.

In addition to maintaining the commitment made by the previous Government to the Secure Training Centres, the 1998 Crime and Disorder Act has also introduced a new custodial sentence for children and young people: the Detention and Training Order, (Sections 73 to 79). This sentence will be available to the Courts from April 2000 in respect of children or young people between the ages of 12 and 17 years for up to a period of two years, with half of the sentence being served in the community. The Order will replace the Secure Training Order and the sentence of detention in a Young Offenders' Institution and it provides for the incarceration of children in a range of institutions including: a Secure Training Centre; a Young Offenders' Institution; a local authority Secure Unit; or a Youth Treatment Centre. The Order, described by the Government as a 'more constructive and flexible sentence', (Youth Justice Board for England and Wales, 1998), will be made available for children as young as 10 should the Home Secretary believe it to be necessary.

New Labour has declared its intention to review the whole range of incarcer- ative institutions for children including local authority Secure Units, Prison Service accommodation, Secure Training Centres and the Department of Health's Youth Treatment Centre, (Home Office, 1997). The *'No More Excuses'* White Paper acknowledges that there has been a 'problem with arrangements' within the penal system and there is a need for improvements in regimes that would 'safe- guard the welfare of young people', consistent with the need to protect the public and staff, (Youth Justice Board for England and Wales, 1998). In the past, the inconsistent standard of care provided across the range of incarcerative institu- tions for children, and the limited availability of places, with the exception of the Prison Service which can always make room for one more, has meant that the quality of life experienced by children and young people on remand or serving a sentence has been profoundly variable. The Summary of the Government's Response to the Home Office Comprehensive Spending Review of Secure Accommodation for remanded and sentenced juveniles in July 1998 found:

> *...little positive to say about the present arrangements for providing secure accommodation for remanded and sentenced children and young people. Regime standards are inconsistent and often poor. Costs vary considerably.*

There is no effective oversight or long-term planning for juvenile accommodation as a whole. In practice, there is no definable juvenile secure estate ... Fundamental change is needed to the way in which the estate is planned and managed if it is to meet the aim of providing accommodation and regimes appropriate to the age and maturity of the young people held in custody on remand and under sentence and which addresses their offending behaviour and wider developmental needs.

(Youth Justice Board for England and Wales, 1998, p 7)

The Youth Justice Board for England and Wales, therefore, has been given the task of managing what is being termed the 'juvenile secure estate'.

The Board is also to be responsible for the creation and maintenance of standards across the new 'juvenile secure estate' and has indicated that there will be a requirement to provide a 'structured and caring environment' within each type of institution conferring 'safety' and 'security' consistent with the principles of the Children Act 1989 and integrated into the rules governing the establishment, (Youth Justice Board for England and Wales, 1998). Across the estate all establishments are to develop clear and consistent objectives and 'vision' and there is to be continuity between the support, assistance and supervision provided to the child both within and outside of secure facilities. Additionally, the Youth Justice Board is to assume responsibility for the commissioning and purchasing of custodial places for juveniles on remand and under sentence across the juvenile secure estate. This will include the need to 'assess the appropriate demand for places' for convicted and remanded children and try to ensure an adequate supply of places of 'appropriate quality', (Youth Justice Board for England and Wales, 1998). Youth Offending Teams will have responsibility for making individual 'placement decisions' and it is envisaged that 'placements' will be made across the range of institutions comprising the 'juvenile estate', depending on the age and maturity of the child or young person. The fact that the majority of 'placements' will continue to be available within the prison sector, however, means that in reality any child who qualifies for prison custody on the basis of age is indeed likely to be sent to prison. Reference has been made to the need to limit the extent of child incarceration and the associated work that needs to be done with the Magistrates Association, the Judicial Studies Board and the Sentencing Advisory Panel to draw their attention to initiatives relating to community sentences 'as an alternative to inappropriate secure remand and custodial sentences', (Youth Justice Board for England and Wales, 1998). Notwithstanding this, it would appear that in response to the widespread observation that 'prison is no place for children' in accordance with the evidence considered above, the government's primary emphasis is directed towards better planning and the provision of 'quality' placements as opposed to abolitionist priorities. There is also the likelihood that such 'reforms', including the level of investment and restructuring which is taking place to bring the 'juvenile secure estate', particularly the prison sector, up to standard will distract attention from, and dilute, fundamental objections that have previously been made to child incarceration *per se*.

Policies and practices in relation to child incarceration in England and Wales place the UK government at loggerheads with the spirit and content of the United Nations Convention on the Rights of the Child. Indeed, despite the 'modernising' and 'humanising' rhetoric of New Labour, its unwavering commitment to the very concept of child incarceration is problematic in this respect. More specifically, the current policy direction determining the New Youth Justice is inconsistent with some of the primary principles and provisions of the UN Convention including:

- The rights of children to protection from all forms of violence, abuse and neglect (Article 19).
- The duty of governments to consider the best interests of the child (Article 3).
- The rights of the child to the highest attainable standard of health (Article 24).
- The rights of the child not to be subjected to cruel, inhuman or degrading treatment (Article 37(a)).
- The duty of Government to provide alternatives to institutional care (Article 40 (4)).
- The duty of Government to use detention or imprisonment as a measure of last resort and for the shortest appropriate time (Article 37 (b)).

Furthermore, despite the plans for the new 'juvenile estate', tension is apparently mounting between the Youth Justice Board for England and Wales and the Prison Service over its ability to deliver, (Scott and Black, 1999). In its second report to the United Nations Committee on the Rights of the Child, the UK government has already stated that whilst it had begun work on establishing a new and separate estate for young prisoners within England and Wales, it will continue to 'place' children and adults together where there was no suitable alternative accommodation, (Second Report to the UN Committee on the Rights of the Child by the United Kingdom, 1999). Principle will inevitably lose out to expedience.

The Children's Society has been a long-term campaigner for the just and humane treatment of children and young people involved in the youth justice system. Along with other child welfare organisations, penal reform groups, civil liberties and children's rights agencies, academics, HM Inspector of Prisons and the erstwhile Chief Social Services Inspector, the Children's Society is concerned about burgeoning forms of child incarceration. The Society established the National Remand Rescue Initiative in January, 1997, to provide an advocacy service directly for fifteen and sixteen-year-old males held on custodial remand. The work of the Initiative has been analysed elsewhere, (Ashton and Grindrod, 1999) and will not be repeated here. In addition to concerns about the harrowing experiences of children within the prison system, however, even the most cursory examination of the life histories of children entering the prison system raise a number of key issues:

- 10 per cent of all children remanded to prison are homeless.
- At least 6 per cent of all children remanded to prison are from local authority accommodation.
- 29 per cent of all children remanded to prison have been excluded from school.
- 37 per cent of all children remanded to prison link alcohol and drug misuse to their offending.
- 27 per cent of all children remanded to prison are black or are from other minority ethnic groups.

(The Children's Society, 1997 and 1998)

The Government's current approach to youth justice treats children and young people as offenders first and as children second. Moreover, it ignores the complex patterns and inter-related problems that such children endure. Across England and Wales children who are amongst the most disadvantaged and vulnerable in the country are being imprisoned, despite the fact that the treatment they will receive is likely to harm them further and compound their problems. It is the easy option to lock up such children and young people because they are seen as demanding, troublesome, resource intensive and, most of all, undeserving. Crowley, (1998), in her study of children who were potential candidates for the Secure Training Centre criticised the 'drawbridge mentality' that sought to lock away the problem and segregate children and young people from their communities:

> *The exclusion of children from normative influences of home, school and youth club can reinforce delinquency. Children and young people find it difficult to invest in and conform to social norms if they are denied access to the accepted ways of achieving them within that society. At a national level and in a range of government policy areas, there is a need to consider practical ways of attaching value and incentive to the integration, rather than the exclusion, of disadvantaged young people.*

(Crowley, 1998, p 59)

Time for a new agenda: beyond child incarceration

In his evidence to the Home Affairs Committee into Alternatives to Prison Sentences in 1998, Sir David Ramsbotham made his opinion clear, reporting that there were too many prisoners in custody who did not need to be there – in particular young offenders and female offenders, (Home Affairs Select Committee, 1998). The Home Affairs Committee subsequently recommended that the government urgently reconsider the use and suitability of custodial sentences for such groups. In responding to criticisms from the United Nations Committee on the Rights of the Child, the Children's Safeguards Review and HM Chief Inspector of Prisons, the Government has continued to concentrate upon improving the site and standard of incarceration, rather than publicly denouncing the use of imprisonment for children and young people. There is a danger that by placing too great an emphasis upon improving conditions inside prisons, and by reorganising and re-naming current provision, this will enable the Government to side step the funda-mental issue. What is required is an unequivocal recognition that the focus of Government policy should aim to divert the overwhelming majority of children from incarceration and to establish a strategically implemented abolitionist agenda. For the small minority of children who present a real danger to themselves or to others, some restriction of liberty within an appropriate, secure, non-prison, setting may be necessary. It is time for the Youth Justice Board for England and Wales to openly acknowledge that state policy since the early 1990s has been an expensive and damaging failure. Since the creation of the juvenile court at the beginning of the last century, politicians, academics and practitioners have sought solutions regarding what to do about young offenders. The reality is that there is not a simple solution to the complex problems facing children and young people who offend. What is clearer, however, is what should not be done. The Children's Society, in its report, *Penal Custody for Juveniles – the Line of Least Resistance*, (1988), refers to a statement made by Le Mesurier in 1931:

> *The difficulty in finding a good alternative is often put forward, but it is not solved by maintaining what is admitted by all to be a bad alternative. When once that is definitely prohibited, human nature, unable to fall back on the rotten line of least resistance, will find new and better alternatives.*

(The Children's Society, 1988, p 1)

This statement is just as pertinent in relation to child incarceration in 2000. It is time that the 'rotten line of least resistance' is finally rejected in order that we may find 'new and better alternatives' to replace the reprehensible practices that char-acterise child incarceration.

References

Ashton, J. and Grindrod, M., (1999), Institutional Troubleshooting: Lessons for Policy and Practice in Goldson, B., (Ed.), *Youth Justice: Contemporary Policy and Practice*, Aldershot, Ashgate.

Children's Rights Development Unit, (1994), *UK Agenda for Children*, London, Children's Rights Development Unit.

The Children's Society, (1988), *Penal Custody for Juveniles: the Line of Least Resistance*, London, The Children's Society.

The Children's Society, (1993), *A False Sense of Security*, London, The Children's Society.

The Children's Society, (1998/9), *Annual Reports of the National Remand Rescue Initiative, 1997 and 1998*, London, The Children's Society.

Crowley, A., (1998), *A Criminal Waste*, London, The Children's Society.

Davis, H. and Bourhill, M., (1997), 'Crisis': The Demonisation of Children and Young People in Scraton, P., *'Childhood' in 'Crisis'*? London, UCL Press.

Department of Health, (1997), *People Like Us: The Report of the Review of the Safeguards for Children Living Away from Home*, London, The Stationery Office.

Department of Health, (1998), *The Government's Response to the Children's Safeguards Review*, cm 4105 London, The Stationery Office.

Department of Health, (1999), *Second Report to the UN Committee on the Rights of the Child by the United Kingdom: Executive Summary*, London, The Stationery Office.

Ferguson, E., (1999), How the Death of Bulger Hardened us to Pity. Observer, October 31st.

Goldson, B., (1997), Children, Crime, Policy and Practice: Neither Welfare nor Justice in *Children and Society*, Volume 11, pp77–88.

Goldson, B., (1999a), Youth (In) Justice: Contemporary Developments in Policy and Practice in Goldson, B., (Ed.), *Youth Justice: Contemporary Policy and Practice*, Aldershot, Ashgate.

Goldson, B., (1999b), Revisiting First Principles and Re-Stating Opposition to Child Incarceration in *Ajjust Now*, No: 44 pp 4–8.

Hagell, A. and Newburn, T., (1994), *Persistent Young Offenders*, London, Policy Studies Institute.

HM Inspectorate of Prisons for England and Wales, (1997), *Young Prisoners: A Thematic Review*, Home Office, London.

Home Affairs Select Committee, (1998), *Alternatives to Prison Sentences: Third Report*, London, The Stationery Office.

Home Office, (1991), *Criminal Justice Act 1991* London, HMSO.

Home Office, (1998), *Crime and Disorder Act 1998*, London, The Stationery Office.

Home Office, (1988), *Punishment, Custody and the Community*, Cmd 424, London, HMSO.

Home Office, (1990), *Crime, Justice and Protecting the Public*, Cmd 965, London, HMSO.

Home Office, (1997), *No More Excuses: A New Approach to Tackling Youth Crime in England and Wales*, November Cmd 3809, London, The Stationery Office.

Home Office, (1999), *Projection of Long Term Trends in the Prison Population to 2006*, London, HM Prison Service.

Howard League for Penal Reform, (1995), *Banged up, Beaten up, Cutting up*. London, The Howard League for Penal Reform.

Liebling, A., (Ed.), (1996), *Caring for People at Risk*. London, Whiting and Birch Ltd.

Littlechild, B., (1997), Young Offenders, Punitive Policies and the Rights of Children in *Critical Social Policy* 53, November, pp73–92.

Lord Bingham of Cornhill, (1997), *Justice for the Young*. London, Prison Reform Trust.

Moxon, D., (1998), The Role of Sentencing Policy in Goldblatt, P. and Lewis, C., (Eds.), *Reducing Offending: An Assessment of Research Evidence on Ways of Dealing with Offending Behaviour.* London, Home Office Research Study 187.

NACRO, (1993), *New Approaches to Youth Crime: Creating More Criminals*, London, NACRO.

Prison Reform Trust, (1993), *Does Prison Work?* London, Prison Reform Trust.

Scott, A. and Black, J., (1999), Youth Justice Board for England and Wales in the *British Juvenile and Family Courts Society Newsletter*, June, 1999.

Sereny, G., (1995), *The Case of Mary Bell: A Portrait of a Child who Murdered*, London, Pimlico.

Tarling, R., (1993), *Analysing Offending: Data, Models and Interpretation*, London, HMSO.

Toynbee, P., (1999), Straw Shakes his Iron Fist at Prison Reform, *The Guardian*, Wednesday June, 23.

White, P., (1999), *The Prison Population in 1998: A Statistical Review*, Research Findings No 94: Home Office.

White, P. and Woodbridge, J., (1998), *The Prison Population in 1997*. Home Office Statistical Bulletin 5/98. London, Home Office.

Youth Justice Board for England and Wales, (1998), *Juvenile Secure Estate: Preliminary Advice from the Youth Justice Board for England and Wales to the Home Secretary*, 17 December, London, Youth Justice Board for England and Wales.

Youth Justice Board for England and Wales, (1999), *Annual Report and Accounts 1999*, London, The Stationery Office.

The United Nations, (1989), *The United Nations Convention on the Rights of the Child*, New York, United Nations.

CHAPTER 8

Corporatism and the New Youth Justice

David Smith

Introduction

There is nothing new in the idea that youth justice policy and practice can be understood in terms of corporatism; what is at issue is the extent to which the Labour government's initiatives in the field have taken the process further than before, and, of course, how one should evaluate the effects and understand the implications of a corporate approach to youth justice. In this chapter I will trace the development of corporatist thinking in policy and practice, and suggest some possible reasons for the emergence of this model, before examining some of the Labour government's key policies on youth justice and the features of these that suggest that the corporatist model has been revived and indeed developed further than under previous administrations. I will argue that, while there are intelligible reasons for being suspicious of these developments and their effects, it would be a mistake to take a wholly negative attitude towards efforts to improve the co-ordination of the youth justice system, and to link it more closely with crime prevention and related policies. The institutional divide between crime prevention and face-to-face interventions with young offenders is, according to Pitts and Hope, (1997), one of the reasons why youth justice policies in England and Wales are less likely to promote social inclusion than those in France; and it is at least worth considering the possibility that a more 'corporate' approach could help to deliver outcomes that liberal or radical penologists have usually seen as desirable.

The origins of corporatism in youth justice

John Pratt, (1989), identified corporatism as the third model of juvenile justice, after the 'welfare' and 'justice' models, and suggested that by the end of the 1980s it had become the dominant model for policy and practice. Arguing that, while justice model thinking had become ideologically dominant over the welfare approach, this was not reflected in the emergence in practice of a full-blown justice-based system. Pratt, (1989, p245) suggested that the features of youth justice which were new in the late 1980s could be understood as *'necessary and essential'*, (original emphasis), elements of corporatism. For Pratt, following Unger, (1976), corporatism refers to a general tendency in 'advanced welfare societies' towards centralisation of policy and greater government intervention, with the aim of reducing conflict among professional and other interest groups and encouraging the emergence of consensus within a coherent and uniform institutional structure. Pratt recognised that corporatism was not the general strategy of the Thatcher government of the 1980s: with its stress on reducing the role of the state and allowing market forces to operate without interference, the overall position, at least formally, was an anti-corporatist one, exemplified in the government's erosion of local authorities' powers, and its efforts to introduce features of the market economy into the provision of welfare services, notably in the field of health. Pratt suggested that these forms of deregulation in the areas of employment and economic policy might actually require a more interventionist and regulatory approach to penal policy, if, for example, the growth of unemployment, especially among young people, was seen to be associated with a growth of crime, and that corporatism provided the mechanism by which this could be achieved.

Pratt identified a number of features of the youth justice policies and practices of the late 1980s to sustain his argument that corporatism had become, in practice, the dominant model. Many of these features, I have argued elsewhere, in fact originated within the professional community of specialist social workers working in intermediate treatment and related projects, (Smith, 1999), and were recognised and supported by the government, and especially by civil servants in the Home Office, as having the potential to contribute to some desired policy objectives, notably greater efficiency in the system's operation and a reduction in the use of custody for young people. Social workers, as several of Pratt's own sources make clear, were often strong proponents of the corporatist approach: they saw it as a means of extending diversion from prosecution, of establishing tight contracts for intervention with young people and their families, and perhaps of enhancing their own discretionary powers at the expense of formal legal processes. The principal example of this practitioner-based corporatism, then and perhaps now, is the juvenile liaison bureau in Northampton, in which, in the interests of inter-agency co-operation and the achievement of policy coherence and predictability, the boundaries between agencies were deliberately blurred, (Cohen, 1985), and consensus was assumed to exist among agencies and staff whose professional backgrounds and priorities might on the surface seem very different, most obviously, between police officers and social workers. The autonomy of individual workers was reduced in the service of wider policy objectives; essentially, those of diversion from the formal system, and of the substitution of community-based for custodial measures. Policy rather than the justice model's discourse of rights was the central source of guidance for practice; and surveillance, as in the 'tracking' schemes that foreshadowed electronic monitoring, and behavioural change replaced punishment as the aim of intervention in cases in which diversion or minimalist intervention was not a practical option.

Pratt, (1989, p 250) also suggests that the corporatist approach requires the maximisation of the social importance of offending by young people, as opposed to the aspirations of the justice model to minimise the problem. Citing Home Office Circular 8/1984, described by Crawford, (1998, p 36) as 'a crucially symbolic milestone in the renaissance of crime prevention', Pratt suggests that corporatism entails an increase in the range of agencies that need to be involved and a more efficient and productive use of resources, which is to be made possible by inter-agency collaboration and the sharing of information across agency boundaries. The circular was also a crucial milestone in the emergence of a formal agenda from central government, and particularly from the Home Office, that was strongly supportive of a corporate approach not only to youth justice but to the criminal justice system as a whole, and was to become a key policy theme of the late 1980s and early 1990s. The essential message of the circular was not so much that offending by young people was a major social problem (it was, after all, a circular on the development of a co-ordinated strategy on crime prevention more generally), as that crime problems were the responsibility not only of those agencies and personnel traditionally thought of as the component parts of the criminal justice system, but of other local authority departments, such as those concerned with housing and education, and indeed of the community as a whole. The circular therefore marked a crucial stage in the development of policy ideas that came to be central themes for Home Office thinking about crime: ideas that revolved around the themes of partnership, community, and consensus among the different parts of the system, (Crawford, 1997). The aims were both to improve the efficiency of the criminal justice process, for example by reducing delays, and to encourage a sense of common purpose that would minimise inter-agency conflict and engender a sense of commitment to shared policy aims. The Crown Prosecution Service, for example, was to be encouraged to conceive of its tasks and to judge its success or failure in achieving them not, as had been lawyers' established practice, on the basis of individual cases, but in terms of its contri-bution to wider policy objectives, (Smith, 1994). In this sense, the circular inaugu-rated a process that placed the successful implementation of policy at the centre of agencies' objectives, one of the key features of corporatism in youth justice according to Pratt, (1989).

Inter-agency co-operation

Another effect of Circular 8/1984 was to encourage the first substantial research into inter-agency co-operation in criminal justice. Youth justice was one of the sites of such co-operation, or the lack of it, investigated as part of a wider ESRC programme on crime and criminal justice issues by a group of researchers in the late 1980s, (for examples of the results and some later reflections, see Blagg et al., 1988; Sampson et al., 1988, 1991; Pearson et al., 1992; Smith, 1994). The researchers' position was that while greater inter-agency co-operation was in many instances desirable, it was considerably more difficult to realise in practice than exhortations from the Home Office, and to a lesser extent other government departments, suggested. They argued that one important reason why difficulties often arose in practice, (Pearson et al., 1992), that seemed not to have been anticipated by policy-makers was that there were inherent and structural power differentials among the agencies at whom the exhortations were directed. The specifically relevant powers were identified as control over resources and over information, the ability to define the problem and make one's definition stick, and the capacity to influence the workload of other parts of the system without the possibility of reciprocal or retaliatory action, (Smith, 1994).

The researchers suggested, (Sampson et al., 1988) that in the literature then available two main positions on inter-agency co-operation could be identified: the 'benevolent' and the 'conspiratorial' perspectives. The former, characteristic of the Home Office, administrative criminology, and some writings of the 'left realist' school, tended to see improved co-operation as an unproblematic good. The latter, characteristic of radical criminologists and sceptical policy analysts, (see, for example, Gordon, 1987), was inclined to see such co-operation as, in extreme versions, merely a front behind which the police could extend their power by the incorporation of other agencies and local authorities into a project of increasing discipline and control over social life. Both positions could also be found among practitioners, who could also argue with some force that official encouragement of co-operation would carry more legitimacy if there were clear evidence that central government departments were co-operating with each other in a way that would provide a model or example for local initiatives. Instead, many argued, the policies of one government department were frequently undermined by those of another. In response to such criticisms, the concept of 'trilateralism' made its appearance at the end of the 1980s, meaning that high level co-ordination of policy should be pursued through regular consultations by ministers and high-ranking civil servants of the three government departments with undeniable responsibilities for the criminal justice system. These were the Home Office, responsible for, among much else, the police, the prisons and the probation service, the Lord Chancellor's Department, responsible for the court system, and the Office of the Attorney General, responsible for the Crown Prosecution Service.

In practice, it was the Home Office, in the form of its senior civil servants, which most consistently and enthusiastically promoted this high-level version of corporatism. One of the results of trilateralism was a series of regional conferences intended to promote more co-operative and considerate behaviour among practitioners, and to complement a series of more thematically organised national conferences, (Smith, 1994). These conferences were initially chaired by David Faulkner, the Home Office civil servant whose 'principled pragmatism', (Rutherford, 1996), was a major influence on the (relatively) coherent and consistent line of criminal justice policy in the late 1980s. Participants were encouraged to identify key areas where better local co-operation would produce a better service, and to think more strategically about the effects of their decisions, including their impact on other parts of the 'system'. Its systemic qualities were usually thought to be more conspicuous by their absence than by their presence. With relatively rare exceptions, who usually came from the legal profession, participants in the thirteen conferences generally expressed themselves as in favour of increased co-operation and a more corporate and over-arching view of their responsibilities to the criminal justice process as a whole. However, during the series of conferences there were examples of policy changes that suggested that it was difficult to maintain such a benevolent spirit in the world beyond the comfortable hotels in which these discussions took place. A modest example was the concession made by the police to the Crown Prosecution Service, that files would be sent to the CPS already typed rather than hand-written, and this meant that police forces had to ask already hard-pressed local authorities for additional funds for clerical support, to be told in many cases that this could not be a priority. In effect, costs were transferred from the CPS to the police: a benefit to one agency was clearly a cost to another. A less modest example was the decision to reorganise the CPS into thirteen administrative areas, which seemed to come as a surprise to representatives of other agencies, and, since there had been much talk at the conferences of the desirability of greater geographical consistency and compati- bility, a theme that reappears in the review of prisons and probation conducted by the Labour government, the appearance of yet another administrative unit seemed to many hard to square with the official espousal of greater 'co-terminousness'. Smith, (1994), on the basis of participation in all the conferences, concluded that they had represented a serious and coherent attempt to modernise the criminal justice process, and that the attempt had largely failed. The centrifugal tendencies identified by Pratt, (1989), such as the devolution of power to 'Next Steps' agencies and the fixing of budget cash limits on an individual agency basis, rather than on the basis of the overall costs of criminal justice within a locality, worked to contradict the centralising, corporatist agenda of the modernisers. By the end of the series of conferences, with Michael Howard shortly due to become Home Secretary, the modernising agenda had been overtaken by a law and order politics of a much more blatantly opportunistic style, (Faulkner, 1993).

The question remains, of course, were the modernisers right? In other words, is inter-agency co-operation the desirable policy end the Home Office declared it to be? The process of modernising criminal justice, if this is taken to mean substituting bureaucratic and administrative values and practices for those of justice, has after all aroused some very fundamental suspicions, (Christie, 1993). Summarising their research, Pearson et al., (1992), argued that neither the benevolent nor the conspira- torial view of the process was adequate. They suggested that inter-agency co-oper- ation in criminal justice, both in practice and in principle, ought to be limited in scope, because conflict is inherent in the criminal justice process, and the interests and priorities of the various agencies and personnel inevitably differ, given that the system is designed to provide checks and balances against domination by one set of interests, as, for example, those of the prosecution. Recognition of the reality and even the desirability of conflict, then, was a necessary precursor to any efforts to improve co-operation, from the level of central government policy to the day-to-day work of practitioners, and it should not be assumed in advance that commonality of aims and interests was an unproblematic good, for example, the police should not be social workers, or *vice versa*. Given this recognition, they argued that increased co-operation held out the promise not only of improving the efficiency of criminal justice, but of crime-related policies more generally, for example by reducing avoidable delays in the process and by bringing greater coherence to local crime reduction initiatives. As well as power differentials across agencies, they identified as important questions for policy the issue of confidentiality, which stands in direct contradiction to the goal of improving the flow of information across agency boundaries, and that of levels and styles of representation. Where in the hierarchy of organisations did inter-agency action stand most chance of success, and how could the tensions between formality and informality be resolved? They also, (Sampson et al., 1991), noted the often overlooked importance of gender in structuring and setting limits to co-operation and mutual understanding among practitioners. Women social workers and probation officers were often very conscious of, and unwilling to tolerate, the routinisation of sexual harassment in the police. The researchers concluded that inter-agency co-operation could produce positive results, identifiable benefits for those enmeshed in the criminal justice system and a greater chance of success in crime prevention programmes, when it was directed at specific, well-defined problems on whose nature everyone agreed, when participants were clear about its purpose, and when the reality of conflict was accepted from the outset rather than repressed or evaded. As an example of successful inter-agency work, they cited joint investigations between the police and social workers of allegations of child sexual abuse. Typically, this work was carried out by women, whose shared commitment to the task enabled them to cross barriers of hierarchy, organisational structure and professional formation, (Sampson et al., 1991). Their qualified endorsement of inter-agency co-operation as a policy aim fell well short, then, of an endorsement of a fully corporatist approach, while also rejecting the simplicities of the 'conspiratorial' position and its rejection in advance of any attempt to promote more considerate and co-operative habits of work across agencies.

Into the 1990s: developing an understanding of corporatism

The work reviewed above has been criticised and developed by, among others, Gilling, (1994; 1996) and Crawford, (1997; 1998; see also Crawford and Jones, 1995). In policy on crime prevention particularly, the key term for the 1990s was 'partnership', found everywhere, from the language used by practitioners working on specific local initiatives, through the work of organisations such as NACRO and Crime Concern, to policy statements at government level. The 'Morgan Report', (Home Office, 1991) on crime prevention envisaged a leading role for local authorities in co-ordinating crime prevention efforts that contradicted the Conservative government's emphasis on reducing the powers of local government, but its advocacy of the 'partnership approach' was nevertheless influential. Adam Crawford in particular has developed an analysis of the meaning of partnership in this context, arguing that the earlier research of Pearson and his colleagues tended to concentrate on surface level conflict and to ignore the ways in which members of inter-agency groups managed and negotiated conflicts at local level. For Crawford and Jones, (1995), the power differentials identified in the earlier research can lead to the denial of conflict rather than its overt expression, as participants convince themselves that apparent differences of interest can be wished away by an 'ideology of unity'. This ideology leads, according to Crawford, (1998), to a failure to resolve real structural conflicts, but it is exactly the set of attitudes and beliefs that corporatism requires, and is exemplified in such well established youth justice initiatives as the Northamptonshire Diversion Units, in which workers seconded from the police, probation, education, the youth service, social services and health, in a model very close to that specified for youth offending teams, are to a large extent expected to work interchangeably and to identify with the diversion team rather than with their organisations of origin.

Crawford, (1997; 1998) is therefore interested in understanding partnerships as a reflection of broader corporatist trends in the implementation of state policy. He argues that the idea of corporatism, as exemplified in crime prevention partnerships, provides a way of making sense of the processes of regulation and control required by the diversification and decentralisation of service provision in the arenas of welfare and criminal justice. Corporatism, as exemplified in crime prevention partnerships, is for Crawford a means of understanding the processes of inclusion and exclusion involved in policy implementation, in which some organisations are given a privileged status as insiders in return for their guaranteed adherence to public policy aims. As Crawford, (1998), notes, it would be a mistake to regard this development as entirely novel. Some non-governmental organisations have long been regarded by central government as sufficiently reliable or 'house-trained' to be incorporated into the policy process and used for the delivery of services, NACRO being the clearest example in both youth justice and crime prevention, (Rock, 1990). Rather, corporatism can be seen as the logical extension of processes in train for some time, such as the marketisation of service delivery and the erosion of the boundaries between the public, private and voluntary sectors, processes identifiable in the sphere of youth justice from the early 1980s.

Earlier accounts of corporatism, then, offer various versions of the processes it entails and the reasons for their emergence. For Pratt, (1989), a corporatist approach to youth justice meant that policy implementation was given priority over considerations of both rights and of welfare. It provided a framework for the specialised, technical management of youth justice processes, enthusiastically taken up by practitioners in the 1980s under the name of 'systems management'. Pratt suggested that, while corporatism was in some ways antithetical to the decentralising, anti-statist thrust of much Thatcherite social policy, its emergence in youth justice could be understood as a necessary counter-balance to deregulation in the sphere of the economy and industrial relations. The research of Pearson and his colleagues, while not specifically providing an analysis of corporatism, examined inter-agency co-operation in a range of criminal justice settings, concluding that there were indeed risks in a thorough-going corporatist approach in which important structural differences could be obscured or denied, but that benefits could be identified from better co-operation that could improve the operation of the criminal justice process, for example, in relation to the experience of victims, and enhance the effectiveness of local crime reduction efforts. They suggested that co-operation was most effective and desirable when agency representatives could agree a common purpose and approach on quite specific, well-defined problems, and that this was where attempts to improve co-operation and mutual understanding might be concentrated. Reflecting on this research in the light of experience of the Home Office's encouragement of a more orchestrated and coherent approach to criminal justice issues at regional level, one direct outcome of which was the Woolf Report's proposal of a national Criminal Justice Consultative Council, supported by Area Criminal Justice Committees, Smith, (1994), suggested that the more global advocacy of co-operation and co-ordination of action which the Home Office sought, and which could well be termed 'corporatism, represented an attempt to modernise and rationalise the criminal justice process. At best, this attempt had a partial success. More notable, however, was the extent to which established interests and traditions were successfully defended and the modernising process resisted, a resistance which was helped by the processes of devolution and cash-limiting which encouraged agencies to seek efficiency gains and economies in their internal organisation and functioning, rather than across the system a whole. One agency's gain was therefore, in many cases, by definition, some other agency's loss, and the failure to implement the corporate approach successfully was more striking than its success. Crawford, (1997), analysed crime prevention partnerships as examples of corporatism, which, he argued, was a necessary, although far from the only, feature of new forms of state policy formation and implementation, such as the growing inter-penetration of the public, private and voluntary sectors, and the contracting-out of services within a culture of market values, with the concomitant stress on accountability and cost-effectiveness. He argued that while the research of Pearson and his colleagues had accurately identified important problematic features of inter-agency co-operation it had underestimated the force, at least in crime prevention contexts, of appeals to ideological unity within new corporate structures that made traditional agency boundaries and allegiances irrelevant.

The strength of corporatist ideology is in fact more impressive in the area of crime prevention with which Crawford was concerned than in other fields of criminal justice activity, including youth justice. Indeed, a main part of the Labour government's case for the reform of youth justice is that current practice is not nearly corporate enough. Goldson, (1999), among others has argued that the period in which John Pratt originally detected corporatist trends in youth justice was the period of greatest effectiveness in policy and practice, and, after all, the end to which corporatism was a successful means was the reduction of the use of custody for young people. The use of custody began to increase again after 1993, precisely in line with a change in government rhetoric that denoted the defeat of the liberal, modernising penology which had promoted inter-agency co-operation. The use of custody increased at the same time as official interest in a corporate approach to youth justice waned. The efforts of the Labour government to promote a more corporate strategy can, then, be seen as efforts to recover the relative coherence, and success, of policy in the late 1980s and early 1990s – efforts, indeed, to modernise youth justice. The tenability of this view of the latest reforms is assessed in the following section, in which various 'corporatist' elements in Labour's youth justice policies are described and analysed.

The corporatism of New Labour

It is easy to regard the policies of the Labour government on youth justice as simply a continuation, and in some ways a more radical extension, of the policies of its immediate Conservative predecessor. The Crime and Disorder Act, with its panoply of new orders, its abolition of the presumption of *doli incapax*, its preoc-cupation with parental responsibility and family discipline, and its enthusiasm for custody for, and electronic monitoring of, children as young as ten, provides ample evidence to support this argument, as noted, for example, by Goldson, (1999) and Bell, (1999). Butler and Drakeford, (1997), have also argued that New Labour's line on juvenile justice is consistent with its predecessor's, and with what John Pratt, (1989), identified as a key feature of the corporate approach, in exag-gerating rather than minimising the seriousness of the problem of youth crime. The similarities with the punitive policies of the Conservative government after 1993 are certainly more apparent than the differences, but there are aspects of the Crime and Disorder Act, and of the guidance and circulars that have accompanied its implementation, that suggest that the new politics of youth justice, including the stress on a corporate approach, also owe something to the policies of the late 1980s and early 1990s. It would be very difficult to argue that Labour has rejected the punitive populism of Michael Howard, although there are nuanced differences of language and rhetoric, but another agenda, which harks back to the modernising thrust of earlier Conservative policy, is also in evidence, and it is within this agenda that the theme of corporatism is most clearly expressed.

The most obviously 'corporate' development is probably the establishment of the Youth Justice Board in September, 1998. The Board has, of course, a 'corporate plan', (Youth Justice Board, 1999), covering three years, and the range of its membership is not unlike that of the Woolf-inspired Criminal Justice Consultative Committee, covering different sets of interests within the criminal justice system as well as the voluntary sector. Importantly, however, the Board has powers and resources, to commission research and make grants to promote good practice, which the CJCC never had, and it seems unlikely that developments in youth justice policy could be introduced that simply by-passed the Board, in the way that criminal justice policy from 1993 to 1997, and subsequently, was developed without reference to the CJCC. This looks, then, like a more serious attempt to develop a corporate strategy.

The Board's first corporate plan, covering the three years 1999–2002, sets out seven objectives for the youth justice system under the overall aim of preventing offending by children and young people. These include speeding up the administration of youth justice, confronting young offenders with the consequences of their actions, encouraging reparation and reinforcing parental responsibility, and ensuring that punishments are proportionate to the seriousness and persistence of the offending. So far, so, broadly, familiar. With the possible exception of reparation, there is nothing here that would have looked out of place in the previous government's youth justice rhetoric. There is, however, a further objective that both suggests a broadening of the policy agenda and in itself provides an encapsulated version of the corporate approach:

> *Intervention which tackles the particular factors (personal, family, social, educational or health) that put the young person at risk of offending and which strengthens protective factors.*
>
> (Youth Justice Board, 1999, paragraph 8).

This indicates a revival of interest in social crime prevention, and a recognition that offending by young people can be explained in terms other than those of wickedness or parental irresponsibility. To be achieved, the objective will also require support and commitment from beyond the boundaries of the youth justice system. Paragraph 5 introduces the theme of links with initiatives beyond youth justice more generally:

> *The Board's work will be taken forward in the context provided by crime prevention work and other social policy initiatives including the work of the Social Exclusion Unit, Drug Action Teams and Drug and Alcohol Action Teams. The Board will promote links between the youth justice plans and local crime and disorder strategies, local action plans on drugs and work in children's services and social and economic regeneration.*
>
> (Youth Justice Board, 1999, paragraph 5).

This is vague, of course, as much talk of 'joined-up government' tends to be, but it points both towards a positive, developmental perspective for corporatism, rather than a simply repressive one, and to the inevitable complexity of effective intervention in complex problems.

The same themes recur in relevant guidelines and circulars on the Crime and Disorder Act and the establishment of Youth Offending Teams, (Home Office, 1998a; 1998b). The 'framework document' for the Act, (Home Office, 1998a) was drawn up not only by the Home Office and the Welsh Office but by the Lord Chancellor's Department, the Attorney General's Office, the Department of Health and the Department for Education and Employment, and presents an impressive list of organisations consulted in the course of its preparation, giving a strong initial message about corporatism at central government level. The Home Secretary's preface tells us that 'Partnership is an essential starting point', and, in language that echoes the exhortations to greater co-operation that were character-istic of the Faulkner era at the Home Office, stresses the need for a 'common aim' and shared responsibility for its achievement. Paragraph 2 lists the agencies and individuals involved in the 'operation of the system', and recognises that they have their 'own traditions and working practices'; but all are said to have 'a common interest in the fair and effective administration of justice ... and in preventing children and young people who have offended from committing further offences'. Paragraph 4 explains the incorporation into statute of the aim of preventing offending. It argues that the 'youth justice system has for too long been seen to be separate from wider youth crime prevention work', and that the new statutory aim 'makes clear the important link that there should be between the work of the youth justice system and wider work to help prevent children and young people offending'. Paragraph 11 cites research on the risk factors asso-ciated with offending by young people, covering family, peer group, educational, personal and economic problems, and concludes that to tackle 'these factors ... requires input from a range of agencies' at both strategic and practical levels; the chances of success will be 'greatest *if all agencies and individuals within the youth justice system work in partnership together*', (emphasis in original). Paragraphs 14.9 and 14.10 refer to Sections 38–39 and 115 of the Act, in encour-aging the pooling of budgets under local authority control by the probation service, the police and health authorities, and making clear that the sharing of information among these organisations and others in the voluntary sector is explicitly allowed in the Act, thus tackling the issue of confidentiality directly. The local authority is given a central role throughout the framework document, and there is at least a hint of the possible development of a local budget for youth justice, a reform often regarded as desirable by critics of the existing system.

The inter-departmental circular on establishing youth offending teams, (Home Office, 1998b), takes a similar line on the virtues of partnership and co-operation under local authority leadership. Paragraph 12 stresses that the task of setting up a local YOT must be approached 'corporately' with the police, probation service and health authorities. Paragraph 15 suggests that the 'inter-agency membership' of YOTs will enable them to identify children at risk and work with their families on a voluntary basis, and to advise the youth service and others on programmes 'which can help to prevent youth offending'. Paragraph 51 specifies that the annual youth justice plan must be consistent with and complementary to the local crime and disorder strategy, the children's services plan, the annual plans of the police and the probation services, the Drug Action Team's action plan, the behaviour support plan of the local education authority, the annual review of the Area Child Protection Committee, and any plan drawn up by the court user group for tackling delays. Paragraph 60 emphasises the prime responsibility of the local authority conceived as 'a corporate responsibility, not something which stems solely from its social services and education responsibilities'.

There is no doubt, then, that the government's approach to youth justice relies heavily on a corporatist strategy. The language of these texts is explicit on the issue, and the government plainly believes that a corporate approach is necessary for the successful implementation of the Crime and Disorder Act. One question prompted by this emphasis is whether such an ambitious extension of the requirements of inter-agency co-operation is feasible. If previous attempts to modernise the criminal justice system failed, is this one more likely to succeed? The initial evaluation of the YOT pilots, (Hine et al., 1999), suggests that the multi-agency character of YOTs can provide an example at the local level of 'joined-up government', but notes, too, that this may make lines of accountability confused, and that some YOTs were proving difficult to manage because some of the seconded workers were treated as still primarily accountable to their 'home' agency management, and not, as Hine et al., recommend, to the YOT manager, who in turn should be accountable to the chair of the steering group. The report also notes that while previous local collaboration among agencies can be helpful, it is important for steering groups to recognise that these must be developed to meet the new demands of the Act, including the statutory duty to develop work in crime prevention. These findings are not surprising, and relate only to the first six months or so of the pilot YOTs, but they suggest that the problems identified in earlier research are still relevant to understanding the challenges facing YOTs, and that more inter-agency working and mutual understanding, a more inclusive corporatism, may be necessary if they are to function as intended.

The second question suggested by the stress on a corporate approach entails a value judgement, as did previous efforts to modernise criminal justice in the interests of efficiency and effectiveness. Is the government right to argue that a corporate approach stands the best chance of having an impact on problems of youth crime? Or should we be suspicious of the erosion of agency boundaries, the loss of checks and balances within the system, or even regard the corporate approach as evidence of the further encroachment of a monolithic and repressive state power, symbolised by the police, on family and community life, with a special focus on the vulnerable and marginalised, the conspiratorial perspective. Without pretending that the issues are clear-cut, it is possible to sympathise with the government's argument that the youth justice system, and young offenders, their families, and their communities, have been ill-served by the lack of co-ordination and coherence that has characterised much, not all, youth justice work over the past decade. This is, after all, close to the position of radical critics such as Pitts and Hope, (1997), whose argument, based on a comparison of youth crime prevention initiatives in London and Paris, calls for more, not less, co-operation among agencies, for a clearer sense of strategic purpose, and for the divisions between direct work with young offenders and developmental crime prevention to be broken down, as a means of linking the youth justice system with a wider consensual politics of social inclusion. It is also close to the argument of Smith, (1999; see also Lobley and Smith, 1999), that programmes for young offenders are more likely to succeed if they are well networked locally and form part of a coherent local strategy on young offenders and young people in trouble. Programmes set up without inter-agency planning and commitment risk isolation, are liable to be diverted from their originally intended target group, may be undermined by autonomous action by the staff of other agencies, such as the police, teachers, social workers, and are likely to impose strains on their staff that better resourcing, such as inter-agency support would provide, could help to reduce. Radical critics of youth justice have, then, in effect argued for a more corporate approach, and it should be remembered that the corporatism of the 1980s was in large measure a creation of practitioners, mostly in social work, even if they have not used quite the same language as the government. There is empirical evidence for the view that a lack of cross-agency commitment can weaken the impact of specific programmes that might otherwise have had the potential to develop creative and innovative work, for example on young offenders' employment opportunities, (Lobley and Smith, 1999).

Conclusion

Although the Labour government apparently feels no qualms about using the term, 'corporatism' is a concept more likely to arouse suspicion than warm endorsement, the opposite effect of a term such as 'community'. Whether it is associated with an increase in state power and the incorporation into the state apparatus of bodies such as trades unions, as in Mussolini's Italy, or more modestly with a loss of professional autonomy and the risk of domination by more powerful organisations, the negative connotations of corporatism are more intuitively obvious than the positive. In this chapter I have argued that corporatism in the sphere of youth justice is not new, that, like much else, it owes much to the practice of youth justice workers in the 1980s, and that the Labour government's enthusiasm for it is part of a revived effort – which was suspended during the period in which Michael

Howard was Home Secretary – to modernise the youth justice system. The corporatist strategy adopted to ensure the successful implementation of the Crime and Disorder Act 1998 does, however, represent a more ambitious and far-reaching attempt than any government has embarked on to ensure, by the use of statute, that a corporatist approach is realised in practice, rather than remaining at the level of rhetoric. Modernisation of the system has become a statutory duty, not a hopeful exhortation. In that sense, youth justice workers will indeed have to make sense of a new policy environment, but its basic contours are familiar, and have been shaped, in part, by practitioners or their predecessors. No-one should be naive enough to believe that corporatism holds no dangers, but a reflex response of opposition is likely to be equally unhelpful to the development of a juster and more coherent system, as well as empirically unjustified. The Labour government's version of corporatism is based, in part, on the kinds of criticism of established practice which youth justice practitioners have themselves made over the years, and it deserves, at least, a serious collective attempt to make it work in practice.

References

Bell, C., (1999), Appealing for Justice for Children and Young People: a Critical Analysis of the Crime and Disorder Bill 1998, in Goldson, B., (Ed.), *Youth Justice: Contemporary Policy and Practice*, Aldershot, Ashgate, pp191–210.

Blagg, H., Pearson, G., Sampson, A., Smith, D. and Stubbs, P., (1988), Inter-agency Cooperation: Rhetoric and Reality, in Hope, T. and Shaw, M., (Eds.), *Communities and Crime Reduction*, London, HMSO, pp204–20.

Butler, I. and Drakeford, M., (1997), Tough Guise: the Politics of Youth Justice, *Probation Journal*, 44, 4, 216–9.

Christie, N., (1993), *Crime Control as Industry*, London, Routledge.

Cohen, S., (1985), *Visions of Social Control*, Cambridge, Polity Press.

Crawford, A., (1997), *The Local Governance of Crime: Appeals to Community and Partnerships*, Oxford, Clarendon Press.

Crawford, A., (1998), *Crime Prevention and Community Safety: Politics, Policies and Practices*, Harlow, Longman.

Crawford, A. and Jones, M., (1995), Inter-agency Co-operation and Community-based Crime Prevention: Some Reflections on the Work of Pearson and Colleagues, *British Journal of Criminology*, 35, 1, pp17–35.

Faulkner, D., (1993), All Flaws and Disorder, *The Guardian*, 11 November.

Gilling, D., (1994), Multi-agency Crime Prevention: Some Barriers to Collaboration, *Howard Journal of Criminal Justice*, 33, 4, pp 246–57.

Gilling, D., (1996), Crime Prevention, in May, T. and Vass, A.A., (Eds.), *Working with Offenders: Issues, Contexts and Outcomes*, London, Sage, pp 222–41.

Goldson, B., (1999), Youth (in)justice: Contemporary Developments in Policy and Practice, in Goldson, B., (Ed.), *Youth Justice: Contemporary Policy and Practice*, Aldershot, Ashgate, pp1–27.

Gordon, P., (1987), Community Policing: Towards the Local Police State?, in Scraton, P., (Ed.), *Law, Order and the Authoritarian State*, Milton Keynes, Open University Press, pp121–44.

Hine, J., Holdaway, S., Wiles, P., Davidson, N., Dignan, J., Hammersley, R. and Marsh, P., (1999), *Interim Report on Youth Offending Teams*, http: //www.homeoffice.gov.uk.

Home Office, (1991), *Safer Communities: The Local Delivery of Crime Prevention through the Partnership Approach*, (the Morgan Report), London, Home Office.

Home Office, (1998a), *Youth Justice: Preventing Offending*, http: //www.homeoffice.gov.uk/cdact/youjust.htm.

Home Office, (1998b), *Inter-Departmental Circular on Establishing Youth Offending Teams*, http: //www.homeoffice.gov.uk/cdact/yotcirc.htm.

Lobley, D. and Smith, D., (1999), *Working with Persistent Juvenile Offenders: An Evaluation of the Apex CueTen Project*, Edinburgh, The Scottish Office.

Pearson, G., Blagg, H., Smith, D., Sampson, A. and Stubbs, P., (1992), Crime, Community and Conflict: the Multi-agency Approach, in Downes, D., (Ed.), *Unravelling Criminal Justice*, Basingstoke, Macmillan, pp 46–72.

Pitts, J. and Hope, T., (1997), The Local Politics of Inclusion: The State and Community Safety, *Social Policy and Administration*, 31, 5, pp 37–58.

Pratt, J., (1989), Corporatism: The Third Model of Juvenile Justice, *British Journal of Criminology*, 29, 2, pp 236–54.

Rock, P., (1990), *Helping Victims of Crime: The Home Office and the Rise of Victim Support in England and Wales*, Oxford, Clarendon Press.

Rutherford, A., (1996), *Transforming Criminal Justice*, Winchester, Waterside Press.

Sampson, A. and Smith, D., (1992), Probation and Community Crime Prevention, *Howard Journal of Criminal* Justice, 31, 2, pp105–19.

Sampson, A., Smith, D., Pearson, G., Blagg, H. and Stubbs, P., (1991), Gender Issues in Inter-agency Relations: Police, Probation and Social Services, in Abbott, P. and Wallace, C., (Eds.), *Gender, Sexuality and Power*, London, Macmillan, pp114–32.

Sampson, A., Stubbs, P., Smith, D., Pearson, G. and Blagg, H., (1988), Crime, Localities and the Multi-agency Approach, *British Journal of Criminology*, 28, 4, pp 478–93.

Smith, D., (1994), *The Home Office Regional Conferences, May 1990: March 1993*, Liverpool, Home Office Special Conferences Unit.

Smith, D., (1999), Social Work with Young People in Trouble: Memory and Prospect, in Goldson, B., (Ed.), *Youth Justice: Contemporary Policy and Practice*, Aldershot, Ashgate, pp148–69.

Unger, R., (1976), *Law and Modern Society*, London, Macmillan.

Woolf Report, (1991), *Prison Disturbances April 1990: Report of an Inquiry by the Rt. Hon. Lord Justice Woolf and His Honour Judge Stephen Tumim*, (Cm. 1456), London, HMSO.

Youth Justice Board, (1999), *Corporate Plan 1999–2000 to 2001–02*, http: //www.youth-justice-board.gov.uk/who/corporate99.html

Acknowledgement

Thanks, for reasons too complex and personal to go into here, to Harry Blagg, Richard Harding and the staff at the Crime Research Centre, University of Western Australia. They know what they have done.

CHAPTER 9

The Courts and the New Youth Justice

Geoff Monaghan

Introduction

The government intends that a reformed youth court will emerge from the radical re-structuring of the youth justice system in England and Wales. Changes being introduced concern procedure, culture, aims, and principles as well as a range of new orders and powers. This chapter identifies the key elements of the new provisions and explores tensions that could become manifest as the court attempts to redefine its role within the New Youth Justice. The chapter is written prospectively and it assumes full implementation of the legislation. Some measures will be piloted before implementation across England and Wales and some may be amended or abandoned in the light of experience. Further, the impact of the Human Rights Act 1998 and judgements of the European Court of Human Rights could be significant in re-directing elements of the government's policy ambitions. Such caveats are important if unpredictable. What is more certain is that the government has shaped a vision of the new youth court.

The new vision

A 'reformed' youth court was outlined in the White Paper, (Home Office, 1997a), which prefaced the Crime and Disorder Act 1998. Earlier, the courts had not escaped criticism from the Home Secretary, Jack Straw. As Shadow Home Secretary, Straw attributed some responsibility to the youth court in accounting for what he perceived to be the failure of the youth justice system. He declared that fundamental reform was necessary, (Lecture to the Royal Philanthropic Society, 27 November, 1995). For Straw, the youth court was part of a system 'trapped in a secret garden, in which a culture of excuse for the performance of the system, its delays, waste, ineffectiveness, and for the offenders themselves, is too prevalent', (Straw, 1996). This criticism, particularly regarding delay and waste, was also reflected in the conclusions of the influential Audit Commission report, *Misspent Youth*, (Audit Commission, 1996).

History suggests that attempts to set new policy and practice objectives through legislative reform can result in contrary outcomes. For example, the Children and Young Persons Act 1969, (and the Criminal Justice Act 1991 so far as the use of custody for children was concerned), did not produce the intended results, (see, for example, Anderson, 1999; Bell, 1999; Goldson and Moore, this volume). Attempting to predict the effect of new legislation on the youth court, including the Crime and Disorder Act 1998, the Youth Justice and Criminal Evidence Act 1999, the Human Rights Act 1998, the guidance on tackling delay, (HM Government Interdepartmental Circular, 1997), and *Opening up Youth Court Proceedings*, (Home Office, 1998a), is a complex and problematic exercise. This is not only because of the inexact relation between legislation and practice outcomes, but is further complicated by the sheer pace of proposed change and the overtly political priorities which underpin the government's youth justice policies, (see for example, Hope and Pitts, 1998; Goldson, 1999). Notwithstanding such complexity however, by analysing the relevant legislation and its associated guidance, it is possible to present a tentative vision of the *intended* new youth court.

We may be expected to anticipate that the youth court, as it passes through the first years of the 21st century, will be located within a 'joined up' youth offending team (YOT) area and will be influenced by an interdependent court users group with some joint ownership of a youth justice plan. Youth court proceedings will focus on preventing offending and will be conducted without delays, with case management methods bolstered by national standards and fixed time limits. The court will need to be trustful of sophisticated assessments and be guided by evidence of what is effective in preventing offending. Court personnel will need to ensure that proceedings are open, informal and involve young offenders in 'round table' deliberations. Without question, the court will be expected to take account of the needs, and perhaps wishes, of victims who may themselves be present. The press will regularly be permitted to identify young offenders and 'naming and shaming' will be commonplace. A shared objective of intervening early in order to 'nip offending in the bud' will prevail. The community will have confidence that court disposals will be implemented by inter-agency work that is rigorously enforced. Remand and bail management will be effective with strong sanctions deployed where there is non-compliance and non-co-operation with programmes, or further offending. Such sanctions will be available through greater powers of the court to remove or restrict children's liberty, both at remand and sentence. Youth court magistrates will no longer be haunted by concerns that custody will expose children to desolate regimes of containment and warehousing as periods of detention will be spent in institutions underpinned by child care standards, education and training; active regimes employing methods of offending-related work that will evidentially reduce levels of recidivism. Further, the youth court will be located within an ambitious inter-agency context facilitating a comprehensive effort to reduce crime and disorder. Local resources will be provided in a transparent and accountable way and the government, through the work of the Youth Justice Board for England and Wales, will ensure effectiveness by applying sanctions where necessary and funding where appropriate. Research and evaluation will inform the development of best practice and contribute to consistency, end 'justice by geography' and eradicate discrimination. Such is the vision, but will all be well in the new 'garden'?

Drawing a line under the past?

In the process of 'reform', surprisingly little of what went before has been removed by the new legislation. Reform in this sense is sedimentary rather than metamorphic. In sentencing children, the only significant orders repealed by the Crime and Disorder Act 1998 are the secure training order and detention in a young offender institution which are replaced by the new detention and training order, (section 73, Crime and Disorder Act 1998). Furthermore, significant amendments to other sentencing options number only two. Firstly, supervision orders with a residence requirement, (section 12AA, Children and Young Persons Act 1969), will be more available through relaxed criteria. Secondly, breaches of conditions on supervision orders may be dealt with by the court imposing any sentence that could have been given for the original offence (including custody) and this results in the repeal of the supervision order as a 'direct alternative to custody', (section 12D, Children and Young Persons Act 1969). The power to commit to Crown Court for sentence, (section 37, Magistrates' Courts Act 1980), where the youth court considers its sentencing powers to be insufficient, is repealed, having been made redundant by the detention and training order which gives the youth court identical custodial powers to the Crown Court – other than for those 'grave' crimes sentenced under section 53 of the Children and Young Persons Act 1933.

More generally, the new legislation does not disturb the sentencing framework provided by the Criminal Justice Act 1991 and this may result in tensions and a lack of clarity. Thus, new orders might be expected to fit into the three principal sentencing bands: 'fines and discharge', 'community sentence' and 'custody'. The principle of commensurate sentencing, 'just deserts', encompassing the right of proportionality, (United Nations, 1989), also remains in place. The Children and Young Persons Act 1933 provides significant principles that apply to the youth court, most notably recognising the child as being in need of protection and establishing arrangements for children that are different to, and separate from, those for adults. Such provisions, together with the 'welfare principle' contained in section 44 of the 1933 Act, and powerfully reflected in the Children Act 1989, that every court in dealing with a child shall have regard to that child's welfare, are not amended.

Possibly the most significant amendment in law is the abolition of the common law assumption of *doli incapax*, (Bandalli, this volume). The value of this doctrine had been reasserted in recent years, (see, for example, Penal Affairs Consortium, 1995; Justice, 1996; Goldson, 1999). However, New Labour regards *doli incapax* as providing an 'excuse' for young children who offend, and as leading to delay in proceedings or 'even making it impossible for the prosecution to proceed', (Home

Office, 1997a). The government was unequivocal in declaring that 'the notion of *doli incapax* is contrary to common sense' (common sense had seemingly supported the doctrine in some form since Saxon times) and abolished it. Thus, under the New Youth Justice, a ten year old child is to be regarded as having the same level of criminal intent and responsibility as an adult, (see Goldson, 1999, pp17–20).

Although the new legislation has left much of the old intact therefore, the revisions and amendments that have been implemented suggest a trend towards the primacy of objectives other than the promotion of children's welfare and rights. This stands in contrast to the current policy direction of the Department of Health which is perhaps best summed up by the words of Sir William Utting in *People Like Us*:

> *Finally, there is the impersonal harm wrought by malfunctioning systems and institutions ... affecting whole cohorts of children in ways which might permanently damage their prospects ... The factor common to this malfunctioning is the substitution of other goals – whether of policy, management, administration or professionalism – for the primary objective of promoting the welfare of children ... Only the best of authorities and institutions are able to see and deal with children as whole people.*
>
> (Utting, 1997, p 19).

New powers and orders – the remand arena

Although the most contemporary legislation does not dispense with the old, it certainly introduces much that is new: there is an array of new powers and orders with which the courts must become familiar. The first new power to be implemented nationally relates to remand arrangements. Here, the new emphasis on reparation, victims and evidence-based practice, which will ostensibly apply to sentencing, is absent. The courts have new powers to remand children as young as twelve into secure accommodation, (section 23, Children and Young Persons Act 1969 as amended). Prior to the Criminal Justice Act 1991, the court could only remand children into custody or secure accommodation in rare circumstances without an application (for a secure accommodation order) or a written report (for a certificate of unruly character) coming from the local authority. The abolition of the unruly character regulations and the introduction of the remand in custody for 15 and 16 year old boys, through the 1991 Act, began to shift real power from youth justice teams and social services departments to the magistrates. The new arrangements represent an even greater shift in power to the court and now it is only ten and eleven year old children who cannot be locked up without an application from the local authority. Thus, whereas previously, decisions were usually preceded by written reports, magistrates are now expected to make crucial decisions on the basis of 'facts' and consultations delivered in a matter of minutes in the court room. Further, the court must grapple with uncertain definitions in forming opinion over what constitutes a 'violent offence', a 'recent history of absconding', 'serious harm' and 'vulnerability'. In the face of robust applications from the Crown Prosecution Service, a probable history of failing to complete a final warning programme and, often, an apparent failure to comply with bail conditions, the new youth court will be placed under ever-increasing pressure to lock children up on remand. Moreover, such pressure will only be exacerbated by the extremely limited range of local authority accommodation or, in some cases, the complete absence of the same. In addition, magistrates and lawyers in the 'adult' court, who do not specialise in dealing with children or youth justice legislation, will be required to deal with such remand decisions regarding children. This situation also occurs in 'special' courts during weekends and on weekdays when there is no youth court sitting. The Children's Society suggests that these problems are common, with as many as 49 per cent of remanded 15 and 16 year olds being remanded in custody by courts other than the youth court, 24 per cent without the knowledge of youth justice services, 43 per cent without an alternative placement being offered and with only 54 per cent of local authorities offering a range of placement types, (Children's Society, 1999). These findings are consistent with those from an earlier study which also highlighted huge regional variations and the dispro-portionate custodial remands of black children, (Association of Chief Officers of Probation and NACRO, 1995). It is not unreasonable to predict that the new remand powers of the youth court will intensify such patterns.

Although the Department of Health has been increasingly critical of local authorities' services for children, there is little other than anecdotal evidence regarding the extent to which local authorities 'allow' children to be remanded into prison service custody due to problems in managing children 'looked after' in community placements or to limit costs. The latter is substantial, ranging from no cost, to the local authority, for prison service accommodation, to more than £2500 per week in a secure unit, and this is a just cause for concern. Countering these issues will be a tough test for the youth court. The Department of Health is pressing into the youth justice system with the 'Quality Protects' agenda, which should result in better services to reduce the inappropriate use of custodial and secure remands, and the new framework for assessment of children in need, laid out in *Working Together to Safeguard Children*, (Department of Health, 1999), which should be applicable to children who enter the youth justice system. The juxtaposition of different assessment frameworks which are emanating from the Department of Health and the Youth Justice Board for England and Wales respec-tively, may cause confusion and reflects the problems inherent in losing focus on children's welfare as the paramount principle. 'ASSET', the assessment tool which is to be widely applied within the New Youth Justice, has a primary focus on offending-related factors. This may displace any emphasis on children in need, and child welfare conceptualisations, to the detriment of appropriately balanced decision making in the court. Best practice will require magistrates to directly challenge inadequate offers of resources and assessments, through YOTs, both in the court room and, strategically, through court user and steering groups. Moreover, such groups will need to be mindful that children who come before the courts will invariably be appropriate candidates for assessment as 'children in need' under the terms of *Working Together*, (see also Goldson, 1998 and 2000).

Even without accounting for new secure remand powers regarding 12 to 14 year olds and 15 and 16 year old females, (section 23, Children and Young Persons Act 1969 as amended), the new youth court begins from a position where custodial remands for children have been rising dramatically in recent years. On a typical day in 1997, for example, there were around 250 boys aged 15 or 16 remanded in prison custody, compared with around 75 for a similar day in 1992, (Home Office, 1997b). In advice to the Home Secretary on the secure estate, the Youth Justice Board for England and Wales attempted to predict the numbers of juveniles who would find themselves placed in secure provisions, both remand and sentence, in 2002/3, and, although this is a difficult exercise, the minimum figure represented a more or less *status quo* scenario and the maximum, a near doubling of current numbers, (Youth Justice Board for England and Wales, 1998). In the face of these trends and predictions, considerable joint effort will be needed if the youth court is to remove children's liberty 'only as a measure of last resort and for the shortest appropriate period of time' as is required by conventional obligations and international standards, treaties and rules, (United Nations, 1989).

A further concern in relation to new custodial remand arrangements for children relates specifically to the issue of 17 year olds. The most recent youth justice 'reforms' have failed to recognise this group as being children for the purposes of remand arrangements despite the unequivocal definitions of the child being a person under the age of 18 years as contained in the Children Act 1989 and the United Nations Convention on the Rights of the Child. Thus, the court will deal with remand decisions for such *children* under *adult* legislation.

Despite the evident need to reverse the trend of locking up more children on remand, (Moore, this volume), and for local community-based services and resources to be wider ranging, of better quality and available to all courts, there are indications that Youth Offending Teams, (YOTs), are being encouraged to reduce efforts traditionally devoted to this end. The second evaluation report on YOT pilots criticises youth justice staff for having:

> *...a cultural hangover which sees social crises in young offenders' lives that are not related to offending as a central feature of work. Remands in custody, for example, have taken up far too much time in some cases and seem to have realised an importance out of all proportion to the need to tackle problems faced by many other referred offenders.*
>
> (Universities of Sheffield and Hull, 1999, p 17).

This seems to suggest that addressing remands in custody is an activity which is not 'related to offending' despite all that is known of the appalling treatment experienced by children in remand settings and the high rates of post-custodial re-conviction. Furthermore, implicit in the above quoted statement is the suggestion that ensuring compliance with the United Nations Convention on the Rights of the Child in limiting custody for children as young as twelve to a 'measure of last resort and for the shortest appropriate period' is a distracting and unnecessary indulgence for YOTs, as distinct from a core professional responsibility.

Given the new emphasis on custodial remands, it is rather paradoxical that the provision of 'bail support' services has become a statutory requirement, (section 38 Crime and Disorder Act 1998), and the development of specific bail initiatives has been a priority for grant aid from the Youth Justice Board for England and Wales. Courts should demand a comprehensive service aimed at reducing secure remands and remands in custody. This service should address the reasons why bail is likely to be otherwise refused. It should provide equal opportunity for children who appear before 'adult' or 'special' courts and should not exclude those aged 17. It should always constitute a 'change of circumstance' when bail has been refused previously.

New powers and orders – the sentencing arena

Previously, the youth court has been the monopolistic source of sentencing young offenders. Diversionary practices based around the police caution and police bail conditions were the only examples of real significance when children could be formally dealt with outside of the court. The New Youth Justice has redefined the role of the youth court however. Although it remains the primary source of sentencing, there are to be new orders which will not lie within its domain. Indeed, certain powers and orders can be applied without the actual commission of an offence, including child safety orders, anti-social behaviour orders, the local child curfew and, in some cases, the sex offender and parenting orders. These may be made in family proceedings and magistrates' courts or by the approval of the Home Secretary, in the case of local child curfew.

It is beyond the scope of this chapter to engage with a detailed analysis of new powers and orders. What is more salient here, however, is to consider how the youth court might make sense of its revised sentencing brief. Magistrates will have to be familiar with a daunting array of sentencing options. In the new youth justice system, a child who admits, or is convicted of, an offence, can potentially be dealt with by reprimand, final warning, referral order, absolute discharge, conditional discharge, a fine, compensation order, reparation order, attendance centre order, drug treatment and testing order, curfew order, action plan order, supervision order, supervision order with requirements (at least five distinct varieties), community service order, probation order, probation order with requirements, combination order, deferred sentence and detention and training order. In addition to these, and as well as ancillary orders and driving licence penalties, the court must also concern itself with parenting orders and financial penalties against parents, (Drakeford and McCarthy, this volume). If this seems to be a complex 'menu', there is the added burden of 'special dietary requirements'. Individual options may be determined by prescribed scoring templates, as in the reprimand and final warning, may be mandatory, with a referral order, may be mandatory unless reasons are stated why not appropriate or reasonable, such as parenting orders, reparation orders, compensation orders, may be restricted by what has gone before, perhaps a conditional discharge, may be restricted by age, by the seriousness of offence, by professional opinion or assessment, with community service and drug treatment and testing orders, and may require consent. Some disposals require specific criteria to be met and some require a pre-sentence or 'sentence specific' report. With exceptions, orders may be combined. Youth court magistrates may be excused should they envy the relative simplicity enjoyed by their colleagues in the 'adult' court and, for that matter, child offenders may feel similarly about their adult counterparts!

Apart from the complexity, and potential confusion, induced by the introduction of new orders and powers, there is the added challenge of new processes and the imposition of 'rationalistic science'. The police are to employ a 'tick box' approach to inform decisions whether to reprimand, warn or prosecute. This is not a direct matter for the new youth court, but it will remain open to the court to take strategic action should police decisions appear to be inconsistent or inappropriate. The first year of piloting reprimands and warnings indicated that decision making, intended to be consistent using a 'tool' designed to be used by any trained police officer, remained uncertain and variable. There were wide variations between pilot areas in the proportion of reprimands to final warnings, with the average being almost exactly 2: 1 but varying from around 4: 1 to almost 1: 1, (Home Office, 1999a). This raises obvious justice concerns in relation to parity, fairness and inappropriate criminalisation, but it will also impact on the workloads of the courts and the new youth offender panels. Children receiving a warning will usually be expected to comply with a 'rehabilitation programme' devised by the YOT. A failure to comply with, or complete, the programme will normally be reported to the youth court in the event of subsequent conviction. This may be the first opportunity for the child concerned to dispute in a judicial setting the facts of any such alleged failure and, as this process is illuminated neither by statute nor official guidance, it will inevitably raise problematic issues for the youth court. Even without such dispute, the court should take account of the extent to which the programme was completed and question whether the programme was indeed realistically achievable, compatible with human rights and commensurate with the seriousness of the offence. As it stands, a failure to comply with a final warning programme is itself intended to be regarded as an aggravating factor in future sentencing, and may lessen bail support opportunities if reported at earlier stages, without judicial finding through breach proceedings.

A further major reform intrinsic to the New Youth Justice is the essential abolition of the conditional discharge as a primary sentence. Except in 'exceptional circumstances', the court may not make a conditional discharge within two years of a warning, (section 66, Crime and Disorder Act 1998). With discharges accounting for over 40 per cent of outcomes in many youth courts the use of other more intrusive sentencing options will clearly increase. The new 'culture' in the youth justice system includes a determination to intervene effectively and at an early stage to 'nip offending in the bud' and this is reflected in the limited range of sentencing and processing options that are not overtly interventionist.

The main replacement for the conditional discharge will be the referral order as provided by Part One of the Youth Justice and Criminal Evidence Act 1999, (Goldson and Haines, this volume). In brief, the referral order will be the primary sentence for children on first conviction and, in all cases where guilt is admitted, will be compulsory unless the offence(s) attract(s) a custodial sentence, an absolute discharge or a hospital order. Home Office statistics, (Home Office, 1997c), suggest that over 40 per cent of sentencing outcomes in youth courts are made in respect of first conviction and it follows that the referral order will comprise a most significant proportion of such outcomes. The order results in 'referral' to a youth offender panel which will determine a 'programme of behaviour' and a 'youth offender contract' with which the child must co-operate. From the perspective of the youth court however, the referral order marks a radical reform in sentencing practice. Essentially, the role of the court is limited to deciding whether the 'compulsory referral conditions' apply. If they do, the only issue that the court must settle is the length of the referral order, from 3 months to 12 months, and this should be proportionate to the seriousness of the offence. The court is effectively obliged to delegate the power of determining the nature and content of the programme and its suitability to another forum, the youth offender panel, and, although it is likely that the court may sometimes pass on its comments, it has no statutory influence over the detail. The youth court magistrate, accustomed to seeking answers as to why a child offended and exercising influence over how best to meet the child's relevant needs and how to prevent further offending, will effectively be rendered powerless. In other cases, where the first conviction follows a finding of guilt, after trial, the full range of sentencing options as discussed above is open to the court, other than referral order. Where there have been mixed pleas, the court *may* make a referral order, at its discretion. It is the application of referral orders, or not, in this discretionary context which will serve to indicate the confidence of the youth court in youth offender panels and its preparedness to voluntarily surrender a significant part of its traditional role, power and influence. A further indication will emerge in cases which are so serious that a detention and training order could be considered. If courts have misgivings about the effectiveness of the panel and/or concerns about delegating their powers then the use of custodial sentences can be expected to increase.

Other than the referral order, the new orders that are available to the youth court include the reparation and action plan orders. The former is not a 'community sentence' under the terms of the Criminal Justice Act 1991, whereas the latter is. Both are intended to be 'restorative' in nature with the focus on reparative, victim-related programmes wherever possible. In line with this, a new form of requirement on a supervision order is also added; a reparation requirement, (section 12A(3)(aa), Children and Young Persons Act 1969, as inserted by section 71, Crime and Disorder Act 1998). With all three orders, the apparent intention of the legislation is for the court to have detail of, and then specify in the order, what form reparation should take. In the case of reparation orders, the reparative element is all that is ordered, whereas for supervision and action plan orders other requirements apply. Within all the interventionist programmes, from final warning to supervision order, there will be a drive towards approaches that are proven, by evidence of 'what works', to prevent further offending, particularly work based on cognitive behavioural models and programmes specific to particular offending related factors, including drug and alcohol factors. With all of the orders that are associated with restorative justice, it is essential for the court to have confidence in the local youth justice services. Where victims are dissatisfied or, worse, feel re-victimised, it is possible that the youth court will bear the brunt of criticism.

The reparation and action plan orders are not only potentially problematic to the youth court in terms of their reparative and restorative practices and the role of victims. Indeed, there are elements of the New Youth Justice with regard to these orders which potentially limit the discretionary and analytical powers of the courts in a way not dissimilar to the referral order. This is particularly apparent in relation to the nature of reports that courts will have in order to inform their deliberations and assessments. Whilst the previous provisions regarding pre-sentence reports essentially remain unchanged, the reparation and action plan orders require, as an alternative, a new 'sentence specific' report. These reports are intended to reduce delay and, as such, will inevitably be less comprehensive than a pre-sentence report. They deal essentially with the components of the proposed reparation or action plan programme and, thus restricted in focus, 'second guess' or even prescribe the sentence of the court receiving them. The evaluation of the piloting of these orders suggests that, overall, the youth court is resistant to this change of reporting and that 'all option' pre-sentence reports are still favoured:

> ...the scale on which this is happening suggests that it may also reflect a more deep-seated cultural resistance on the part of magistrates to embrace the new approach that is set out in the Act ... This reflects a traditional 'craft guild' approach which views the process of sentencing as a uniquely personal skill in which each case has to be judged on its own merits by the particular bench sentencing on the day.
>
> (Sheffield and Hull Universities, 1999, p 23).

The argument for limiting the use of the pre-sentence report is seemingly associated with reducing delay and this is conceptually problematic. The implicit suggestion that judging each case on its merits is outdated and in need of 'modernisation' is not only unsupported by evidence but presents a fundamental challenge to the independence of the courts and the delivery of justice. It is implied that magistrates should adopt a more 'corporate' approach, almost unquestionably accepting the assessments conducted by YOTs on the one hand and 'binding the hands' of colleagues at future hearings on the other. The purpose of a pre-sentence report has been to inform and enlighten the sentencing bench by way of a comprehensive professional analysis of the specificities of individual cases. Approaches other than this have tested the Higher Courts on appeal and pitfalls have been found in practices which bind future courts.

Despite the expanded and developed range of sentencing options available to the court, I have argued that in other respects the discretion of the youth court will be checked. Moreover, the expanded range of disposals is likely to present additional problems. Indeed, the court will perceive the similarity between programmes under the terms of final warnings on the one hand, and referral, reparation, action plan and supervision orders on the other. Where offending is repetitious, there may be resistance to making another order which is perceived as a re-run, albeit under another guise, of work that has already been tried, tested and 'failed'. With the prominence of YOT staff in the administration of programmes, it may also seem that the same professionals are involved and such tensions will be particularly pertinent in cases where a 'failure to respond' is perceived, with or without breach proceedings. Youth courts are familiar with repeat supervision orders, with varied requirements, but this had been falling into disrepute, often frustrating magistrates and contributing to perceptions of courts without adequate powers. The new system risks similar criticism once the 'new clothes' become transparent and it suggests a sentencing arena with more snakes and fewer ladders. The challenge here lies in ensuring that programmes are of differential intensity and focus through the system and in preserving real opportunities for more intensive programmes for the most serious child offenders. Whether the result will be seen as a 'tariff' or a 'menu' is uncertain. The term 'tariff' has been much used but has no clear definition, it suggests a linear passage towards more intensive and punitive orders for more serious offences or repeat convictions. 'Menu' suggests a model with each offence or episode considered on its specific merit, with the sentence reflecting what will be effective and most suitable, with account taken of the previous history only so far as it is relevant. For example, re-offending after an action plan order could be dealt with by way of a reparation order or a conditional discharge, if that would best resolve the matter, rather than a more punitive, or 'up-tariff', use of a combination order or custody. However, such an approach is fundamentally contested by the new youth justice system which presses for a more purist 'tariff' model, fixed in place at reprimand, final warning and referral order stages:

For repeat offenders, punishments should also be progressive. Young people who ignore the help offered them, and continue to offend regardless, should be in no doubt about the tough penalties they will face.

(Home Office, 1997a, p 15).

The detention and training order – the custodial arena

Here comes the candle to light you to bed
Here comes the chopper to chop off your head

(Oranges and Lemons, Nursery Rhyme)

Where offending is not 'nipped in the bud' and children 'ignore the help offered them', stronger custodial sentences are provided. The detention and training order allows sentences from 4 months to 24 months to be made in the youth court and, as provided for by section 73 of the Crime and Disorder Act 1998, it applies to children from ten to seventeen years of age, inclusive. Whilst there is a case for dealing with even 'grave' offences in a further reformed youth and family court arena, especially as the Crown Court may be found to be an unsuitable venue for children in the light of judgements of the European Court of Human Rights, this would surely require qualified and specialist 'judges', or some equivalent, to safely administer the significantly greater powers that would need to be available therein. In that context, it remains a sobering thought, regarding the way children are treated in England and Wales, that youth court magistrates have been given greater powers to lock up a twelve year old, up to two years for a single offence, than those enjoyed by their colleagues dealing with an adult, who are protected from being sentenced by unqualified peers to more than 6 months for a single offence or twelve months for two or more offences.

The custodial criteria are less stringent than those which previously applied for the short-lived secure training order as provided by section 1 of the Criminal Justice and Public Order Act 1994. Crucially, there is no longer a criterion relating to previous orders. The general restrictions on custodial sentences continue to apply but for children aged under fifteen the Crime and Disorder Act 1998 requires the court to form an 'opinion' that the offender is 'persistent'. For those under 12, there is an added 'opinion' to be formed that only custody would protect the public from further offending. The definition of 'persistent' is not provided by the legislation and it may be some time before a consistent approach is achieved. To confuse this issue, there is a definition of 'persistent offender' that the government 'adopted' with regard to 'fast-tracking' proceedings, (HM Government Inter-departmental Circular, 1997). The problems of defining persistent offenders were highlighted by the Howard League with the conclusion that the government's definition was too wide and would 'label children as "persistent" when they are not', (Howard League, 1999).

The tentative 'vision' of the new youth justice system and the future youth court set out at the beginning of this chapter suggested that magistrates will no longer be haunted by the prospect of desolate regimes of containment and warehousing when considering incarceration of children. The proposals of the Youth Justice Board for England and Wales regarding its role in commissioning and purchasing within the 'secure estate' and the developments of standards, regimes and programmes, on the face of it, represent considerable improvement, certainly with regard to Prison Service institutions. Child protection procedures are also being introduced, to an extent, although there is still no clear statutory requirement for this. However, it will take considerable time and financial investment to achieve such stated objectives. In the early years of the new century, there will be a substantial risk that a sense of reassurance as to conditions for children in custody will prematurely prevail in the courts and elsewhere. It is ironic that 'better', 'child care' orientated custodial conditions are likely to exacerbate what experienced magistrate, Sarah Curtis, describes as the increase in 'tolerance for locking up children', (*The Guardian*, 8 September, 1999). But there will almost certainly be a gap between political rhetoric and operational realities in custodial institutions. It will be difficult, even assuming enormous commitment, to move from the sort of conditions currently prevalent in young offender institutions to the Board's proposed regimes which would require radical reform which is not achievable by mere cosmetic change to existing facilities. The recent report of Her Majesty's Chief Inspector of Prisons on Feltham YOI is introduced by a condemnation of conditions and treatment of children and young prisoners as 'in many instances, worse than when I reported on them two years ago and reveal a history of neglect of those committed to their charge and a failure to meet the demands of society to tackle the problem of offending behaviour', (Home Office, 1999b). The Chief Inspector challenged the staff at Feltham and Prison Service Headquarters as to 'whether they would be happy for their sons, or the sons of any of their friends, to be on the receiving end of the treatment and conditions described in the report which are unacceptable in a civilised country', (ibid, preface). This provocative and penetrating question is one that must trouble many youth court magistrates and has a long history dating back to 1899 when the world's first children's court was charged with the challenging aim of administering justice 'like a just and kind parent', (Allen, 1999). Feltham Young Offender Institution is not an isolated example and general deterioration within the prison estate for children has been identified by Her Majesty's Chief Inspector of Prisons:

> From our visits to every single establishment holding young prisoners there is no doubt that the quality of regime provision has been eroded.
>
> (Home Office, 1998, para. 2.25).

The detention and training order allows children to be incarcerated in greater numbers, at younger ages and for longer periods. The question as to whether the ambitious improvements in conditions and treatment programmes within the new 'secure estate' are actually implemented and, even then, whether they produce positive results, awaits the test of time. In the meantime, the human rights agenda demands that the incarceration of children is kept to the minimum and the youth court will need to develop its new 'culture' with this in mind.

The new youth court: a formidable challenge

In addition to each and all of the complex challenges set out above, the new youth court will also be under increasing pressure to achieve its performance targets in the swift administration of justice, a key government objective. This involves making use of early first hearings, with court personnel having prepared in advance, and sentence often concluding on this occasion. Clerks will be active in case management, making directives to streamline preparation for trials. Magistrates will be trained for early administrative hearings. Statutory time limits and national standards will be applied.

The court will also be operating within a 'modernised' culture of 'openness'. It will have to consider allowing the press to identify children (perhaps attracting considerable opposition with regard to children's rights, welfare and protection) and may be expected to target those who did not plead guilty at the earliest opportunity, if at all. It might admit victims, their supporters and, in some cases, the public at all stages of proceedings and yet it will also be required to conduct proceedings in the most informal, participative and non-adversarial manner as possible. The 'key objective' of 'equipping magistrates to seek information effectively from young people about the reasons for their offending, and to discuss with them how these might be addressed', (Home Office, 1998a), will almost inevitably be impeded and compromised by the reduction in privacy inherent in 'opening up' youth court proceedings.

Apart from these procedural and cultural changes, the youth court will have greater powers of punishment in sentencing and restriction of liberty on remand. The orders that it makes will contain more requirements, which may often control children's lives around the clock, will be more interventionist in nature, and will threaten the important principle of proportionality. The expanded range of powers and orders, together with more intensive restrictions on the child's liberty in the community, will almost certainly result in more 'breach' issues and there will be a risk that children are removed prematurely from their families as a result of 'failures to comply' rather than actual 'increased danger to the public'. Paradoxically, however, the court's power and discretion is diminished at other points of the justice process. This is almost exclusively at the 'front door' with the police controlling reprimands, warnings and initial bail decisions; with restricted capacity to impose conditional discharges and with the requirement to make a referral order, reparation order and/or parenting order in many cases.

The various tensions and complexities that have been explored here, together with shifts in power and discretion, suggest that the position of the youth court in the wider youth justice system has moved more toward the overtly punitive limb of the justice process, as opposed to the limbs of prevention and early intervention. The youth court is likely to struggle with the issue of principles of children's welfare and rights within this new context.

The 'vision' of the new youth court expressed at the beginning of the chapter is not so harmonious with the wider re-structuring of the youth justice system as may first appear. The extent to which the 'vision' is realised or is fundamentally distorted and undermined comprises a formidable challenge for youth court magistrates and related personnel.

References

Allen, R., (1999), A Kind and Just Parent in *Safer Society, Number 4*, London, NACRO.

Anderson, B., (1999), Youth Crime and the Politics of Prevention in Goldson, B., (Ed.), *Youth Justice: Contemporary Policy and Practice*, Aldershot, Ashgate.

Association of Chief Officers of Probation and NACRO, (1995), *A Crisis in Custody*, London, NACRO.

Audit Commission, (1996), *Misspent Youth: Young People and Crime*, London, Audit Commission.

Bell, C., (1999), Appealing for Justice for Children and Young People in Goldson, B., (Ed.), *Youth Justice: Contemporary Policy and Practice,* Aldershot, Ashgate.

Children's Society, (1999), *National Remand Rescue Initiative: National Co-ordinator's Summary for 1998*, London, The Children's Society.

Department of Health, (1999), *Working Together to Safeguard Children*, London, The Stationery Office.

Goldson, B., (1998), *Children in Trouble: Backgrounds and Outcomes,* Liverpool, The University of Liverpool Department of Sociology, Social Policy and Social Work Studies.

Goldson, B., (1999), Youth (In) Justice: Contemporary Developments in Policy and Practice in Goldson, B., (Ed.), *Youth Justice: Contemporary Policy and Practice,* Aldershot, Ashgate.

Goldson, B., (2000), 'Children in Need' or 'Young Offenders'? Hardening Ideology, Organisational Change and New Challenges for Social Work with Children in Trouble. *Child and Family Social Work, Vol. 5 No. 3.*

HM Government, (1997), *Tackling Delays in the Youth Justice System: Inter-departmental Circular*, London, The Stationery Office.

HM Government, (1999), *Second Report to the UN Committee on the Rights of the Child by the United Kingdom 1999*, London, The Stationery Office.

Home Office, (1997a), *No More Excuses: a New Approach to Tackling Youth Crime in England and Wales*, London, The Stationery Office.

Home Office, (1997b), *Prison Statistics: England and Wales*, London, The Stationery Office.

Home Office, (1997c), *Criminal Statistics: England and Wales*, London, The Stationery Office.

Home Office, (1998a), *Opening Up Youth Court Proceedings,* London, Home Office.

Home Office, (1998b), *Young Prisoners: A Thematic Review of HM Chief Inspector of Prisons for England and Wales*, London, Home Office.

Home Office, (1999a), *Delivering the Aim: News from the Youth Justice Pilots: Issue 3,* London, Home Office.

Home Office, (1999b), *HM Young Offender Institution and Remand Centre Feltham: Report of an Unannounced Full Inspection,* London, Home Office.

Hope, T. and Pitts, J., (1998), Hanging Tough in Worcester: New Labour and Youth Justice, paper presented to *ESRC Criminal Justice Policy Seminar,* 16 October.

Howard League, (1999), *Child Jails: The Case against Secure Training Centres,* London, The Howard League.

Justice, (1996), *Children and Homicide: Appropriate Procedures for Juveniles in Murder and Manslaughter Cases,* London, Justice.

Penal Affairs Consortium, (1995), *The Doctrine of 'Doli Incapax',* London, Penal Affairs Consortium.

Sheffield and Hull Universities, (1999), *Youth Justice Pilots Evaluation: Second Interim Report on Youth Offending Teams,* Universities of Sheffield and Hull.

Straw, J. (1996), Challenges of the Future: Taking the Criminal Justice System out of its Secret Garden, transcript of a speech in *Justice of the Peace and Local Government Law,* Vol.160, pp 853–5.

United Nations, (1989), *The United Nations Convention on the Rights of the Child,* New York, United Nations.

United Nations, (1995), *Concluding observations of the Committee on the Rights of the Child: United Kingdom of Great Britain and Northern Ireland,* New York, United Nations.

Utting, Sir W., (1997), *People Like Us,* London, The Stationery Office.

Youth Justice Board for England and Wales, (1998), *Juvenile Secure Estate: Preliminary Advice from the Youth Justice Board for England and Wales to the Home Secretary,* London, Youth Justice Board.

CHAPTER 10

Community Safety and the New Youth Justice

Richard Hester

Either way, the relationship between the criminal and the 'law abiding' community is problematic, since the decision has to be made whether the criminal can or should be excluded from the community or reintegrated within it

(Worrall, 1997, p 48).

Introduction

In this chapter I hope to develop three principal points. First, crime and disorder strategies/community safety initiatives are conceptually problematic. So too is the notion of youth justice. Indeed it may be said that there is an intrinsic tension between community safety and youth justice. However, there may be room for some optimism by searching beyond the 'rhetoric of fear' and discovering how these apparent opposing discourses may, in practice, have more in common than is at first apparent. Second, that evaluation occupies an important space within the current political, policy and practice contexts with regard to youth justice. Moreover, whilst there is merit to evaluation, there are also major problems with it, particularly if what passes for 'evaluation' is reductionist, simplistic, short-termist and thus obfuscates (or even denies) aetiological complexity. In this sense evaluation might serve crude auditing and political imperatives without being of any real value to practice or the development of genuine knowledge. Such problems with evaluation are located broadly within the context of managerialism, and more specifically, within the context of the present government's 'modernising' agenda. Third, with this in mind, I will propose a model for effective community safety based upon a synthesis of community safety and youth justice priorities which addresses the 'anthropoemic', (Young, 1999, p 56) tendencies of 'get tough' rhetoric.

The problem of meaning

Before pressing on it is perhaps necessary to clarify a couple of points that relate to definitions and language. As Nellis, (1999a; 1999b), has stated, language matters and in this sense the meaning of 'youth justice' and 'community safety' requires attention. This has become more topical in light of the debate around the renaming of the Probation Service, (see Travis, 1999). 'Youth justice' in this chapter is used as shorthand for the formal processes that are activated in respect of 'troublesome young people'. The term is not necessarily employed to imply systemic or indeed 'just' processes and the many problems associated with the very concept of 'youth justice' are recognised. The term 'youth justice system' for example is not only problematic because of a:

> *...disparate collection of agencies and government departments operating to different boundaries, different aims and objectives, different information systems.*

> (Boateng, 1999, p 4).

but by virtue of its inference of justice. The view that the youth justice system is patently unjust and riddled with potentially conflicting ideologies and discourses is not news, (Goldson, 1999; Goldson and Chigwada-Bailey, 1999 and Worrall, 1999). However, for the purpose of discussion here I intend to limit the scope of my analysis to the tensions between 'community safety', 'crime and disorder reduction', and 'youth justice'. In order to do this I will review some of the emerging ideas in relation to the means by which we might evaluate these apparently conflicting responses to youth crime. I hope as well to demonstrate that this apparent conflict may actually be the basis for a positive response to youth crime.

I use the term 'community safety' for what otherwise has been described by the government as 'crime and disorder prevention/reduction', (Home Office, 1998b). It is worth remembering that the alternative term 'community safety' was in fact first advocated by the Home Office's Standing Conference on Crime Prevention, (Morgan, 1991), with a view to broaden a concept too readily seen as the sole responsibility of the police. This need for an all-inclusive term is not without problems however, and it has been argued that 'community safety' is in danger of becoming meaningless, (Ekblom, 1994; Gilling, 1996). Indeed, McLaughlin, (1994), has described the term 'community safety' as a 'free floating signifier', (quoted in Hughes, 1998, p 100), thus implying a looseness in its connectivity with anything specific. The power of the term however lies in its value in broadening an otherwise narrowly defined debate on how we are to reduce crime and its causes. Here four issues are particularly noteworthy. First, it describes what it is that practitioners in the field aspire to do, to make communities safe. Second, it provides a framework for social crime prevention. Third, it implies 'community based' solutions. Fourth, it is a helpful alternative to the notion of disorder which is conceptually more problematic than community safety itself. During the development of *Crime and Disorder Reduction Strategies* across England and Wales in 1998/9 for example, 'disorder' effectively covered anything that local communities defined as a problem. This often included general complaints about young people 'hanging around', litter and road traffic issues and was partly a result of the guidance published by the Home Office, (1998b, 1.43) which provided that 'within reason, nothing is ruled out and nothing is ruled in'.

It would be erroneous however to suggest that the term 'community safety' is only problematic in terms of its all-embracing ambitions. An association between community safety and communitarianism is problematic if it uncritically engages with such exclusionary concepts as 'zero tolerance', (see Bowling, 1999), and ill defined notions such as 'family values'. Whilst not all would agree that the communitarian ideal, (Etzioni, 1995), is personified in the term 'community safety' particularly as interpreted by New Labour, (Ryan, 1999), there are those who do, for example Worrall, (1997), and Hughes, (1998). If the key aim of communitarianism purports to, 'restore communities without allowing Puritanism or repression', (Etzioni, 1995, p 2), the fact remains that in times and places where there is fractured consensus, attempts to create a spirit of community might involve the exclusion of those unable or unwilling to 'belong'.

Community safety and justice: signposting the challenge

As Radzinowicz, (1991), and Garland, (1999), remind us, there has been a developing rift between criminology and criminal justice policy. In Garland's view this rift is, in part, created by changes associated with the social conditions of late-modernity which might include consumerism, individualism, 'distantiation' and the 'sequestration of experience', (Giddens, 1991), coupled with recent political events. As Ryan points out in the context of the current Labour government penal policy making:

> *This mobilisation has largely been understood in terms of managing or manipulating fear. Whilst this discourse has provided us with many insights, our argument is that if we interpret the changing attitudes of the state towards the role of the public in penal matters in another way, as more about acknowledging loss and re-engaging the public voice(s) than simply managing or manipulating fear, we are better placed to understand New Labour's populist appeal and how this connects with what has been defined as the new criminology.*
>
> (Ryan, 1999, p 1).

The recent political events that have shaped criminal justice policy are perhaps symbolised most potently in the reaction to the death of James Bulger in 1993 and characterised by John Major's call to 'understand a little less and to condemn a little more' shortly afterwards. The historical detail of how Major's vision manifested itself in the youth justice and crime reduction debate by both Conservative and New Labour governments is described with clarity by Anderson, (1999), and will not be repeated here. What is evident and worth repeating however, is that we are faced with some interesting challenges in the next few years, not least those codified in the *Criminal Justice System Strategic and Business Plans, 1999–2002*. These are: to reduce crime and the fear of crime and their social and economic cost, to dispense justice fairly and efficiently, and to promote confidence in the rule of law (Home Office, 1999, p 4). In theory, although these aims should complement each other, Anderson, observes that such:

> ... 'schizophrenic' (sic) new arrangements ... appear to be driven by conflicting policy objectives. To put it more bluntly, current youth crime policy appears equally committed to preventing the social exclusion of children and young people at risk and increasing the exclusion of those who go on to offend.
> (Anderson, 1999, p 83).

So on the one hand we have a commitment to reduce crime through community and multi-agency involvement and on the other, commitment to an 'efficient' criminal justice system which, it is hoped, will lead to growing public confidence in the rule of law. Unfortunately this latter commitment is further impeded by the tension between criminological theory and a highly retributive discourse based on 'public opinion' described, in part, by Radzinowicz, (1991), and Garland, (1999). However, it is the conflict between efficient criminal justice and community involvement that lies at the heart of the communitarian problem. Methods designed to strengthen communities may equally result in defining stronger boundaries between those who are 'on the inside' and those who are not. Those who do not or will not fit in to this new 'responsible regime' must logically be excluded. If 'community safety' and 'youth justice' imperatives are potentially antagonistic then it may be worth investigating the current debate on evaluation to indicate the exact sites of possible ideological conflict.

Evaluating 'success'

Contrary to the impression that evaluation in the crime reduction field occupies a space completely devoid of theoretical direction, and is itself under researched, there is ample evidence of a growing interest in this subject, (Martinson, 1974, and 1979; Nuttall, 1992; Ekblom, 1994 and 1998b; Gilling, 1997; Pawson and Tilley, 1997; Hough, 1998; Hough and Tilley, 1998; Crawford, 1998 and Hughes, 1998). The task of evaluating community safety is difficult not least because of the aetiological complexity of crime itself, but also the myriad of activities that have developed under its banner. For example, the breadth of such 'community safety' initiatives extends from schemes designed to support vulnerable people by fitting locks to doors and windows to groups set up to improve the literacy of parents of children in high crime areas, (Poole, 1999). How these very different activities impact on crime is, of course, also likely to vary. Pawson and Tilley's, (1997), advice to engage in 'realistic evaluations' does however provide a helpful way through the maze of aetiological gridlock and Ekblom has argued that it is indeed possible to 'draw diverse findings and theories together', (1998a, p 2).

The quest for an effective evaluative tool has been influenced as much by geographers as criminologists. Early on in the development of the evaluation debate on 'community safety' the emergence of Geographic Information Systems (GIS) could be observed as a rising star. This technique allows events such as a 'recorded crime' or reports of 'nuisance youths' to be electronically plotted on a map having been initially 'geo-coded' using a road name, grid reference or postcode. A process of spatial analysis can then be used to identify so-called 'hotspots'. Particularly noteworthy in this respect was the work of Hirschfield and Bowers, (1997 and 1998). Of further interest is the work undertaken by partnerships developed between the Metropolitan Police and a number of London Boroughs. GIS provides possibilities for stunning colour maps to be produced looking at 'hot spots' or 'hot points', colour contours of crime intensity, cluster analysis, kernel density fitting, network analysis, spatial interpolation and visibility analysis of CCTV cover. The degree of sophistication of this analysis is presently located in a few areas such as Merseyside and London, other areas being content with simple mapping. However, the development of this activity is guaranteed given the technical and operational improvements associated with GIS software. What this increased efficiency does not do however, is to capture the continually changing variables that play a part in producing the 'crime and disorder event', (Ekblom, 1998a). Thus the value of the blue dot plotted on the map, the event itself, is both fixed spatially, and granted a kind of uncritical essence as though it were free of any kind of social construction or material context. This is not to denigrate the use of GIS. Indeed the application of spatial analysis in respect of unemployment, benefit claims, health and the distribution of 'known offenders' can be extremely helpful in beginning to understand some of the complex aetiological linkages. The difficulty arises when the connections between these factors are either under or overemphasised and crudely presented. Similarly, an over reliance on technical spatial analysis (and indeed statistical analysis) will be dangerous if it takes no account of the detailed process of crime recording and reporting for example. A fundamental priority within the present government's criminal justice policy not only requires that it is 'tough on crime' but also proves such 'toughness' by the next general election. This urgency of proof has a profound impact on the relationship between community safety and youth justice as well as influencing strategies that are being developed to monitor their respective effectiveness. This 'urgent perspective' is situated in a problematic that is, at best, constrained within the limited parameters of explanations of crime loosely coalescing around notions of strain theory, communitarianism and social exclusion. At worst it is limited to demonstrating that the ambitious targets set out in the Government's *Criminal Justice System Strategic Plan*, (Home Office, 1999), are indeed being met by the development of strategies which have the 'bulimic', (Young, 1999), intention and effect of simultaneously including and excluding offenders from communities. The derivation of this perspective however can be linked to a wider discourse.

On one level the sweep of managerialist business language, (Clarke and Newman, 1997), characterised by such Orwellian Newspeak as 'best value', 'business excellence' and 'benchmarking' may encourage a 'dumbing down' of evaluative projects. What at first sight looks like an impressive list of crosscutting initiatives, linked to changes in levels of recorded crime, may in fact turn out to be paper based taxonomies that bear no relationship to real changes in service delivery. 'Crime-and-disorder-partnerships' may then congratulate themselves on a job well done and hope that the spotlight moves elsewhere before anyone asks any difficult questions about aetiological relationships. Another problem will be the influence of undue pressure on the recording and classification of crime and police 'command and control data'. For example, targets to reduce 'nuisance youth complaints' may invoke close scrutiny of recording systems by the police leading to the re-classification of previous 'nuisance youth' complaints to 'minor traffic', 'criminal damage' or something similar. In this way nuisance youth problems are solved and next year's target becomes 'minor traffic'. Perhaps the most insidious problem, however, will be that of the potential displacement of 'difficult-to-measure-activities', for example, long-term 'early years' interventions, by those that are more easily subjected to analysis, for example, the development of CCTV in town centres. Coupled to this the displacement effects caused by the attractiveness of short-term rather than medium or long-term activities can further distort an evaluative programme. In both cases the loser in a battle of priorities would be social crime prevention measures, the benefits of which potentially take longer to materialise. (For a fuller discussion of the dangers of applying Performance Indicators in evaluating crime reduction see Tilley, 1995).

Notwithstanding the problems and complexities associated with evaluating community safety, it is ironic that it is evidence, the result of effective evaluation, that is to be the cornerstone of the new youth justice practice. Looking across to the probation service, the idea of evidence based practice, 'what works' by another name, 'has been formally adopted as the central tenet of the service's work in cutting crime', (Lockwood 1999, p 8). The Inspectorate of Probation Report *Evidence Based Practice: A Guide to Effective Practice*, (Chapman and Hough, 1998), devotes ten pages, (of a 110 page document) on the subject of evaluation and another nine on 'getting evaluation done and used'. Differentiating between outcome and process evaluation, the report focuses on some methods of assessing changes in recidivism rates based on the premise that:

> ... *reduction in crime and contributing to public protection are now clearly stated as the aims of probation. This means that the ultimate success of probation supervision must be judged against the criterion of reduced re-offending.*

(Chapman and Hough, 1998, p 95).

This very specific example of an attempt to measure success is worth looking at more closely. Those involved in youth justice debates on 'net-widening' in the mid eighties may question the effects of such a blunt evaluative tool. A particular concern would be the possible incentive for Probation Officers, or more likely still, their managers, to include potentially more 'successful' candidates in the probation 'net', leaving the more 'difficult' candidates to custodial disposals. This rather simple example highlights the difficulty of embarking on an overly restrictive and crude evaluative programme with the parameters set so tight as to seriously jeopardise the quality of outcome analysis. A number of difficulties may be summarised which either weaken serious attempts to evaluate effectiveness or directly contribute to ineffectiveness. They are firstly, a focus on Key Performance Indicators such as reconviction rates for clients of Youth Offending Teams, (YOTs) and the Probation Service. Key Performance Indicators may well be used as crude evaluative tools if they are related to additional resources or used to compile simplistic 'league tables'. Secondly, the development of new provisions that are not based on evidence of success or usefulness (so far) such as Parenting Orders, Anti Social Behaviour Orders and Child Curfew Orders set an unhelpful example for those attempting to relate a 'what works' agenda to practice. Thirdly, Objectives outlined in the *Criminal Justice System Strategic Plan*, (Home Office, 1999), and *Tackling Drugs to Build a Better Britain*, (Cabinet Office, 1999), resemble more of a wish list than a reflection of reality and may prove not only to be a hostage to fortune for the current government but an additional pressure to practitioners who in turn may feel they need to cast an optimistic spin on results that appear to be failing these 'demanding' targets.

Approaches to the evaluation of community safety and youth justice reflect the tensions and political context of their existence. Serious attempts to understand the impact of new schemes compete with centrally driven, and funded projects, aimed to prove that certain approaches/initiatives/court orders do in fact 'work' over ever shortening periods of time. On the one hand the government appears to be committed to piloting initiatives and to learn from experience and yet on the other hand, certain ideas like Anti Social Behaviour Orders seem to be enjoying a degree of political backing out of all proportion to their potential to reduce crime and disorder. The dilemma for the government is clear: in order to stay in power it needs to show progress in the criminal justice field by the next election and however genuine its commitment to inclusion appears to be, short term remedies may actually store up problems for the future and work against 'projects of inclusion'.

Synthesising youth justice and community safety

The government's agenda of getting 'tough on crime', and its causes, may, para-doxically, be detrimental to the development of community safety. One of the reasons for this, as I have discussed, is the apparent conflict between 'youth justice' and 'community safety', or 'tackling offender' versus 'tackling offence', approaches to crime prevention. In addition to this inherent tension, the process of developing Crime and Disorder Reduction Strategies arguably leads to a police-led and very particularised crime focus. This need not be the case. In the county of Warwickshire for example, all of the five *Crime and Disorder Reduction Partnerships* included a significant element of social crime prevention in their strategies. Furthermore, a model for youth justice and community safety might address the need for a wide holistic analysis of crime and anti-social behaviour and the potential causes of these problems. More importantly, such a model could indeed exist within the current legislative framework.

Recently a number of criminologists from the University of Bristol School for Policy Studies organised the rather ambitiously titled conference 'Zemiology: Beyond Criminology' (12th-13th February, 1999). The conference focussed on the idea that Zemiology, the study of harm, would address some of the inherent problems associated with criminology, notably its lack of 'ontological reality', and its narrow focus caused by its conceptual enclosure by law. The conference attempted to highlight some of the difficulties thrown up by crime-based audits resulting from the Crime and Disorder Act 1998, (Home Office, 1998b), and the problems associated with locally derived strategies. This inward looking process was exposed as having two key drawbacks. First, by focussing on locally perceived problems of crime it may be easy for local communities to attribute an unfair proportion of blame on themselves and to assume that the solutions therefore are to be found within. Second, and related to the first, is a 'tyranny of the majority' problem: an appeal to simple, and often retributive, solutions to complex problems. This is similar to the point made by Ryan when he concludes in the context of New Labour that '... re-engaging the public voice(s) is problematic, and does not necessarily imply a more progressive politics', (Ryan, 1999, p 1).

To an extent, of course, communities need to be at the heart of solutions to crime and disorder. Interestingly, this has been achieved in Northern Ireland and whilst the involvement of paramilitary groups may be thought to be problematic there is much to be learned from the considerable achievements that have been made in terms of engaging the community. At a seminar organised on 17th June, 1999 by the Home Office and the National Network for Community Safety, Alice Chapman, Director of the Community Safety Centre in Belfast, reinforced this point. She pointed out that community groups in Northern Ireland were generally much more active in directing community safety initiatives than they were on the British mainland. However, not all of the potential causes of crime are to be found in communities. Indeed many, such as the effects of 'the global market' on employment prospects, are beyond the power of national governments let alone local government partnerships. There is therefore a need to clarify the limits of what communities can do, and how they can help to reduce crime and disorder. It is this need for a clarification of the role of 'communities', along with an understanding of their potentially constructive relationships with projects developed under the umbrella of Youth Offending Teams and Youth Justice Plans, that is central to a working model which synthesises 'youth justice' and 'community safety'. In order to achieve their principal aim, that of preventing offending by children and young persons, Youth Offending Teams must engage in a dialogue with those responsible for developing crime and disorder strategies. They will need to map out the boundaries between Youth Offending Teams and the broader and more socially based agenda for community safety. Moreover, if 'youth justice' and broader 'community safety' priorities can be integrated and synthesised then they must be underpinned by a set of shared objectives.

Including young people

There is perhaps a subtle irony in the fact that one of the central tenets of evidence based practice, (Chapman and Hough, 1998, p 6), is the 'responsivity principle'. Responsivity in the context of a 'Modern' Probation Service, (Home Office 1998a), may have a different feel to it than the youth justice worker/ client relationship of the late eighties and early nineties. If this is the same as 'being where they're at' and listening to, and indeed taking account of, young people's views, then this is encouraging. Certainly in the context of the recent *Crime and Disorder Reduction Strategies* there has been some imaginative activity in this respect where young people have been involved in producing videos, organising conferences, recruitment initiatives, peer education, youth forums and so on. For example, on 22nd October, 1999, LARIA, (Local Authorities Research and Intelligence Association), organised a seminar on consulting young people covering 'classic research techniques' and 'hybrid' approaches to consultation. The need to 'communicate effectively with children and to enjoin their active collaboration', according to Smith and Sparks, (1999, p 1), is a premise on which the new provisions of the 1998 Crime and Disorder Act are based. In order to achieve effectiveness, Youth Offending Teams will need to think through carefully what is meant by 'responsivity'. The resulting effect could be the development of an area of effective practice that is 'young person centred'.

The fact that over the years young people in many different forms have been cast as demons is well established. Young, (1999), suggests that there are a number of reasons for societies to 'essentialize the other' and argues that such processes provide ontological security, they legitimise both privilege and deference, they allow us to blame the other, and provide a basis for projection, (1999, p 104). If the boundary between YOTs and community safety is to be managed effectively then it may be necessary to develop a 'position' on young people that is consistent with the conviction 'to treat young people as part of the solution not part of the problem', a phrase used by Alun Michael and a number of Home Office officials during the developments of the 1998/9 'Crime Audits'. There is some evidence of this in many areas in relation to community safety but Youth Offending Teams will need to develop a 'youth positive culture' in order to counteract the demonising tendencies that have deep roots.

Preventive socially focussed crime reduction

The word protection as in 'protecting the public' exudes connotations of defence rather than prevention which sit uncomfortably alongside the concepts of 'community safety' and 'youth justice'. In this sense, a discourse dominated by protective priorities as opposed to preventive concerns will be problematic. Defensive community safety almost certainly has a role to play: it must form a part in a suite of measures designed to reduce crime. However, such an emphasis must not be allowed to subsume social projects and therefore lead to 'fortress cities, brutally divided between fortified cells of affluent society and places of terror where police battle the criminalised poor', (Hughes 1998, p 140). Indeed, the fact that Youth Offending Teams are there to reduce offending, or more accurately re-offending, suggests that strategies need to be focussed on assisting the offender and preventing the potential offender from formal involvement in the criminal justice system. It will help if those involved in both 'systems' share, as much as is possible, common views on the balance of prevention and protection. There are, of course, difficulties in widening the net of intervention as I discussed earlier and this is well known to those in the youth justice field (Goldson, this volume). In this context Muncie warns that:

> ... by drawing the less problematic young people into an extended social
> control network at an earlier age, Labour has revealed how a logic of
> 'prevention' and 'risk management' is quite capable of being used to justify
> any number of repressive and retrograde means of dealing with young
> people in trouble.
>
> (Muncie, 1999b, p 59).

That is not to say it has to happen like that. Non-stigmatising interventions such as Behaviour Support Plans and 'early years' support are being developed by local authorities which can and do promote prevention in relation to those 'at risk' without widening the repressive net. We just need to be aware of the dangers and ensure that benign measures do not produce unintended repressive and retrograde outcomes.

Drug misuse and the Drug Action Teams

Closely associated with public concern that young people are 'going off the rails' has been the burgeoning anxiety over the link between drugs and crime. Public awareness of this issue has been further increased by the recently published report by NACRO, (1999), which highlighted the estimated cost to victims of drug related crime as £2–2.5 billion. Similar concerns have also been raised by Edmunds, May, Hearnden and Hough, (1998, iv). The evidence of a strong connection between problem drug use and a wide range of criminal activity may be established, (NACRO 1999, p 12), but considerable confusion remains as to the precise detail of the relationship, (see MacDonald, 1999 and Newburn, 1999). The common relationship often raised in *Crime and Disorder Reduction Strategy* public consultation and other such fora crudely link addictive drug misuse, usually heroin, and acquisitive crime. This is seen by many police officers, and others, as one of the major factors of concern and as a result features in a number of *Crime and Disorder Reduction Strategies*. During the week of the Labour Party Conference in 1999 a number of articles discussing the legitimacy and accuracy of this relationship within the context of newly proposed mandatory drug tests, appeared in *The Guardian* newspaper and elsewhere, (see for example Travis, 1999a and 1999 b; Bennett 1999; Ward, 1999). I mention this only to reflect that the issue of drug misuse is complicated by differing organisational and political perspectives. Whilst the NACRO report proposed the need for more prevention and treatment, Jack Straw announced in September, 1999, (Travis, 1999b), that mandatory drug testing and denial of bail for heroin and cocaine users would be introduced. In parallel with this debate the Ten Year National Strategy in relation to drugs includes both enforcement and treatment, (Cabinet Office, 1999), and it will be interesting to analyse retrospectively the proportion of resources allocated to treatment and prevention as opposed to enforcement.

The current political emphasis on enforcement may suggest that the government is wedded to a solution for drug misuse based on highly prescriptive, and in some cases over ambitious, targets and objectives. This approach, whilst mirrored to some degree by the creation of the Youth Justice Board for England and Wales has not, at the time of writing, been applied to the *Crime and Disorder Reduction Strategies*. The more organic, slightly idiosyncratic *Crime and Disorder Reduction Strategies* based on local agreements are an alternative approach to the highly centralised prescriptive approach to youth justice and drug misuse. The former seem to be working well although it is probably fair to say that neither approach has been allowed sufficient time for firm conclusions to be drawn. Whether or not better co-ordinated drugs education in schools has an impact on reducing drug misuse, the problem will remain a central one for those involved in the delivery of youth justice and community safety as will the development of treatment services for those who develop drug misuse problems. It is probably too early to say whether Drug Action Teams have been effective or not as MacGregor, (1998), suggests. However, moves to further criminalise drug users through mandatory testing seem like another exclusionary tactic based on a misconception of the complex relationship. It may actually end up hindering the work of Drug Action Teams to achieve their targets. Quite apart from the issues of diversion versus drugs prevention; holistic approaches versus compartmentalism; and the problems of 'joined up working', highlighted by Newburn, (1999, p 620), in respect of the Drug Action Team /youth justice interface, the fundamental issue must be the delivery of a range of preventative and treatment services available and appropriate to young people.

Families
Families appear to be at the centre of the New Labour communitarian ideal in respect of crime prevention. A lot of this makes sense and few would argue that providing parents with support in bringing up their children may impact positively

in reducing the likelihood of youth offending. However, a 'sledgehammer' is not needed to aid this process. Bringing up children, like cooking a small fish, needs to be done with care. It is an art, not a science. This is an area where state responses to youth crime are at their most contradictory. Demonising parents, like demonising children, will exacerbate a situation that for many parents is already complex and strained, (Drakeford and McCarthy, this volume). Many very positive parenting projects, some linked to literacy and college accreditation, have been shown to attract parents who can recognise the benefits of support given in a focussed and non labelling way, (Poole, 1999). However, given the introduction of Parenting Orders, the struggle to ensure that parenting is not something that is to be undertaken at the direction of a court of law will become increasingly difficult. The translation of the idea of mandatory parenting classes seems to be at the heart of this issue. A recent report in The Guardian, (Freely, 1999), suggests that it is the quality and nature of the approach which may be critical in the difference between a measure which will exacerbate tensions in the families and those which will help. It is my guess that in those areas where non-stigmatising parenting projects already exist, the development and use of the new Parenting Orders, if indeed they are used at all, will be more successful than in those areas where they do not. Youth Offending Team managers and those responsible for co-ordinating community safety will need to map out existing resources in this respect. Where there are gaps in provision this will need to be developed, either as part of the Crime and Disorder Reduction Strategy or as a local authority's response to section 17(1) of the Crime and Disorder Act 1998. In either case it will be essential that parenting classes themselves are not seen as the only solution but will be coupled with material support as well as being incorporated into a more socially inclusive environment.

Conclusion

The Home Secretary's remarks over the last few years on 'squeegee merchants', 'beggars' and 'Travellers' and his views that 'society has been inflicted with a crime breeding 'excuse culture'', (Muncie 1999a, p 148), should concern all those who believe in pluralism, liberal democracy and inclusion. However, to focus on the Home Secretary would be to reduce complex issues to the level of personalised politics, even if this particular Home Secretary, in the context of overseeing *Crime and Disorder Reduction Strategies*, has extended the meaning of 'hands on' *in absurdum*. Similarly, to focus on some of the more retributive rhetoric surrounding the Crime and Disorder Act 1998 may also fail to identify how some partnerships are interpreting youth justice and community safety in very positive ways. Whilst Muncie, (1999a), provides an excellent analysis of the characteristics of the government's agenda and suggests that the Crime and Disorder Act will 'only serve to exacerbate the problems it purports to address and to deny young people access to those very rights it claims to protect', (ibid, p 172), there are at least notions of inclusion within this agenda, as yet little evidenced, which may act as a counterpoint to what appears to be an overall punitive and excluding discourse.

There is some evidence that the interpretation of the community safety agenda at a more local level can embrace inclusion as a principle for policy development. Local community based initiatives however, are not without problems and could be prone to take an introspective view of crime and disorder, ignoring structural inequalities over which they have little control, in particular the growing economic inequality in Britain since the 1960s. The additional powers of Anti Social Behaviour Orders and Local Child Curfew Schemes, are likely to be targeted at poor communities and by definition they will thus be disproportionately deployed in respect of Black children. This raises important questions around the perceptions of justice in a post-Macpherson Britain. There is a need for strategic leadership from central government: an agenda that 'includes a little more and excludes a little less'. Perhaps an agenda that attempts to understand a little more about the causes of crime, and one that spends less time on the classification of risk assessment.

Looking at the ways in which community safety partnerships and Youth Offending Teams are attempting to measure success there are some interesting ideas emerging in relation to tying initiatives into targets that are socially and educationally inclusive. In parallel to this there are developments that indicate some insensitivity to the social constructions of crime, problems of exclusion and the need to support not only those at risk of offending but those at risk of reoffending. Training in community safety will be an urgent requirement for local policy makers and practitioners. However, some questions still remain. Will the joint training courses provided by the Crime Prevention College, Local Government Association and National Police Training College address the difficulties of bringing these two discourses together and the lessons learned from attempts to evaluate community safety and youth justice? Will the launch of the new National Occupational Standards for Community Safety bridge the gap between community safety and 'advanced and specialist work with offending behaviour'?

There is an opportunity for practitioners to influence policy in youth justice much in the same way as practitioners influenced the debate in the early eighties. Added to this, support from practitioners in community safety, drawn from a variety of disciplines and diverse backgrounds, may assist a process whereby the gap between the youth justice and community safety agenda is bridged. It will be an altogether more difficult task to bridge the gap between social policy in this area and the wealth of experience that is currently held by practitioners and academics in the field. We cannot turn the clock back nor should we desire to do so. Young, (1999, p 199), observes that the solution to social exclusion in late modernity does not lie in nostalgia. Contemporary society is where we live, 'dark heart', (Davies, 1998), and all. Realistically, repairing the damage will need to include some element or focus on the short-term view. However, a betrayal based on acceptance of short term oppressive solutions which in turn is based on the premise that the social solutions in place will take a long time to 'kick in', is a promise that has been broken too many times before. It resonates uncannily with the old meta-narratives of oppression. There is no doubt that the present government faces a difficult dilemma in this respect as a failure to deliver on law and order appears not to be an option. In order to avoid the dystopian vision outlined by Hughes, (1998), where communities end up as 'fortress cities' with rampant privatism and growing social exclusion, we need to take the idea of social inclusion seriously. Perhaps the first step will be to undertake realistic evaluations that can tie together the apparently incompatible ideas of social, political and economic inclusion with that of protecting the public.

References

Anderson, B., (1999), Youth, Crime and the Politics of Prevention in Goldson, B., (Ed.), *Youth Justice: Contemporary Policy and Practice,* Aldershot, Ashgate.

Bennett, C., (1999), The Menace of Blair's Drugs Ignorance, in *The Guardian* September 30th 1999, G2: 5

Boateng, P., (1999), Reducing Levels of Crime and Disorder, in *Criminal Justice Management, July, 1999,* Manchester: Partnership Media Group.

Bowling, B., (1999), The Rise and Fall of New York Murder: Zero Tolerance or Crack's Decline?, in *The British Journal of Criminology,* Vol.39 No.4: pp 531–54

Cabinet Office, (1999), *Tackling Drugs to Build a Better Britain: United Kingdom Anti-drugs Co-ordinator's Annual Report 1998/99, United Kingdom Performance Targets for 2008 and 2005, National Plan 1999/2000,* London, Cabinet Office.

Chapman, T. and Hough, M. (1998) *Evidence Based Practice: A Guide to Effective Practice,* HM Inspectorate of Probation, London, Home Office.

Clarke, J. and Newman, J., (1997), *The Managerial State,* London, Sage.

Crawford, A., (1998), *Crime Prevention and Community Safety: Politics, Policies and Practices,* Harlow, Longman.

Davies, N., (1998), *Dark Heart: The Shocking Truth about Hidden Britain,* London, Vintage.

Edmunds, M., May, T., Hearnden, I. and Hough, M., (1998), Arrest Referral: Emerging Lessons from Research, *Drugs Prevention Initiative Paper 23,* London, Home Office.

Ekblom, P., (1994), Proximal Circumstances: A Mechanism-based Classification of Crime Prevention, in *Crime Prevention Studies,* Vol. 2: pp185–232.

Ekblom, P., (1998a), *Community Safety and the Reduction and Prevention of Crime: A Conceptual Framework for Training and the Development of a Professional Discipline,* www.homeoffice.gov.uk/cdact/cstrng5.htm, London, Home Office.

Ekblom, P., (1998b), *The Conjunction of Criminal Opportunity: A Tool for Clear, Joined-up Thinking About Community Safety and Crime Reduction,* London, Home Office.

Etzioni, A., (1995), *The Spirit of Community,* London, Fontana.

Freely, M., (1999), Teaching Mothers a Lesson in *The Guardian,* September 29th: G2.8.

Garland. D., (1999), The Fate of Modern Criminology, Plenary presentation at the *British Criminology Conference* hosted by Liverpool John Moores University July 13th (unpublished).

Giddens, A., (1991), *Modernity and Self-identity: Self and Society in the Late Modern Age*, Cambridge, Polity Press.

Gilling, D., (1996), Crime Prevention in May, T. and Vass, A., (Eds.), *Working with Offenders: Issues, Contexts and Outcomes*, London, Sage.

Gilling, D., (1997), *Crime Prevention, Theory Policy and Politics*, London, UCL Press.

Goldson, B., (1999), Youth (In) Justice: Contemporary Developments in Policy and Practice, in Goldson, B., (Ed.), *Youth Justice: Contemporary Policy and Practice*, Aldershot, Ashgate.

Goldson, B. and Chigwada-Bailey, R., (1999), (What) Justice for Black Children and Young People?, in Goldson, B., (Ed.), *Youth Justice: Contemporary Policy and Practice*, Aldershot, Ashgate.

Hirschfield, A. and Bowers K.J., (1997), The Development of a Social Demographic and Land Use Profiler for Areas of High Crime, *British Journal of Criminology*, Vol.37 No.1: pp103–20.

Hirschfield, A. and Bowers, K.J., (1998), Monitoring, Measuring and Mapping Community Safety, in Marlow, A. and Pitts, J., (Eds.), *Planning Safer Communities*, Lyme Regis, Russell House Publishing.

Home Office, (1998a), *Joining Forces to Protect the Public: Prisons-Probation,* London, Home Office.

Home Office, (1998b), *Guidance on Statutory Crime and Disorder Partnerships. Crime and Disorder Act 1998*. London, Home Office.

Home Office, (1999), *Criminal Justice System Strategic Plan 1999–2002,* Home Office, Lord Chancellor's Department, Attorney General's Office.

Hough, M., (1998), *Evaluating Community Safety Projects,* London, Local Government Information Unit.

Hough, M. and Tilley N., (1998), *Getting the Grease to the Squeak: Research Lessons for Crime Prevention*, London, Home Office.

Hughes, G., (1998), *Understanding Crime Prevention: Social Control, Risk and Late Modernity*, Buckingham, Open University Press.

Koch, B.C.M., (1999), *The Politics of Crime Prevention,* Aldershot, Ashgate.

Lockwood, H., (1999), Evidence-based Practice: Effectively Redefining Practice. *Criminal Justice Management, July 8*, Manchester, Partnership Media Group.

McLaughlin, E., (1994), *Community, Policing and Accountability*, Aldershot, Avebury.

MacDonald, Z., (1999), Illicit Drug Use in the UK: Evidence from the British Crime Survey in *The British Journal of Criminology* Vol.39 No.4: pp 585–608.

MacGregor, S., (1998), Have Drug Action Teams Increased the Safety of Communities? in *Drugs and Community Safety: the Strategic Challenge*, Report of a Local Government Drugs Forum Conference held on 10th December, 1997. London Home Office.

Martinson, R., (1974), What Works? Questions and Answers about Prison Reform, in *Public Interest*, Vol.35: pp 22–45.

Martinson, R., (1979), New Findings, New Views: A Note of Caution Regarding Sentencing Reform, *Hofstra Law Review* Vol.7: pp 234–58.

Morgan, J., (1991), *Safer Communities: The Local Delivery of Crime Prevention Through the Partnership Approach,* London, Home Office.

Muncie, J., (1999a), Institutionalised Intolerance: Youth Justice and the Crime and Disorder Act, in *Critical Social Policy*, Vol.19 No.2 : pp147–73.

Muncie, J., (1999b), Auditing Youth Justice, in *Prison Service Journal*, No. 126: pp 55–60.

NACRO, (1999), *Drug-driven Crime: A Factual and Statistical Analysis*, London, NACRO.

Nellis, M., (1999a), Politics, Probation and the English Language in *Vista: Perspectives on Probation,* Vol.4 No.3: pp 233–40.

Nellis, M., (1999b), *A Question of Degree: The Diploma in Probation Studies and Effective Probation Training*. A Paper presented to the National Probation Research and Information Exchange Conference, Manchester 11th-13th May 1999 (unpublished).

Newburn, T., (1999), Drug Prevention and Youth Justice: Issues of Philosophy, Practice and Policy in *The British Journal of Criminology*, Vol.39 No.4 pp 609–24.

Nuttall, C., (1992), What works?, in *Proceedings of the Annual Conference of the Association of Chief Officers of Probation*.

Poole, M., (1999), *Breaking the Cycle: Widening Parental Participation in Education,* unpublished MA Thesis The University of Nottingham.

Pawson, R. and Tilley, N., (1997), *Realistic Evaluation,* London, Sage.

Radzinowicz, L., (1991), Penal Regressions, in *Cambridge Law Journal*, Vol.50 No.3: pp 422–44.

Ryan, M., (1999), Penal Policy Making Towards the Millennium: Elites and Populists; New Labour and the New Criminology, in *The International Journal of the Sociology of Law*, 1999 Vol. 27, pp1–22.

Smith, M. and Sparks, R., (1999), *Conversations About Punishment: Children as Penal Commentators*, (unpublished paper).

Tilley, N., (1995), *Thinking about Crime Prevention Performance Indicators*, Police Research Group Crime Detection and Prevention Series: Paper No.57 London, Home Office.

Travis, A., (1999a), Testing Time for Crime in *The Guardian*, September 29th, 1999: 23.

Travis, A., (1999b), Figures Undermine Straw's Drug Case in *The Guardian*, October 1st, 1999: 12.

Travis, A., (1999c), Straw's Tough Probation Order in *The Guardian*, December 8th, 1999: 8.

Ward, L., (1999), Police to Get New Drug Test Powers in *The Guardian* September 27th 1999: 1&3.

Worrall, A., (1997), *Punishment in the Community: The Future of Criminal Justice,* Harlow, Addison Wesley Longman.

Worrall, A., (1999), Troubled or Troublesome? Justice for Girls and Young Women, in Goldson, B., (Ed.), *Youth Justice: Contemporary Policy and Practice,* Aldershot, Ashgate.

Young, J., (1999), *The Exclusive Society*, London, Sage.

CHAPTER 11

Victims of Crime and the New Youth Justice

Brian Williams

Introduction

Victims of crime are a politically popular group, and an increasingly powerful one. Politicians have been quick to take account of these facts, and the balance between offenders and victims has altered correspondingly. The Labour government elected in 1997 showed no sign of reversing the 'vicious incarceration spiral', (Dignan, 1999a, p 53), favoured by its Conservative predecessor, and its ministers have consistently emphasised the importance of punishing offenders, holding young offenders and their parents responsible for crime, and improving the level of victims' satisfaction with the criminal justice process, (Home Office, 1997; Dignan, 1999a). This raises some concerns in respect of the rights of young offenders.

This chapter reviews recent legal and policy changes affecting young offenders and their victims, and raises some practical and ethical issues in relation to Reparation Orders and the other new Orders. The pace of change in youth justice has been extremely fast since 1997, and there is a danger that politically motivated changes are implemented without proper preparation or evaluation. Practitioners are in a position to influence such evaluative work, if they make appropriate demands upon the local researchers funded by the Youth Justice Board for England and Wales and point out the contradictions they come across in their daily practice. Some of the evidence needed for such debates is provided here.

Victims: the new order

Youth Offending Teams' new responsibilities in respect of victims of crime have their origins in the Major government's *Victim's Charter*, (Home Office, 1990; 1996), first published in 1990, (Mawby and Walklate, 1994). It set out some suggestions about how agencies working with adult offenders might make their procedures and practice more sensitive to the needs of victims of crime. It was a weak, tentative document and it was widely ignored. This caused considerable resentment among victims' organisations, with good practice developing in isolated pockets and nothing changing at all elsewhere. Political pressure was brought to bear, and the *Charter* was strengthened and reissued in 1996, (Home

Office, 1996). The new version made explicit demands on the police, probation and prosecution services. In particular, it required the police to keep victims informed of the progress of cases against 'their' offenders, and it introduced a system under which victims' views are sought before people serving long prison sentences are released.

The police have been dilatory in implementing the new requirements in some parts of the country, but they have done so diligently elsewhere, (Mawby and Walklate, 1994; Williams, 1999). There is a view in some quarters that it is a good idea to treat victims well, because this will improve their performance as witnesses at court. Where this idea has taken root, the service provided by the police to victims has improved correspondingly. Elsewhere, it seems to be a matter for individual officers' discretion whether they keep victims informed of developments in criminal cases. For many busy police officers, it is a relatively low priority (Williams, 1999).

Probation officers were charged with a new responsibility for ascertaining victims' views as part of the parole process in relation to more serious adult offenders, defined, for these purposes, as those sentenced to four years' imprisonment or longer. Although the new system did not give victims a veto on offenders' release, it has changed the balance of power between victims and serious offenders. Victims' concerns influence parole conditions in many cases, and offenders are no longer allowed to go and live near their victims on release in cases where victims are expressing serious concerns, or making threats. Pre-Sentence Reports (PSRs) are also changing in response to the *Charter*. PSR authors are now required to include information about the impact of offences upon victims, where this is available, and probation officers and youth justice workers increasingly try to instil victim awareness in the offenders they supervise. This occurs both in individual interviews and in group work settings.

The new victim orientation was a substantial cultural change for probation and youth justice staff, who had traditionally seen themselves as part of an offender-orientated service, (Kosh and Williams, 1995). In some ways, such change was overdue: many workers have welcomed the new emphasis on victims because it makes it possible to confront offending behaviour more effectively. It also brings into the open issues such as male violence, preventing male workers from colluding with abuse by arguing that it is irrelevant to the individual's supervision plan, (see Mullender, 1996, p 211). In group work with sexual offenders, too, the new emphasis on victims has been welcomed because it provides legitimation for current thinking about offenders' attitudes to victims and the need to unpick these as part of a group work or individual supervision programme, (Beech, 1997; Spencer, 1999).

The change was painful in practice, however, because it was introduced hurriedly, without much warning, and at a time of substantial financial cuts in the probation service. Untrained, overburdened staff were suddenly allocated victim contact work in some areas, and there were predictable difficulties. That said, these have mostly been overcome remarkably quickly. In many areas, probation work with victims is now a specialism, and staff have been able to build up expertise and a network of contacts with other agencies. Although still under-staffed and particularly short of qualified probation officers, the service seems to be keeping on top of this demanding new work, (Crawford and Enterkin, 1999).

These developments form part of the background to the new concern with victims in youth justice. Pre-Sentence Reports for the Youth Court have also changed, to incorporate information about victims, and the Crime and Disorder Act 1998 introduced Reparation Orders (discussed below). Probation staff with experience of working with victims have become members of some Youth Offending Teams, and YOTs will be able to draw upon the probation experience in developing their practice.

Another major contextual issue is the growing popularity of family group conferences, (Jackson, 1999). Drawing upon traditional Maori ideas of justice, the family group conference provides opportunities for 'reintegrative shaming', (Braithwaite, 1989). Bringing together offenders, victims, the family and supporters of each, and a trained co-ordinator, the family group conference aims to resolve the issues between the offender and victim. The aim is to confront the offender with the consequences of the crime, and then move on. Offenders are given an opportunity to put right some of the wrong they have done, and to take pride in having the courage to do so. The role of the professional social worker is reduced in order to leave the resolution of disputes and offences within the community in which they arise. The family group conference approach was first used in the UK in the context of child welfare cases. The professionals seem to have found it hard, at least at first, to stand back and let the participants make their own decisions, and agencies do not always find the resources necessary to implement conferences' decisions. Nevertheless, family group conferences are generally agreed to have achieved at least a limited success in the context of family cases, (Lupton and Nixon, 1999).

Conferencing was also used in New Zealand and Australia with offenders from 1989, and experiments began in England in the mid-1990s, (Spencer, 1997). The best-publicised of these, sponsored by Thames Valley Police, was hailed as a great success, although the claims made about reductions in reconviction rates were somewhat implausible. Family Group Conferences for young offenders were championed by penal reform agencies as well as the police, and the pilot projects were promoted and supported by NACRO and the Family Rights Group, (NACRO, 1995). These developments occurred at a time when there seemed little hope of positive change in the law relating to young offenders. Instead, elements of the New Zealand model were incorporated into the existing youth justice system. In the Thames Valley, the model was substantially adapted. Since 1998, the cautioning system there has incorporated 'Restorative Conferences' which are police-led rather than employing independent co-ordinators to balance the interests of the various parties, (Jackson, 1999). This approach has subsequently been supported by the Home Secretary, (Dignan, 1999a).

When youth justice legislation was introduced by the new government in the form of the Crime and Disorder Act 1998, it showed little sign of being influenced by developments in New Zealand. However, it was closely followed by the Youth Justice and Criminal Evidence Act 1999, which introduced Youth Offender Panels for first offenders who plead guilty. The Panels, which will be piloted in 2000–2001 and fully implemented in 2002 or 2003, incorporate some elements of the Family Group Conference approach. However, these restorative approaches are grafted onto the existing bureaucratic, conflictual Youth Court system, rather than replacing it, (Haines, this volume).

Victims and the new youth justice

Reparation Orders
Reparation Orders and other restorative measures were thoroughly piloted in four Youth Offending Teams during the 18 months prior to the implementation of the 1998 Act, and the initial findings of an independent evaluation were made available to the pilot areas at a relatively early stage, (Dignan, 1999). They raised a number of important policy and practice issues.

The probation experience had shown the importance of adequate preparatory training before staff trained to work with *offenders* became responsible for *victim* contact, (Williams, 1999a). Workers needed to think about and debate the implications of the new victim orientation. Agencies, in turn, had to adapt procedures to make them more appropriate for work with victims. The practicalities of working with victims had to be considered, and in many cases new resources were required. Such resources were not necessarily provided in practice, however, (Jackson, 1999). Reading between the lines of Dignan's evaluative study, it would appear that the pilot schemes upon which he particularly focused got off to rather a difficult start. Some of the prerequisites for effective work, such as appropriate staff training, were not in place. Some of the issues on which clarity was needed from the start were still being addressed almost a year after the beginning of the pilots. For example, the interim report draws attention to the lack of sufficient trained mediation and reparation workers, difficulties with confidentiality, failure in some cases to consult victims about reparative interventions, and insufficient preparation prior to reparative interventions, (Dignan, 1999). Most of the practice issues should perhaps have been anticipated. Rigorous procedures and clear agency policies might have prevented some of the problems. However, they should not arise to the same extent in future, as many of the issues are covered by the new National Standards for Youth Justice, (Youth Justice Board, 1999).

The experience of the pilot projects may help others to avoid making some of the same mistakes. For example, Dignan draws attention to the need for time to be spent in preparatory work with both victims and offenders before setting up reparative activities. He points out that court staff and sentencers need to be convinced of the value of these preparations. While there is widespread recognition among the professional and voluntary agencies of the need to prepare victims and offenders for contact with each other, this concept needs 'selling' to the courts. This is therefore another group requiring training in the principles underlying reparation, if Reparation Orders are to be successfully introduced. Dignan suggests that the need is for training in 'the restorative justice ethos that underlies the Crime and Disorder Act'. This is debatable however.

Sentencers will only allow sufficient time for proper preparation for reparation if they understand why it is required. Convincing them that victims should be given time to decide whether they want to get involved in reparation is likely to be a substantial task. It challenges the government's policy of rewarding courts for 'fast tracking' and dealing with cases more quickly, (Williams, 1999b). It also requires a focus on victims' needs which is relatively new in the Youth Courts, and which may on occasion raise issues about the appropriate balance between the rights of victims and those of young offenders. It is all very well to assert, as the Restorative Justice Consortium does, (1998, p 9), that 'Criminal justice processes should allow adequate time for victims to decide whether to participate in a restorative justice programme'. In practice, victims' needs may have to compete with those of others, including offenders. In any event, Youth Offending Teams will clearly need to debate these issues with Youth Court magistrates and clerks at an early stage. If victims feel that they have been steamrollered into taking part in reparation, it is unlikely to be very successful, (Tudor, 1999; Jervis, 1996).

However little time is available to prepare for reparative activities, Dignan's recommendation that 'victims should routinely be consulted' is disturbing. It suggests that, in the pilot schemes he studied, this was not always the case. He goes on to recommend that 'Courts must ensure that victims have been consulted and have given their consent *before* requiring an offender to undertake any form of direct reparative activity to a victim'. This strongly implies that the rights of victims and offenders alike have been ignored in the pilot areas, at least on occasion. The Crime and Disorder Act clearly states that 'a reparation order shall not require the offender … to make reparation to any person without the consent of that person', (s. 67 (5) (b)). Similarly, there are references in Dignan's report to offenders being asked to apologise to victims where there had been no finding of guilt. There are important principles at stake here. If the courts' enthusiasm for reparation leads them to impose Orders illegally, defendants should be encouraged to appeal. The new National Standards make it clear that victims' wishes must always be respected.

Where reparation schemes propose to assess young people prior to conviction, this should be resisted. As one researcher put it, reflecting upon the experience of the pilot areas:

> *It would be lamentable if a system designed to empower children and their families actually served to disavail them of some of their fundamental civil rights.*

(Jackson, 1999, p 141).

Reparation Orders are administered by inter-agency Youth Offending Teams. There has been a tendency to assume that the police have the most expertise in working with victims, and some pilot and 'shadow' Youth Offending Teams left the police representative in the Team to do the development work. This is a risky strategy for a number of reasons. First, because the record of the police in supporting victims and keeping them informed of the progress of cases is extremely patchy, (Williams, 1999). Second, because there is a need to involve victim support agencies in the planning of reparation work, and in many areas relationships between the police and some of these agencies are poor, except in the case of Victim Support. Youth Offending Teams need to establish good relations not only with Victim Support, but also with other local victim agencies such as Women's Aid refuges, Rape Crisis centres, racial equality campaigns, Support After Murder and Manslaughter groups, and so on. These groups tend to come into conflict with the police, because they are campaigning organisations as well as service providers, (Williams, 1999b). Establishing initial links with them might not be a task best undertaken by police officers. Third, there is a case for building upon the existing skills and experience of health, probation and social work staff within Youth Offending Teams. If they do not have direct experience of working with victims of crime, they will in many cases have transferable skills. Arguably, they all need to understand the principles underlying reparative work. Staff with such an understanding will be better equipped to protect the interests and rights of offenders and victims. A service co-ordinated by a Youth Offending Team member would seem likely to be better able to integrate provision than one which had been handed over to another agency such as the police, (Williams, 1999a; Fordham, 1999).

In certain areas, Youth Offending Teams have attempted to 'contract out' their work with victims to voluntary organisations. Allocating such work to local victim agencies is opposed by Victim Support national office on the grounds that the local statutory services should take full responsibility for the duties which have been allocated to them by law. Victim Support also argues that it is not for victims or their representative organisations to take on the role of working to change the attitudes of offenders, (see Reeves and Wright, 1995). In some areas, however, existing mediation schemes were willing to take on the work, (as in Sheffield and Wolverhampton: see Dignan, 1999). Teams may have reservations about the appropriateness of handing such potentially controversial, sensitive and demanding work over completely to voluntary agencies. It can, however, be done effectively in partnership. The experience of mediation schemes has been important in developing reparative work in some of the pilot areas, not least because of their clarity about ethical issues. For example, they have resisted offering reparative interventions to obviously unwilling victims. They have also been clear about the circumstances in which mediation may be appropriate – broadly, where victims are likely to find it helpful in resolving the emotional effects of offences. 'They are interested in receiving acknowledgement of their experience, an apology and an assurance that the offence will not be repeated by the offender', (Fordham, 1999).

There may be much to be said for ensuring that all youth justice staff develop victim awareness, which is likely to influence the way in which they carry out the 'core' work of the Youth Offending Team. For example, direct work with victims has changed the ways in which many probation officers prepare Pre-Sentence Reports and carry out individual and group supervision. Many youth justice workers are initially very apprehensive about becoming involved in work with victims, but in practice they go on to find it rewarding and professionally helpful. Unfortunately, despite the phased implementation of the Crime and Disorder Act 1998 and the opportunity to learn from the pilot areas, many Youth Offending Team staff have had little time to prepare for implementing the new Orders. It is hardly surprising that in some Teams people have tended to 'keep their heads down' and concentrate on what they see as the core tasks: court duty, report preparation and individual supervision.

In some Youth Offending Teams, the former youth justice workers and probation officers, as qualified social workers, have been left to get on with this core work while others have developed the new court Orders. This may lead to subsequent conflict, if decisions have been taken without consultation, or if issues of professional ethics have been neglected. There may also be a perception that the new staff from health, police, education, youth service and the voluntary agencies get all the 'glamorous' tasks while the social and probation workers get on with the routine job.

Action Plan Orders
Action Plan Orders place young offenders under supervision for three months. They may include certain conditions, one of which is 'to make reparation specified in the requirements or directions to a person or persons so specified or to the community at large', (Crime and Disorder Act 1998, s. 69 (5) (f)). It is explicitly stated that direct reparation can only be ordered where the victim consents to it, (s. 69 (8)). The Orders are presumably intended to be more focused and intensive than a Supervision Order, given their relative brevity. They were introduced as a replacement for repeated cautioning, (Jackson, 1999). It would therefore seem important to limit the extent of the demands made upon young people who are

placed on such Orders. Otherwise, there is a danger that a brief reparative intervention may be seen as having been tried and failed, pushing individuals 'up-tariff' if they appear in court again subsequently. The Restorative Justice Consortium, (1999, p 13) argues that:

> *Criminal justice agencies need to recognise that successful reform cannot be initiated immediately or on all occasions. Given the immensity of some of the problems underlying crime, attempts at reintegration need to be made at each point of intervention, even if previous attempts have failed.*

This seems sensible and straightforward in principle, and it goes some way towards justifying the recurrence of reparative provisions at different stages of the youth justice process under the Act. However, there is more than enough evidence that intervening too soon can lead to young people being labelled in an unhelpful way, (Pitts, 1999; Goldson, 1997). Indeed, the Audit Commission in *Misspent Youth*, (1996), explicitly called for greater use of cautioning, which the 1998 Act abolishes altogether, and more diversion, which is replaced with a plethora of new court Orders, including those discussed here.

The inclusion of reparation in Action Plan Orders is a matter of some concern to experienced practitioners, because it requires the investment of considerable resources, and sucks young people into the formal criminal justice system, at an early stage. Rigorous gatekeeping will be needed to ration the proposing and making of conditions of reparation.

Reparation as a condition of Supervision Orders

The Crime and Disorder Act 1998 also provides for reparation as a new condition in Supervision Orders, (under s. 71). This accords with the principle of attempting reparative interventions at every non-custodial stage in the system, as discussed in the previous section. It also provides a further cause for breach proceedings, with a provision in such cases for re-sentencing the young person for the original offence. In some cases, this may mean that young people are propelled into custody for failing to undertake reparative work. It will therefore be very important that PSR writers ensure that there are good grounds for proposing such conditions. Supervisors will need to ensure that reparative interventions are well planned and that young people are properly supported in seeing them through. The consent and involvement of victims will be important in appropriate cases, and the wholehearted commitment of the young person will be required.

Pre-Sentence Reports

While the law in respect of Pre-Sentence Reports remains unchanged, new National Standards to be issued by the Youth Justice Board make it clear that all PSRs must include a section headed 'Effect on Victim'. The National Standards in respect of adult offenders go into more detail, requiring that the 'Offence

Analysis' section of every PSR should 'assess ... what is known of the impact on any victim' and 'assess the offender's attitude to the offence and awareness of its consequences, including to any victim'. The expectation that Pre-Sentence Reports should explore young offenders' attitudes towards their victims, and include some information about the level of loss or damage sustained by victims, has developed gradually in recent years. It has come to be commonly agreed that at least the impact of the offence upon the victim should always be described if the information is available. The good practice guidance issued by the National Association for Youth Justice, for example, says that the 'Offence Analysis' should include the young person's perception of the offence:

> *...taking account of the impact on the victim; the actual harm, damage or cost of the offence; any expressed remorse or guilt...*
>
> (NAYJ, 1998, para. 8 (b) (iv) of 'Pre-Sentence Reports' section).

The availability of information has been a persistent problem, however. Bundles of documents provided to report writers by the Crown Prosecution Service (CPS) should include detailed information obtained from victims, but this is not always available in time to be included in a PSR and discussed with the young person who is the subject of the report. It is not appropriate for report writers to approach victims directly for information, and there is, as yet, no provision for separate victim impact statements to be prepared, although there have been recent experiments with such documents in respect of adult offenders. Local arrangements for obtaining information from the CPS therefore need to be improved where this remains a problem.

It is important that victim information is used with care. It would be wrong for offenders to be punished more severely because of the unanticipated vulnerability of a particular victim. Courts may legitimately take into account the deliberate selection of victims who, for one reason or another, are obviously vulnerable. If, for example, an offender targets confused elderly victims for offences of theft by deception, this is likely to lead to a more severe sentence. But it is easy to envisage situations where two similar offences might result in very different sentences because of the availability of victim information in one case and not the other. Likewise, it is conceivable that two identical offences might have widely differing levels of impact upon their victims for reasons of which the offender was unaware. For example, the theft of a car belonging to a shift worker might make them vulnerable to losing their job. Domestic burglary has a significant, long-term impact on a minority of victims. Some victims suffer little loss because they are insured, while others cannot afford insurance. Should 'their' offenders be treated more severely as a result? Clearly not, except perhaps where compensation is concerned. Report writers need to be circumspect in using victim information, taking care not to draw unjustified conclusions from it. Where possible, victim information should be put in context: if the documents show that a victim was particularly vulnerable, it may be appropriate to show that the offender was unaware of this fact.

In many cases, a Pre-Sentence Report will be dealing with a small number of offences which are part of a larger picture. Reports writers are used to dealing with this situation, but it raises new questions in relation to victims. Clearly, only those victims affected by the offences for which the young person is currently before the court can be consulted about the possibility of making Reparation Orders. Dignan, (1999), found that some courts were reluctant to adjourn cases for consultation with victims before making Reparation Orders, and negotiations between Youth Offending Teams and magistrates in liaison meetings may be required before this will change. The likelihood that some cases will involve a number of victims complicates matters further.

Racially-aggravated offences
The Crime and Disorder Act 1998 introduced the concept of 'racially-aggravated offences', (in sections 28–32 and 82). The new offences are racially-aggravated assault, criminal damage, harassment and a variety of public order offences. Although this has been broadly welcomed by penal reform and race relations organisations, (Iganski, 1999), the new offences carry substantial fines and imprisonment as well as community penalties. This would seem likely to mean that some young offenders who would previously have been placed under supervision will instead be fined or, in more serious cases, by-pass community penalties altogether. The government seems to have decided to take 'declaratory' measures in order to 'crack down' on racially-motivated offenders, creating the impression that something is being done, (Brennan, 1999; Iganski, 1999), without thinking through the consequences of making more severe sentences available to the courts.

Much will depend in practice upon the willingness of the police and crown prosecutors to identify racially-motivated offences as such. There is some evidence that levels of understanding of the new provisions are poor – indeed, in some areas, white young people have already been prosecuted under the new provisions for offensive remarks made to police officers. Previous provisions for harsher sentencing in the case of racially-aggravated offences have been inconsistently applied, (Sibbitt, 1997; Iganski, 1999). Further problems arise from the Act's failure to change the existing case law on the definition of an 'ethnic group'. At present, Jews and Rastafarians enjoy legal protection, albeit limited, which is denied, for example, to Moslems, (Brennan, 1999).

If the new offences under sections 28–32 of the Act are used appropriately, this will provide greater scope for intervention by Youth Offending Teams. Racist motivation is consistently played down by the police, crown prosecutors and defence lawyers, (Home Office, 1994; Dixon and Okitikpi, 1999), and the fact that victims of violence or criminal damage are black is often simply not seen as relevant. In some parts of the country, however, dealing with racially-motivated offenders has recently come to be seen as part of the work of crime prevention partnerships, (Edwards, 1999). The Macpherson report on the inquiry into the murder of Stephen Lawrence stressed the need for inter-agency partnerships in countering racist violence, not least in order to ensure that information about organised racism is shared, (Macpherson, 1999). Youth Offending Teams clearly have a part to play in formulating and implementing local strategies, and in providing appropriate group work as a condition of supervision. Staff working with racially-motivated offenders need to be well-informed and well supported. Training materials which have recently been prepared for use with adult offenders, (Kay et al, 1999), and for youth workers, (Lorenz, 1996), can perhaps be adapted for individual and group work with young offenders.

Victim awareness work is likely to be difficult to undertake with young offenders with entrenched racist views. Some workers will not wish to attempt it in one-to-one supervision. There are also likely to be difficulties in bringing groups of racially-motivated offenders together. It is probably more appropriate to include issues of racially-motivated offending and the effects upon victims in general sessions on victim awareness. Black YOT members and black service users should not be put in the position of having to take responsibility for challenging the racist views of white offenders. There is experience of good practice in victim awareness work with individual adult offenders and in groups which addresses race issues on which Youth Offending Teams can draw, (Kay et al., 1999).

Referral Orders
Under the Youth Justice and Criminal Evidence Act 1999, most young offenders prosecuted for the first time will be referred to a Youth Offender Panel, which will:

> *...provide a constructive forum for the young offender to confront the consequences of crime and agree a programme of meaningful activity to prevent any further offending.*

> (Home Office, 1999).

The exceptions are offences which merit only an absolute discharge, and offences so serious that custody is being considered, along with Hospital Order cases. The intention is that Panels will be introduced, after piloting, in 2002 or 2003. They will include a single representative of the local Youth Offending Team and at least two local community representatives. Victims who wish to do so will be invited to attend Panel meetings to discuss offences and the details of reparation packages with young offenders. Offenders' parents will be 'expected' to attend, along with 'other influential adults', but no lawyers will be involved. Whether or not victims take part, there is an expectation that the programmes agreed by Panels will include some form of reparation, although this will be indirect in many cases, (Home Office, 1999). Referral Orders will last for three to twelve months, and they cannot be combined with any other sentence, although they can include compensation orders and exclusion from football matches.

These arrangements have clearly been influenced by Family Group Conferences, but they are different in a number of important ways. Although the power of youth justice professionals is likely to be somewhat reduced by the involvement of community representatives, Panel meetings seem unlikely to be as focused on the community resolution of offences as Family Group Conferences. The Youth Offending Team is given the responsibility of monitoring individuals' compliance with the packages of compensation, reparation, community work, attendance at courses or groups, school attendance, being at home by a particular time and other conditions agreed by Panels. The Youth Offending Team representative will presumably also be responsible for taking breach action in cases of non-compliance: there are re-sentencing provisions in such cases. The implication that parents can be compelled to attend also reinforces the preoccupation with 'parental responsibility' which has characterised so much recent political discourse about youth offending, (Brown, 1998; Jackson, 1999; Drakeford and McCarthy, this volume). Whereas Family Group Conferences assume the willing involvement of young people's families, the underlying assumption with Referral Orders is that this may need to be coerced. By implication, young offenders' families are seen as part of the problem rather than contributing to the solution. Similarly, the blanket requirement that reparation should be part of every programme agreed by Panels reduces the flexibility of the process in favour of a more standardised approach. It seems that reparation is seen as such a good thing that all first offenders should partake in it.

In practice, some victims will not want to take part in Youth Offender Panels. The experience of victim-offender mediation and reparation to-date suggests that careful provision needs to be made to ensure that victims are not 'bounced' into unwilling involvement in reparative activities, (Dignan, 1999; King and Piper, 1995). The ways in which attendance at Panels is presented to victims and other participants will clearly be very important. There should be no direct or implied pressure to attend. Unfortunately, the trend towards fast-tracking young offenders through the system creates pressure to deal with cases quickly. Youth Offending Team representatives will need to be particularly vigilant in ensuring that this does not translate into pressure on victims who would prefer to stay away, to become involved in Panels. It is also important that sufficient time is given to preparing victims for Panel meetings where they do agree to attend. Many victims will need time to think about whether or not to attend. This may be hard to guarantee in the era of accelerated youth justice, but the new National Standards at least require staff administering restorative conferences to undertake recognised training courses. This may well influence the arrangements for Panel meetings, (Home Office, 1999; Youth Justice Board, 1999).

Witness protection

As well as introducing changes to the way in which young offenders are dealt with, Part Two of the Youth Justice and Criminal Evidence Act 1999 also provides new protection to vulnerable witnesses and victims, including young people. Complainants in cases relating to sexual offences, and all witnesses aged under 17, will be eligible for a range of special measures. These include screens which prevent the witness seeing the defendant, cross-examination and evidence using video, the removal of lawyers' wigs and gowns, and the giving of evidence in private. Child witnesses will also be eligible to give evidence through an approved intermediary in certain cases. Eligibility for all these special measures is decided at pre-trial hearings. Restrictions on reporting of cases involving alleged juvenile offenders and witnesses will also be extended, (Home Office, 1999a).

These changes result from a consultation exercise carried out in 1998, (Home Office, 1998; Scottish Office, 1998), and the law has been amended unusually quickly. No implementation dates have yet been announced, and some of the new measures are to be piloted first. Some provisions, such as those relating to cross-examination by live video link, may have to wait until funding has been found to adapt court-rooms. The legislation contains a provision for courts to sit 'at a place appointed' with live video link facilities. This need not be a court-room and need not even be within the court's Petty Sessional Division area, (Baird, 1999). These arrangements seem unlikely to be much used, however: they would cause courts considerable inconvenience.

The increased reporting restrictions and some of the other measures probably arose from Home Office concern about criticism of the UK's treatment of young offenders by international agencies. In certain cases, the practice in Youth Courts in England and Wales contravened international conventions to which the government had signed up, (Howard League, 1999). All the same, these changes will significantly improve the rights of young people appearing in court, whether as witnesses or defendants. They make it unlikely that the abuses of procedures which occurred in the Bulger case, (Scraton, 1997), will be repeated while the legislation remains in force. Generally speaking, they improve the position of vulnerable witnesses without impinging upon the rights of offenders. Sadly, the same cannot be said of most of the other changes reviewed above.

Victims, young offenders and the new youth justice

The discourse of 'restorative justice' has become fashionable in youth justice circles. In reality, there is no real prospect of genuinely restorative justice being introduced in England and Wales. A youth justice system based on conflict between the prosecution and the defence remains substantially unaffected by the addition of reparation as an extra sentencing option. In New Zealand, the formal criminal justice system is largely by-passed by restorative processes which replace court hearings. In England and Wales, however, these processes are 'bolted on' to an otherwise unchanged retributive sentencing system. Reparation thus becomes part of the 'tariff' of formal interventions, rather than an alternative to them. Whether or not one believes, with John Braithwaite, (Braithwaite and Mugford, 1994, p168), that Family Group Conferences 'narrow ... the nets of social control' in Australasia, it is clear that they will not do so here. As Gordon Hughes has pointedly written,

> *It has as yet to be shown that re-integrative shaming will not be mobilised against the most vulnerable sections of ... society and indeed be employed for trivial offenders without any reduction in the use of traditional custodial sentences.*

> (Hughes, 1996, p 35).

There is a real danger that the practical effect of the range of new court Orders will be that more young people are criminalised, both by becoming part of the caseloads of Youth Offending Teams and by being made subject to such Orders. This has important implications in terms of labelling: placing more young people under statutory supervision means widening the net of social control and increasing the proportion of minor young offenders with criminal records, (Goldson, this volume). Further down the road, those who fail to meet the demands of these Orders will have to be returned to court. More young offenders facing breach action is bound to lead to a further increase in the use of custodial penalties, (Monaghan, this volume). The rhetoric of restorative justice should not disguise the punitive intent underlying this legislation, although many people have welcomed what they see as the 'diversionary' provisions of the Crime and Disorder Act: senior agency managers interviewed about the legislation expressed a wide range of views about its implications. A good proportion said that the Act encourages diversion, despite the net-widening aspects discussed earlier, (see Bailey and Williams, forthcoming). In reality, it switches resources from intensive work with persistent young offenders to:

> *...massive over-involvement with petty and minor delinquents, and a major growth of residential and custodial sanctions which inevitable create disaffected youth who re-offend more.*

> (Jones, 1996, p 5).

Involving victims of crime in youth justice can only be justified if their rights and those of offenders are protected, and if there is a real possibility that both groups will benefit from their involvement. There are signs that victims have, once again, been cynically used to improve the presentation of punitive criminal justice policies, (Elias, 1993; Williams, 1999b). Changes which are not based on respect for the rights of both parties cannot honestly be characterised as promoting restorative justice.

Some academic commentators have nevertheless suggested that a restorative justice ethos underpins the government's youth justice policies and legislation, (see Dignan, 1999; Spencer, 1997; James and Raine, 1998). The legislation seems to reflect a desire to appease both the restorative justice lobby and just deserts campaigners. If it were intended to put restorative justice principles into practice, the new legal framework would have avoided the creation of so many new court Orders, each backed with punitive responses to failures to comply. It would, instead, have placed victim-offender reparation at the front end of the system. It would have accepted the need for delay in dealing with offenders in order to allow time to build consensus around restorative solutions to the problems they create. Most of all, it would have marginalised the courts, the prisons and the secure units, and it would have fundamentally changed attitudes towards victims in the criminal justice process. There is little sign of any commitment to such strategies on the government's part.

The new emphasis on reparation does, all the same, open up some space for discussion of these issues. In practice, it also allows youth justice workers to engage with victims, and to make victim awareness more central to their work with young offenders. In the longer term, the experience of implementing Reparation Orders and the panoply of other reparative interventions may lead to a reappraisal of the place of the victim in the youth justice process. Practitioners meanwhile face the task of making sense of these new Orders and operating them in ethical ways, a job made no easier by the confusion about the true purpose of the legislation.

References

Audit Commission, (1996), *Misspent Youth: Young People and Crime*. London, Audit Commission.

Bailey, R. and Williams, B., (forthcoming) Inter-agency Partnerships in Youth Justice. Sheffield: University of Sheffield/Community Care Social Services Monographs.

Baird, V., (1999), Youth Justice and Criminal Evidence Act 1999: Part 2, Legal Action December, 1999, pp 15–6.

Beech, A. R., (1997), Community-based Sex Offender Treatment Provision: An Evaluation by the STEP Team in Holden, C. and Hayman, S., (Eds.), Treating Sex Offenders in a Custodial Setting. London, ISTD.

Braithwaite, J., (1989), *Crime, Shame and Reintegration*. Cambridge, Cambridge University Press.

Braithwaite, J. and Mugford, S., (1994), Conditions of Successful Reintegration Ceremonies: Dealing with Young Offenders, *British Journal of Criminology*, 34 (2) pp139–71.

Brennan, F., (1999), Racially Motivated Crime: The Response of the Criminal Justice System, *Criminal Law Review* January pp17–28.

Brown, S., (1998), Understanding Youth and Crime: Listening to Youth?. Buckingham, Open University Press.

Crawford, A. and Enterkin, J., (1999), Victim Contact Work and the Probation Service: a Study of Service Delivery and Impact. Leeds, University of Leeds Centre for Criminal Justice Studies.

Dignan, J., (1999), Draft Interim Report on the Reparative Work being Undertaken by Youth Offending Teams. Sheffield: University of Sheffield.

Dignan, J., (1999a), The Crime and Disorder Act and the Prospects for Restorative Justice, *Criminal Law Review* January.

Dixon, L. and Okitikpi, T., (1999), Working with Racially Motivated Offenders: Practice Issues *Probation Journal* 46 (3) pp157–63.

Edwards, R., (1999), Working with Racially Motivated Offenders, *Probation Journal* 46 (1) pp37–9.

Elias, R., (1993), Victims Still: The Political Manipulation of Crime Victims. London, Sage.

Fordham, C., (1999), Personal communication with the author from member of staff at Sheffield Youth Offending Team, 29th November.

Goldson, B., (1997), Children in Trouble: State Responses to Juvenile Crime, in Scraton, P., (Ed.), *'Childhood' in 'Crisis'?*. London, UCL Press.

Home Office, (1990), *Victim's Charter: A Statement of the Rights of Victims of Crime*. London, Home Office.

Home Office, (1994), *Racially Motivated Crime: A British Crime Survey Analysis*. Research and Planning Unit Paper no. 2. London, Home Office.

Home Office, (1996), *The Victim's Charter: A Statement of Service Standards for Victims of Crime*. London, Home Office Communications Directorate.

Home Office, (1997), *No More Excuses: A New Approach to Tackling Youth Crime in England and Wales*. Cm. 3809. London, HMSO.

Home Office, (1998), *Speaking Up for Justice: Report of the Interdepartmental Working Group on the Treatment of Vulnerable or Intimidated Witnesses in the Criminal Justice System*. London, Home Office.

Home Office, (1999), *Referral Orders: a Short Guide*, Home Office Juvenile Offenders Unit website http: //www.homeoffice.gov.uk/yousys/referral.htm.

Home Office, (1999a), *Youth Justice and Criminal Evidence Act Part 2*: Criminal Evidence, Home Office website http: //www.homeoffice.gov.uk/yjceact/crimevint.htm.

Howard League, (1999), *Protecting the Rights of Children*, briefing paper prepared for the UN Committee on the Rights of the Child. London, Howard League for Penal Reform.

Hughes, G., (1996), Communitarianism and Law and Order, *Critical Social Policy*, 49 pp17–41.

Iganski, P., (1999), Why Make 'Hate' a Crime?, *Critical Social Policy*, 19 (3) pp 386–95.

Jackson, S. E., (1999), *Family Group Conferences and Youth Justice: the New Panacea*? in Goldson, B., (Ed.), Youth Justice: Contemporary Policy and Practice. Aldershot, Ashgate.

James, A. and Raine, J., (1998), *The New Politics of Criminal Justice*. London, Longman.

Jervis, B., (1996), *Developing Reparation Plans through Victim-offender Mediation by New Zealand Probation Officers*, in Galaway, B. and Hudson, J., (Eds.), Restorative Justice: International Perspectives. Amsterdam, Kugler Publications.

Jones, D., (1996), *Tough on Crime and Nasty to Children*, Prison Report 36 pp 4–5.

Kay, J. et al., (1999), *From Murmur to Murder: A Resource Pack for Probation Officers and Others*. Birmingham, West Midlands Probation Training Consortium.

King, M. and Piper, C., (1995), *How the Law thinks about Children*. Second edition. Aldershot, Arena.

Kosh, M. and Williams, B., (1995), *The Probation Service and Victims of Crime: A Pilot Study*. Keele, Keele University Press.

Lorenz, W., (1996), *Practical Activities for Anti-racist Work* in Aluffi-Pentini, A. and Lorenz, W., (Eds.), Anti-racist Work with Young People. Lyme Regis, Russell House Press.

Lupton, C. and Nixon, P., (1999), *Empowering Practice? A Critical Appraisal of the Family Group Conference Approach*. Bristol, Policy Press.

Macpherson, W., (1999), *The Stephen Lawrence Inquiry Report*. Cm. 4262. London, HMSO.

Mawby, R. I. and Walklate, S., (1994), *Critical Victimology: International Perspectives*. London, Sage.

Mullender, A., (1996), *Rethinking Domestic Violence: The Social Work and Probation Response*. London: Routledge.

Muncie, J., (1999), *Youth and Crime: A Critical Introduction*. London, Sage.

NACRO, (1995), *Family Group Conferencing*, NACRO Briefing. London, NACRO Youth Crime Section.

NAYJ, (1998), *Policy and Practice Guidelines for Youth Justice*, revised edn. Leicester, NAYJ.

Pitts, J., (1999), New Labour, New Youth Justice System?, *Howard League Magazine* 17 (2) pp 6–7.

Reeves, H. and Wright, M., (1995), *Victims: Towards a Reorientation of Justice*, in Ward, D. and Lacey, M., (Eds.), Probation: Working for Justice. London, Whiting and Birch.

Restorative Justice Consortium, (1998), *Standards for Restorative Justice*. London, National Council for Social Concern.

Scottish Office, (1998), *Towards a Just Conclusion: Vulnerable and Intimidated Witnesses in Scottish Criminal and Civil Cases*. Edinburgh, Scottish Office Home Department.

Scraton, P., (1997), Whose 'Childhood'? What 'Crisis'?, in Scraton, P., (Ed.), *'Childhood' in 'Crisis'?*. London, UCL Press,

Sibbitt, R., (1997), *The Perpetrators of Racial Harassment and Racial Violence*. Home Office Research Study no. 176. London, Home Office Research and Statistics Directorate.

Spencer, A., (1999), *Working with Sex Offenders in Prisons and Through Release to the Community*. London, Jessica Kingsley.

Spencer, S., (1997), Family Group Conferencing: A Promising Way Forward for Juvenile Offenders?, *Childright*, May, pp12–13.

Tudor, B., (1999), *Reparation and the Victim's Perspective: The Drive towards a More Positive Focus*, paper given at Thames Valley Crime Intervention Service Information Day, 6 September.

Williams, B., (1999), *Working with Victims of Crime: Policies, Politics and Practice*. London, Jessica Kingsley.

Williams, B., (1999a), Initial Education and Training for Work with Victims of Crime, *Social Work Education*, 18 (3) pp 287–96.

Williams, B., (1999b), The Victim's Charter: Citizens as Consumers of Criminal Justice, *Howard Journal of Criminal Justice*, 38 (4) pp 384–96.

Youth Justice Board, (1999), *Draft National Standards for Youth Justice*. London, Youth Justice Board.

Acknowledgement

The assistance of Carol Fordham and Alison Reeve with the research for this chapter is gratefully acknowledged.

Index

193